GET REAL

about

LOVE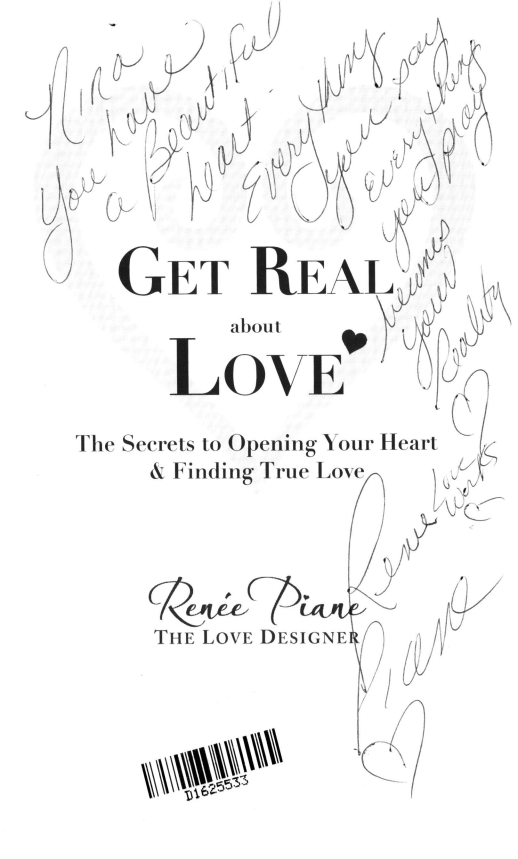

The Secrets to Opening Your Heart
& Finding True Love

Renée Piane
THE LOVE DESIGNER

D1625533

WHAT OTHERS ARE SAYING ABOUT GET REAL ABOUT LOVE♥

"*Get Real about Love* should be required reading for women AND men at any stage of their love life. It's filled with profound insights into human mating psychology and provides specific advice for dealing with the many complexities and hurdles of the mating game. Get it, read it, and learn its lessons from a true mating master!"

– **David M. Buss**, Ph.D., Author of *The Evolution of Desire: Strategies of Human Mating*

"*Get Real about Love* goes right to the heart of the matter: it's internal preparation, not external manipulation, that opens the gate and invites true love to enter your life. Renée Piane has a gift for shining light on the path to a lifetime of authentic love."

– **Michael Bernard Beckwith**, Author of *Life Visioning*

"Renée Piane's *Get Real about Love* advice is the real deal for successful singles around the world!"

– **Dr. Wendy Walsh**, Author of *The 30 Day Love Detox*, www.DrWendyWalsh.com

"Renée Piane is a Godsend to single men and women who are navigating the rapid waters of the dating world. She walks her talk, she truly cares, and her advice is rock solid. I've been referring my matchmaking clients to Renée for over a decade for image consulting and dating coaching, with rave reviews. She's the real deal."

– **Julie Ferman**, Master of Matchmaking, www.JulieFerman.com

"We searched far and wide to find the best love coach in the business to help our clients with dating challenges. Hands down, Renée will surely fire up your love life with her years of dedication and experience. Her passion and wisdom in *Get Real about Love* will be the wake-up call you need to find real love!"

– **Kenneth Agee**, International Marketing director at www.SinglesAdvice.com and www.Loveme.com

"Renée Piane is one of the most genuine and love-inspiring people... and love healers I know. This book is a must read if you're truly looking for real and sustained love. Renée is a combination of passion, healer and sage. Her insights and experiences touches every person who has ever been in a love relationship, and hopes to find the love of their lives."

– **Ruth Klein**, Business & Book Brand Strategist, Author of six bestselling books; *Time Management Secrets for Working Women and De-Stress Diva's ™ Guide to Life*

"*Get Real about Love* is filled with powerful messages that will inspire busy singles to open their hearts to true love. Renée Piane shares her personal journey and the processes she used to heal herself and attract her amazing husband. Now it's your turn."

– **Dr. Marcy Cole**, Ph. D., Holistic Psychotherapist

Renée's work is truly transformational! *Get Real About Love* is a compelling love journal, inter-woven with solid guidance and effective tools to heal the wounds of our love history and establish new patterns to attract real and lasting love. This a must-read for anyone who is ready for a serious relationship based on true love.

– **Meloney Hudson**, Author of *Sexy, Spirited and Strong: Becoming a Positive Energy Woman*

"I've never met anyone so committed to helping people find true love as Renée. Her *Get Real about Love* wisdom will heal and transform your heart."

– **Julie Spira**, Best-selling Author of *The Perils of Cyber-Dating: Confessions of a Hopeful Romantic Looking for Love Online*

"What a jewel Renée is and her *Get Real about Love* book is an inspirational guide that is full of deep wisdom. If you are thinking that it is too late for you or that love is something that happens to others, this book is for you. Thank you, Renée, for your positive attitude, your huge heart and for introducing me to my amazing husband at your Valentine's event."

– **Dr. Nancy B. Irwin**, Author of *YOU TURN Changing Direction in Mid life*

"Renée is a ball of energy, a leader, a love trainer and role model for many. She's an inspiration, an excellent speaker and is an innovator with her *love lineage* process. It's been my pleasure to work with her as one of my coaches in my Vision Board Book. She has made a real contribution to its success as a bestseller. Reading her powerful work will help you achieve your love vision."

– **Joyce Schwarz**, Author of *The Vision Board Book*

"*Get Real about Love* offers profound wisdom that reveals the principles Renée Piane practiced to manifest the love of her life. This book is sure to change your heart forever."

– **Cynthia Charis**, M.S., Transformational Healer

"Renée Piane is a powerful catalyst for transformation. I have been blessed to work with many brilliant teachers and coaches and she is in a class by herself. I cannot recommend her more highly. Anyone who has the opportunity to work with her should jump at the chance."

– **Wendy Kram**, Film & Television Producer, *Mad Money*

"Renée Piane is one of a kind. I call her the 'love whisperer.' She opened my mind, body and soul. After following all of her steps & rituals, I met the most incredible man who is my soul mate and now my husband. Renée not only opens hearts, she heals them and I am grateful that I followed her priceless advice. Anyone who has the privilege to work with her can expect epic and outstanding things to happen in their lives. If you're looking for love…you know who to call…Renée Piane."

– **Niki Shadrow Snyder**, Project Pop Drop, Columnist, Style Expert, *Hollywood Weekly Magazine, Public Speaker*

"The healing wisdom of Renée's work is simply phenomenal! Seeing the amazing results everyone gets out of her books and classes is mind-blowing. I HIGHLY recommend that if you are a single busy woman looking to FINALLY call in the love you want in your life, from the most empowered, clear, alive place—DO this heart-healing work! It changed my life and I am in love with my magnificent life partner!"

– **Lynn Rose**, International Speaker Trainer, www.LynnRose.com

"Singles of the world will be elated, motivated and believe that love can be achieved at any age with *Get Real about Love*. This is a MUST for people who have given up on love. It's important to slow down and take time for love."

– **The late Rhonda Grayson**, Producer CNN Atlanta,
Executive Producer of *Health Styles*

"Renée Piane I love this book! I had no idea that I was acting out certain behaviors from childhood, not only in romantic relationships, but in ALL of my relationships. *Your Get Real about Love* approach helped me to pinpoint the stuck patterns, address them and change them for the better. If you're ready for a real shift, Renée's heart-healing work will change your life!

– **Kimberly Lou**, Executive Life Management and Fitness Coach,
Author of *Hit It & Quit It*, www.KimberlyLou.com

GET REAL about LOVE
The Secrets to Opening Your Heart & Finding True Love

By Renée Piane

For more information about Get Real about Love ©, please contact us at our website at www.reneepiane.com or the address or phone number below. To order more copies give us a call for information about distribution and wholesales prices.

Interested distributors contact: Renée Piane Enterprises, LLC

Love Works Publishing
4712 Admiralty Way, Suite #721
Marina del Rey, CA 90292

Office:+1-310-827-1100
www.ReneePiane.com

© Copyright, October 2014, All Rights Reserved
Printed in the United States
ISBN # 978-0-9678964-2-7
Library of Congress Cataloging-in-Publication Data
Piane, Renée
Get Real about Love
"The Secrets to Opening your Heart and Finding True Love"

1. Opening your heart to love—Relationships. 2. Self-awareness—Motivation. 3. Examining the past—Healing rituals. 4. Dating advice 5. Designing a new love life—Meet your soul mate.

SPECIAL THANKS TO MY AMAZING TEAM OF ARTISTS

Front Cover Photography: Odessy Barbu

Makeup and Hairstyling: Octavio Solis

Stylist: Niki Shadrow Snyder

Back Cover and Dedication Photography,
Makeup and Hairstyling: Maria Rangel

www.MariaPhotography.com

Family Photo: Paul Huston

Book Layout and Design: Tessa Smith

Book Cover Design: Victoria Graham with
contributions from Katherine Gu

Structural Editing: Lisa Schneiderman

Line Editing: Joseph J. Campanella

Book Polishing: Victoria Graham

Love and Support: My husband, Joseph W. Campanella

DEDICATIONS

This book is dedicated to my extraordinary husband, soul mate and best friend, Joseph Campanella. I dreamed of meeting someone like you my whole life and you were worth the wait. Your passion for life, kind heart and dedication to our love, family and the community is unsurpassed. You are a model of strength, passion and love for all that know you. I thank you for your love and support while I share my passion with the world. I am the luckiest girl in the world to have you as my life partner. You are my dream come true! I know our love story will inspire others to believe in love.

The book is also dedicated to the amazing women in my love lineage and Rhonda Grayson who all guided and inspired me to write this book. Your spirit lives on inside of me and in the generations to come.

Contents

FOREWORD

"It is my honor and pleasure to introduce Renée Piane's powerful guidebook for manifesting the love of your life. *Get Real about Love* is more than a pathway to your soul mate. It is a book that asks you to be honest with yourself, first and foremost, and find happiness within before seeking it without. And perhaps most importantly, this book provides an intimate glimpse into the life of a wise and courageously honest woman, a woman totally committed to being herself and enjoying every minute as she passionately and happily lives the life she has created, a life dedicated to helping everyone fulfill their most intimate dreams.

I teach my students and clients that to love is to fully participate in the face of change, impermanence, and death. Renée lives this definition. She teaches all of us that love, for yourself, your higher power and your intimate partner, is the key that opens the treasure chest of your life.

Renée is popularly known as the Love Guru and the Love Designer. The truth is, *Get Real about Love* will convince you that she is all that and much more. She is a wonderful balance of compassion and technology, insight and action, feminine and masculine. She deeply cares about people and, through her book, she will help you every step of the way to identify and fulfill your dreams of *true love*.

Her expertise is like a diamond that shines pure light on those who sincerely seek their soul mate. A major facet of Renée's brilliance is her insistence on honesty as the basis of any love relationship, whether with yourself, your higher power, or your intimate partner.

Again and again, she advises women and men to be honest with themselves, first, and then with others, particularly an intimate partner. Then, as a living example of all that she teaches, she proceeds to do exactly what she recommends. She withholds nothing and opens her life for all to see, making herself completely vulnerable in service of her message. While sharing her personal experiences of how she removed her roadblocks to finding *true love,* Renée graces you, dear reader, with the essential keys needed to live the way you've always wanted and manifest the love of your life.

Renée asks questions that lead you deeply into yourself where you discover what has prevented you from experiencing the joy you deserve, and she explains what is necessary for life-long relationship happiness. To insure that happiness, she asks you to make several powerful promises to yourself, for example, "I vow to *get real* and to speak my truth from this day forward knowing my words are a powerful force."

I love her insistence of honesty and transparency as a foundation of *true love.* Her principles resonate deep within my mind and soul. If you want measurable results in your love life, Renée gives you step-by-step instructions for doing just that and so much more.

In my classes I teach that in order to love and be loved, you must know what you feel, want and think which, is the essence of your personal identity. Renée agrees and wants you to know who you are, because it is not possible to be loved without taking the risk of revealing your identity, that is, what you feel emotionally, want, and think Renée makes it clear that getting real about love means stepping outside of the box. It means learning and revealing what you honestly want in all areas of your life.

As I teach in The Destination Method, love is one of seven virtues, each one is a powerful goodness. Love is a goodness that comes in many forms, self-love, love of relatives, love of friends, love of family, and soul mate love. But Renée makes it absolutely clear that Love is the greatest virtue, and then she provides a road map to the destination you have longed for.

Love is prized by all human beings, not only because it is necessary for us to fully enjoy our personal life and experience *true love,* but because love, in the spiritual sense, is the experience of oneness or unity with all that exists, the foundation of lasting peace and happiness.

The information in this book embraces every level of love as it helps you to unfold and move forward. So, enjoy your journey with Renée, as she makes grounded sense of the physical, emotional and mental aspects of love, all the while embracing the fragrance of spiritual love, thus helping you to celebrate each step as you *Get Real about Love.*

– **Dr. Robert Dee McDonald**, Creator of The Destination Method®, *Tools of the Spirit,* Founder of The Telos Healing Center, TelosCenter.com

ACKNOWLEDGEMENTS

What an adventure it is to write a book! My heart is full of gratitude for so many people who were on the sidelines cheering me on. Thanks for all the loving support and encouragement from my husband, my dearest friends (you all know who you are), my amazing family and clients as well as business associates from all walks of my life. With all of your support, this dream is now a reality. A special blessing goes to my parents for always believing in me and supporting me to live my dreams.

Without the assistance of a team of angels and artists, this book would not be in your hands right now. I need to give special thanks to Lisa Schneiderman for helping restructure this book into the new *Get Real about Love* Series and supporting my vision. Thank you for being so loving and patient with me during some of my challenging *wake-up* calls.

I also want to acknowledge several people for their editing assistance and awesome insights, which includes: Lori Shapiro, Maria Garcia Crocker, Herb Friedman, Sheida Pisheh, Pam Buongiorno, Lynn Isenberg along with my amazing final editor Joey Campanella.

A huge thankyou goes out to Victoria Graham for the final cover design and her hawk eye detail polishing in the final editing stages and Tessa Smith, my master interior layout designer. I must also mention the artistic talents of the amazing Katherine Gu, who helped me design my original graphics and marketing materials over the last few years.

I am so blessed to be surrounded by love and to be alive to share my heart-healing work with the world. I'm eternally grateful for my "angel healing team" of doctors and spiritual practitioners especially Dr. Cheryl Joy Bratman, Mark Fishman and Dr. Prosper Benhaim, who supported me through my health challenges. Finally, I thank you God for guiding me to help people open their hearts and find *true love*. I get to live my mission to spread more love on the planet. LOVE WORKS!

INTRODUCTION

Are you ready to find the love of your life? If you picked up this book, something was tugging at your heart to read it. You came to the right place because I know what it takes to help *you* manifest *real love*. I'm proud to say after almost two decades in the love business and years of serious love investigating, I've helped thousands of people find *true love*. Now it's your turn! I knew that one day I would pass on these lessons of love and heart expanding true stories. I am ready to share my secrets and my personal journey with successful, busy *wonder women* and *super men* who are ready to create a new *love story*. I believe we all have special assignments and gifts to share in the world and this is my true calling. It warms my heart when I receive messages from happy clients who have found love at last!

This book is part memoir and part honest love guidance that will surely wake you up to *get real* with yourself and your heart. Just know that divulging my personal love journey makes me feel a bit vulnerable, but I'm more passionate than ever to share my truth. I am going to be raw and real with you. I had a life threatening health *wake-up* call while I was in the middle of writing this book that made a major impact on the direction of my message. My body and soul forced me to unplug from the normal pace of my busy life and slow down to reflect on the important things: LOVE, family, faith, good health, happiness and living in the now.

Luckily, I'm fully recovered and now my goal is to help you *get real* and live life to the fullest because every moment is sacred. My life is dedicated to helping people reinvent their love lives and I'm committed to making your dreams come true!

From the outside looking in, other people saw me as a successful and attractive *wonder woman*. I was so busy focusing on my career that I didn't meet the love of my life and get married until I was in my forties. For years, I had walls protecting my heart and it wasn't until I did this powerful work on myself that

I became open to receiving *true love* and created the life I had always dreamed of as a *little girl*. I am on a mission to share how you can transform any imprints from your past and finally let love into your life!

So, why trust me with your heart? Like many of you, a part of me had lost faith in love after experiencing the disappointments and frustrations in the game of love. Once I finally met the love of my life, everyone wanted to know what *secrets* I had learned after all those years in the single's world. How did I find *real love* after forty? Because I healed myself, it has become my life's work to inspire you to *believe in love* no matter what your past experiences may have taught you. Let's just say that my pain led me to my passion! I am excited to introduce you to my work, which just might be the missing link that has blocked your heart from love...until now.

You could be just getting back in the dating game after a breakup, divorce or dating someone who you know isn't your match but think it's better than being alone. You could be a single parent pondering if love is even possible for you. You may have a great career, awesome friends and have finally made it to the top and wonder...where is that special partner to share all of your success? You might be doubting yourself and have anxiety about getting back out there since you've heard it's so hard to find *true love*. If you feel there is a void in your love life, or that your past has kept you from being successful in relationships, your intuition has led you to pick up this book and *Get Real about Love.*

As the President and Co-founder of *Rapid Dating*, and a Love Designer, I have successfully matched thousands of couples and counseled many suddenly single people getting back in the dating game after countless heartaches and disappointments. I have been working in the dating trenches with singles of all ages and it's an honor to have this opportunity to work with YOU.

This series is an inside-out love process that most of us never learned growing up. I coach successful people who spend most of their time working, yet are still not fulfilled in their personal lives. I have listened to clients on a daily basis say how hard it is to meet great partners but they are not properly taking care of their own hearts. Many people are just too busy and claim that "someday soon" they will *take time for love*. I see and hear it all the time in my business: hectic schedules, broken hearts, people yearning for love and rushing into relationships to fill the void. Some clients spend hours ruminating over their faults, insecurities and fears, rather than focusing on a new vision. Often, they attract unhealthy situations and keep repeating the same behaviors expecting different results. They call me for a quick fix, but many of them don't want to take the time to stop, reflect and get clear on what could be holding them back from finding a healthy relationship.

I am here to encourage you to *get real* about your love life and create an *action plan*, especially if you want to have children. It's important to be happy with your own life and to choose a life partner with the right tools and a better understanding of yourself. If not, you may be so busy that you commit to the wrong person or rush into a marriage for fear of being alone. Or, you could stay in a dead-end relationship wasting precious years of your life. I've been there and done that. I only wish I would have had a love guide to help me through all the challenges and issues most singles face. I have a direct *get real* approach in my coaching. I weave in true stories to help you relate to some of the experiences and open your eyes to see the truth.

I developed this step-by-step process that enabled me to heal my heart from the battle scars of generations of amazing women in my lineage who dealt with infidelity. Their broken relationships caused a lot of stress and forced them to work several jobs to support and raise their kids as single mothers. This workaholic gene became a running theme that weaved into my family tree. These women were my role models and I learned at a very young age that I should be self-sufficient and not rely on anyone else to take care of me. I could feel their pain and I continued this pattern to make sure I was in control of my life. Later, I discovered that these themes became the primary imprints and affected my ability to trust most men. Yet, deep down inside, I still wanted to share my life with a special partner; someone who would love, cherish and adore me. When I finally treated my heart as sacred, I was able to call in a partner who honored me the way I was honoring myself. I can promise you that once you fully open your heart, magic will happen in your life. My dreams came true, and now it's your turn!

I call myself a Love Designer because I have successfully helped many disappointed and frustrated singles reinvent their lives and *get back in the game of love*. I want you to learn from my experiences in order to help you avoid some of the same "mis-takes" that I made. I will help guide you to reflect on your past love lessons and then draft a blueprint for your future. Make a promise to unplug from your busy life each day in order to really get in touch with the deeper part of yourself. With no set of "rules," we will create your unique love plan based on your soul's choice and your ultimate love vision.

If finding *real love* someday is a part of your dream, I invite you to commit to this body of work, which comes from the depths of my soul. Make a commitment to your heart in this moment that your special someday is now!

HOW MY LOVE JOURNEY STARTED

Before we get started on your journey, I thought you might like to know some history on how my crazy love journey started. I am 100% East Coast Italian and grew up in a very large, traditional and loving family in Wilmington, Delaware. Some people say my family is like a combo of the characters in the movies *My Big Fat Greek Wedding* and *Moonstruck*. We did everything BIG! There were lots of holidays, birthday celebrations, amazing food, hugs, love, drama, and of course big hair. When my friends came to our parties, they were always amazed and had never experienced anything quite so extravagant. Since we owned a large catering company and three Italian restaurants, taking care of people, feeding them and celebrating life were huge parts of my heritage. Their love and devotion to our family and their never-ending service to the world was woven into the fabric of my soul along with my siblings. We grew up raising money for my father's favorite charity, The Little Sisters of the Poor. My father was like the Leo Buscaglia of catering, always out spreading the love. He and my mother were very charismatic and people that gave back to the community. I had a blessed life growing up with my cousins and our huge extended family.

Ever since I was a child, I was in love with romance stories, playing dress-up, acting in the theatre and writing about boys in my *Holly Hobby* journals. I also had an extrasensory perception about people and a fascination with angels and other mystical things. Who knew back then that I'd be using these skills to help people find love. My parents told me of the many times that I woke them up to come see the angels in my room at night. They always assured me that the angels were sent to guide and protect me. I was lucky to have such open-minded parents who supported me over the years. Around age 12, I told my mother that I would get gut feelings and frequently see visions about people, including my grandmother who had passed on that year. I later discovered that my mother and other members of my extended family had these same intuitive gifts. However, she told me not to tell anyone else about this *secret* because she worried that people would think I was different. Hmm, I wonder why?

I was also influenced by other intuitive people in my life including our nurturing and very spiritual housekeeper, Elizabeth Proctor. My mother confided in her about my angel visitors. Elizabeth told her that I had been given a gift to heal people's hearts and would be teaching and inspiring people someday. She was sure that God had a plan for me. I'll never forget the day I overheard her sharing her predictions in the kitchen saying, "Ree-nay will be moving away from home someday and marrying later in her life to a man who has a child … and she won't have any children of her own." She claimed, "She's got God's work to do and she will not be getting married until she is *old.*" I always wondered … how old would I be?

In high school, I began working as an assistant at my cousins' popular salon and quickly realized that the beauty business was perfect for my personality. I became a licensed cosmetologist specializing in hair design, color and makeup. I loved making my client's look and feel beautiful as I transformed them with complete image makeovers. As a stylist and a bridal consultant, I had the opportunity to get to know people very intimately. They would reveal their hearts and souls to me, especially about their dating experiences and relationship challenges. I would touch people's heads and be able to see into their hearts and would often get clear messages to pass on to them. I learned Reiki and began practicing the various healing modalities on my clients to relax them while styling their hair. I started getting a reputation for being a "love advisor" and healer at the salon. Consequently, my schedule would book out weeks in advance and I soon realized this was a part of my calling. I always attracted interesting clients who were into spiritual studies which led to more in-depth research of the mind, body and spirit connection. The floodgates of my soul were opened and I was following my heart.

During that time, I experienced *true love* in my small hometown. I was in a serious relationship for eight years with my high school sweetheart. He was a great guy but he had a serious drinking problem. So six months before my wedding, I knew I had to make a life-changing decision. We went for premarital counseling since he was often jealous and not willing to face his addiction to alcohol. After a few months, I knew he wasn't going to change or follow our counselor's advice. We had started to grow apart and he was not comfortable with my spiritual growth or success. I thought everyone would be upset with me if I canceled the wedding. Although I loved him and his wonderful family, I knew in my heart that he was not the right life partner for me. I prayed for guidance and my answer came in an unexpected way.

One night, we snuck into my parent's room while they were out of town and fell asleep on their bed. In my slumber, I felt someone pulling on my big toe and I was sure we had just been busted by my parents. As I slowly opened my eyes, I was awakened by my late grandmother, who was standing at the bottom of my bed surrounded by a glowing light. She had her hands on her hips and said with a strong tone, "Do not marry him Renée, or you will be unhappy for the rest of your life! He drinks too much and he is never going to stop. You *must* cancel the wedding!" I told my parents when they got home about her surprise visit. I knew I had finally received the sign I was looking for. Now I had to end our eight-year relationship and even though it was the right decision, it was incredibly hard to do.

A few days later, we got together for dinner and I told him I wanted to cancel the wedding and returned my engagement ring. My decision surprised him and both of our families. I had hidden his drinking problem long enough and I needed to listen to my intuition as well as my grandmother's message. He moved on and was engaged within a year. Years later, I told him about the vision and, as it turns out, my grandmother was right. He was still drinking and got divorced after being caught with another woman.

After the breakup, I was still so young and naïve, and went out with a series of men who were more skilled in the dating game. I experienced a few bad heartbreaks along the way. A few years later, I met a charismatic man who swept me off my feet. Our passionate and rocky relationship was on and off for almost three years until my father blatantly asked him if he intended to marry me during one of our traditional Sunday night spaghetti dinners. He quickly replied, "No Mr. Piane, I am not ready yet." I was in shock realizing we had just ended our relationship in front of my entire family. I recall wanting to throw my pasta in his face! Needless to say, it was a very awkward breakup. As he was leaving, I remember my grandfather saying in his broken Italian accent, "You're a bum," then spitting on his shoe. I was so embarrassed! I walked him out and as I hugged him goodbye I was in total disbelief at what had just happened. There had been some clear signs along the way that he was not "the one," but this was still one hell of a way to end a relationship. He was also aware of the visions I had, which he later admitted scared the life out of him. Our break up ended up being a blessing in disguise. He was a free spirit and never committed to much of anything in his life. He also had the dangerous combination of good looks, charm and sex appeal that could've kept me addicted.

After many tears, I was guided to take a much needed two-week vacation to California. During my visit, I had many magical connections with men asking me out as well as some new business opportunities. I felt right at home and loved the warm weather. Since I was very interested in self transformation, I was thrilled to be meeting people that seemed more aligned with my expanded way of thinking. I went back to school to study psychology, sociology, marketing and TV production, while reading powerful books by Dale Carnegie, Louise Hay, Dr. Wayne Dyer, Leo Buscalia, Rumi, Les Brown, Norman Vincent Peale, Doreen Virtue and many other great spiritual authors. I felt that moving to Los Angeles would expand my social and spiritual life. I was ready to move on and re-invent my life after living in my small, conserva-

tive hometown. Given that there were so many signs guiding me at the end of my trip, I decided to take a leap of faith and create a new life in Los Angeles, the City of Angels. I told my mother that I kept getting clear messages to move and she said, "Honey, follow your heart and your angels will guide you." That's when my new adventures began.

After my move, I set out to find a spiritual community to join and visited many churches services that just didn't feel like the right fit. I went to the lectures on the *Course in Miracles* when Marianne Williamson was just starting out. Then, I was led to the *Agape International Spiritual Center* with the renowned Reverend Michael Beckwith in 1988. It was a small community back then, with fewer than seventy people and I knew I had found my new spiritual home. This magical center was trans-denominational and embraced people from all religions. I began taking classes to expand my spiritual studies and joined the Agape choir. I met many life-long friends there and we created mastermind/visioning groups. I knew that my soul was led out west to fulfill my destiny as a messenger to help people with love. These powerful teachings confirmed that I was on the right path and supported as I did my "angel" work.

I started to attend networking events and made some great contacts. I began working at a popular Beverly Hills salon and part-time as a bridal consultant for the Riviera Country Club in Los Angeles. My expertise in the beauty industry was soon recognized. I was asked to speak at various seminars and began offering image makeovers as well as beauty tips while teaching at a well-known modeling agency.

I began consulting with many singles who expressed they were lonely and looking for love. I could understand their plight and became inspired by a talented man that I was casually dating to produce a monthly show called *Love Works*. I was interviewing singles, psychologists and authors in the dating field and realized this work was my sweet spot. I also did "man on the street" live interviews about love, sex and dating. I then expanded into radio and co-hosted my first show *Love on the Edge* with Richard Hatch.

After a year of looking for places to meet successful singles, I saw there was a need to connect people in the city. So, I took a leap of faith and began hosting *Love Works* community-building cocktail mixers. At each event I gave out a *Love Works Angel Award* to a prominent business owner who was making a difference in the community. These events drew hundreds of professionals, both single and married, and I matched them up for love, business and friendship. I discovered that I was a natural matchmaker from the start. I was out "making magic" every day and meeting a lot of men!

I was then introduced to a production team of like-minded souls and we created another show called, *The Good News Network*. We reported all the good news and people making a difference in the community. We continued to give out *Love Works Angel* awards and helped inspire people to get involved to spread more love in Los Angeles. There were great organizations involved and exciting interviews with many famous stars. I was having a blast making a difference with our dream team.

Once I began to share my craft in the media, I knew I had found other new passions: motivational speaking and storytelling. Beginning with the Learning Annex in Southern California, I started teaching men's seminars called *The Smart Man's Guide to Dating, Attracting and Understanding Women*. I spent more than seventeen years facilitating various love seminars and singles panels while expanding my coaching and image makeover services. Back then, there was no such thing as a "dating coach." Personal ads and video dating were the most popular ways to meet people. I helped people brand and market themselves to attract the right match.

New doors opened and I began consulting with some of LA's most popular matchmaking companies. It amazed me how many people expected us to match them with their soul mate even though their hearts were not entirely healed. This is when I knew my *get real* coaching and seminars would make a difference.

Soon after, I was flown to New York and got hired to produce segments and interview single men for a show called *Men Across America*. Men, men, men! It was a perfect job for a single woman looking for the answers to what men really wanted. I felt as though I was working towards a doctorate in relationship studies while being open to meeting my special man in the process. That's when I realized it was time for me to put everything I had learned about love and dating into a series of books. While out in the field doing research, I was also studying to become certified as an NLP practitioner and hypnotherapist. These experiences inspired me to write my first book, *Love Mechanics*. This book offered men the "power tools" to build successful relationships with women and combined all my work up until that point. My goal was to represent the strong and independent *wonder women* of the world and to teach men to understand how we tick. This was a huge undertaking, but I was determined to lead the way for all my frustrated allies out there!

As I was completing my book in early 2001, I was offered a partnership with an amazing woman to launch the first non-denominational speed dating company in America. I jumped at the opportunity. By April, we had launched *Rapid Dating* in Los Angeles and it was an immediate success. We were featured on numerous talk shows, local news segments, in national newspapers and magazines. Since I was still single, I was also hoping this was going to be the way for me to find my *true love*. The five-minute rapid dating business was a perfect match for me.

We traveled to major cities launching events while we were training event leaders and creating media buzz. I now realize the valuable education I received by hosting hundreds of events and personally working one-on-one with thousands of singles in their 20s, 30s, 40s, 50s, and even their 60s. I had the chance to observe and learn about many different cultures as well as understand the various dating rules of different generations. It was fascinating!

I surely had my share of fun and success during these times. I dated some amazing men and a few bad boys while I was building my business, yet I still hadn't found *true love* for myself. On many of my TV interviews and radio shows, the host would ask the big question: "You help so many other people find love, what about YOU? If you are so good at helping other people *tune-up* for love, why aren't you hitched?" I would always reply, "I am ready for love, and once things slow down a bit, I will find him. I am not worried, and I know he is out there getting ready for me!" Since work was my focus in life, my family was concerned that the one thing I didn't do was *take time for love*.

As I expanded, I did have love and a few serious relationships, yet I still needed to heal that part of me that still mistrusted men. I made it very challenging for men to get close to me since I was so busy, yet I kept promising myself that someday soon I'd slow down long enough to find *true love*. Sound familiar? As it turns out, the coaching work and the research I was doing was actually what I needed to open my own heart and break through the barriers that kept me from attracting *real love*. So now, after all these years of research and winning the International Dating Coach Award, I feel it is my duty to help people find love. I am sharing my story and *secrets* so you can create your new *love story*.

NOW YOUR LOVE JOURNEY BEGINS

I'm so glad your heart is open and you're reading this book. It proves you are ready to call love into your life. My mission is to help you *Get Real about Love* and become aware of the signals you're sending out. You will gain insights and assurance that both sexes desire to love and be loved. You will get back on track with increased self-awareness, energy and connection to your higher self. You get to design your love life based on your lifestyle choices, core beliefs, vision and goals. First, you must love your life, honor yourself and get clear on who you are and what makes you happy.

There will be only honesty and wisdom that comes from my years of experience in the love industry. You might say that I have been engaged in the ultimate type of *prince training* for men. Women have asked me for years to share what I have learned from working with men so closely, and those who have read advanced copies of this book say that they wished I had written it sooner.

Many of my clients, who had not been in the dating scene for a while, were a bit rusty after being in long-term relationships or marriages and needed some guidance in their daily lives. I have witnessed some amazing results from personalizing my coaching programs for each client by combining this inner work with daily rituals, heart-healing exercises and visioning processes.

I know that deep down in your soul, no matter if you are the president of a company, a famous TV host or movie star, a super salesperson, a popular motivational speaker, a professional businessperson, doctor, surgeon, attorney, banker, judge, therapist, nurse, TV producer, writer, musician, model, graphic designer, event planner, artist, fitness guru, chef, painter, author, photographer, musician, teacher, spiritual healer, super mom (or dad), newly-divorced, unemployed, widower, or you're single on the quest for your soul mate, you want *true love*. At the end of the day, we all want an amazing partner to share our life with, right?

This book was written from a heterosexual perspective since that has been my experience. The *Get Real about Love* process applies to all forms of love and I encourage everyone to embrace love in whatever form they choose. If you're a man reading these lessons and *secrets*, keep in mind they also apply to you. If you're gay or lesbian, this process is applicable, because there are masculine and feminine energies in every relationship.

From my heart and soul to yours, if you make the commitment to *Get Real about Love*, you will create success with all your relationships and have a fulfilling life in the process. It's time to get started on your journey by first committing to yourself that this time around you are going to lovingly take your heart into your own hands. I will help you design your life with powerful intentions, and once you *get real* with yourself, you will be transformed forever. Throughout the book, you will see Secret Keys ⚷ to emphasize certain points for reflection. I am excited for you and I am here to support you on this magnificent journey. So, let's explore your life and help you open your heart and find *true love*.

THE GET REAL ABOUT LOVE TOOLS

The following is a list of what you will need as you go through your Love Design process:

1. An open heart and a commitment to yourself to *Get Real about Love* and get ready for the love of your life.
2. A special journal or notebook dedicated to this heart-healing work.
3. A heart-shaped crystal or stone that represents your heart. You will be using this "love anchor stone" during some of our Love Design rituals.

4. Special music that moves you or a collection of your favorite upbeat songs to lift your energy and slower tempo music for moments of meditation and reflection.
5. A device to record your voice as you read and complete the exercises.
6. A Commitment to your Love Design Process. Sign your *Get Real about Love* vows below and let's get started. Hold onto your heart…your life will never be the same.

GET REAL ABOUT LOVE VOWS

Take your *Get Real about Love* vows now by holding your heart stone in your left hand and place your right hand over your heart while proclaiming out loud:

- I vow and commit to myself that I _____ will take time to *get real* and be 100% honest with myself about what has blocked me from opening my heart and finding *real love* in my life.
- I vow that I will make this *get real* process a priority in my life.
- I vow to do the inner reflection it takes to go deep and discover more about my *love lineage* and my *true love* vision.
- I vow to create new daily rituals and habits to support my *action plan* to *get real* and *get ready for love*.
- I vow to *get real* and to speak my truth from this day forward knowing my words are a powerful force.
- I vow to check in with my heart every day and follow my instincts.
- I vow to live in the moment during this life-changing adventure.
- I vow to be loving and kind to myself as I navigate through this heart opening process. And so it is!

Sign your name _____

Date your Love Journey began: _____

Let's begin this process by examining your role models of love.

CHAPTER I
ROLE MODELS OF LOVE

"Your task is not to seek for love, but merely to seek and find all the barriers within yourself that you have built against it."
– Rumi

WHO TRAINED YOU ABOUT LOVE & RELATIONSHIPS?

I don't know about you, but I never had official love training or dating classes when I was younger. Did you? Let's face it, most of us were not guided by our parents when it came to understanding love, dating and sex in our early years. Also, depending on your age, most schools were not educating us on such intimate and private topics.

Most little girls started our education with the magical fairy tales we were told like *Cinderella, Sleeping Beauty, The Little Mermaid* and *Aladdin*. We were taught that our prince would come someday, sweep us off our feet and we would live happily ever after. We graduated from those seemingly harmless fairy tales to the ever-present fantasies we absorbed in soap operas, romance novels and chick flicks. Then after years of reading magazine articles like "Cosmo's Magic Tests and Formulas" or "Discovering Your Soul Mate in Ten Easy Steps," our minds were filled with unrealistic expectations. Young boys and girls were given completely different pictures about love as they were growing up.

The average time parents and children spend together is less than an hour a day because of the demands of modern life, according to a study conducted for Virgin Holiday and Universal Orlando Resort. Seven in ten parents say that when they do get together time is spent in silence in front of the TV because they are busy reading, playing computer games or simply too tired to talk. Many parents believe their kids will learn the information they need about sex and dating at school, on television or the Internet. What a joke!

My knowledge about love started by observing my family, the nuns at my all-girl Catholic academy, and sneaking around at home reading books hidden in my mother's room. I also found rolled up *Playboy* magazines hidden in my brothers' mattresses that they had borrowed from my dad's office. None of these were the greatest guides to follow. However, those became some of my earliest role models growing up.

Fortunately, I got more guidance than most because I was so precocious and asked many questions. For example, I had heard about oral sex from my older brother's friends. Since I didn't know anything about sex, I innocently inquired at school. In 7th grade sex-education class, I asked an elderly nun if oral sex was a sin. You can imagine how much my question alarmed her and she immediately excused herself in a tizzy. She never returned to class. Years later, I was told that my questions and inquisitive nature had sent that poor nun back to the cloister! The nuns at the academy still talk about it today and even teased me about it at my wedding.

In contrast, my mom was cool and open about sex. She acted as the counselor to all of my friends and even her own sisters, who were constantly coming over with relationship challenges. My sister Theresa, who is four years older, was a strong role model for me as were my older brother Bobby and his buddies, who were always at the house. My investigative nature gave me more insight about boys and sex than most young girls my age. Unfortunately, we had grown up with divorce and a lot of infidelity in my family, so my "research" started early. As you continue to read, you will see how this became a big part of my story.

So, who taught you about love? Many people were brought up in single parent homes or didn't receive any guidance at all. Some of us were lucky to have fabulous role models for relationships and were given support along the way. Others had bad programming about love from observing their parents fight, separate, or get divorced. Sound familiar? Where did you get your guidance? As you begin this internal look into your life and examine your primary models of love as you grew up, you need to ask yourself, "Who were your primary role models for relationships?"

Perhaps it was your parents, grandparents, siblings, teachers, school peers, or coaches who were your role models. For many women, they were based on Hollywood love stories, dramas in the tabloids, romance novels, movies, or soap operas. Now we have instant access via the internet and the crazy role models of reality television. Every day we are being bombarded with information overload and messages in all forms of media that influence us to buy or do things that make us feel sexier, happier, or more confident. But is this information influencing us in the right direction towards self-love and empowerment, or is it is brainwashing us?

Many people marry at a young age due to family pressure before they ever really know themselves. We often follow the path of our parents or heritage and get married too young because of tradition, often ending up disappointed and divorced. Becoming aware of your modeling will help you powerfully choose the right life partner without feeling the obligation to take such a leap just to please your family. We don't have to follow the outdated traditions or conditioning from the generations who walked before us. We have to design our own path to love and change the patterns from our love lineage.

According to the Forest Institute of Professional Psychology, the current divorce rates are 50% of first marriages, 67% of second and 74% of third marriages[1]. Many of my clients who are currently divorced often share that they wished they had understood more about love and relationships when they were growing up. If that was the case, they may have chosen a more suitable life partner for marriage.

This inner work will prevent you from desperately dating and help you to slow down and reflect from an empowered place before getting back into the

---

1   Hooglander, Ingrid M. "Do 50% of American Marriages Really End in Divorce?" *Brandon Divorce Help*. Brandon Legal Group, 15 Sept. 2011. Web. 01 Sept. 2014.

game of love. You will be taking care of your heart and practicing more self-love while you design the lifestyle you want. I only wish that I had learned this information when I was younger. It would have saved me from going through all of the growing pains and anguish it took to learn these life lessons.

Most people want fast results and often rush into relationships without much thought. Some singles feel pressured by their families to get married "before it's too late" and are injected with fear from the old school rules of the past. We all need to *take time for love* and really listen to our gut instincts. By doing so, it will help to clarify if we are ready to be in love, have a long-term relationship, casually date, or have the desire to raise children.

⚷ *The choice of a life partner is one of the most important decisions you can make in your life. Learning about yourself and taking time to do the inner work is the first step in attracting your perfect match.*

You need to discover your dream vision and understand where you are in your life at this time in regard to relationships. Some men and women feel pressured to have children when they know they are not cut out for raising kids, which to me is one of the most important jobs on this planet! Some people choose to be single and never marry. This is your life and you can design your love life any way you want. Remember, you are the creator of your unique Love Design. Just slow down and *get real* with your heart.

MEN'S LACK OF PRINCE TRAINING

But wait! What about all the men in the world. Women always ask me "Where do men learn about love and where is my *prince charming*?" After years of teaching my seminars and interviewing hundreds of men nationwide, I finally woke up to the fact most men had not been given any official *prince training* or taught the information that we thought they knew. Most women, like myself, *assumed* that they had magically learned this love formula as young men. Boy, were we ever wrong!

Men and women are brought up to believe vastly different philosophies about love and romance. Yet, we expect men to intuitively know how to love a woman and be prepared for marriage and commitment, right? I don't think so! I've coached hundreds of men about what women really want and this topic makes their heads spin. Many have expressed that no one taught them love skills. As boys and young men, they are just expected to figure it out. Yes, it is sad but true... I have discovered that no one ever gave most of the men in the world *prince training,* although I am doing my best one man at a time!

Many women believe that men know what we expect them to say or do in most situations. We constantly get disappointed and frustrated when they do not follow the "fairy tale" we have manufactured in our minds and lived with for so long. I now know that these so-called "rules" and high expectations need to be managed by women and understood by men. By doing so, we will all be communicating more effectively, preventing disappointments, and creating a new reality in the game of love.

We must wake up and be realistic about some men's lack of love training. It's time to end the complaining and create something new with our feminine energy. We all need to learn about ourselves so we can convey our true essence when we interact with each other. Let's become a part of the solution and create more empowering relationships.

Countless women have told me that they felt men were holding out on them when it came to love and communication. Based on my extensive personal research, most men are more open to coaching or counseling after they've experienced pain from a breakup, a divorce, or years of rejection. Since they tend to be very private and sensitive when it comes to *matters of the heart,* men often lack support from their family and friends. Just as we have our *little girl* inside of us, men have that *little boy* side of themselves as well. Some men are just too macho, egotistical or embarrassed to admit that they actually need some guidance. All the while, we are in dreamland with high expectations that would be impossible for *Superman* or even *Prince Charming* to fulfill.

Most men learn about women by observing, but where did they get their information about love, dating, and sex from? Did they learn about women in high school or college? Conversations with their father, mother, or siblings?

From their drinking buddies on poker night? Did they learn from watching online porn or reading magazines such as *Playboy* or *Penthouse?* From one of their ex's? Perhaps they learned it from trial and error or from the guys they hung out with while watching or playing sports…you get the idea.

Unfortunately, the media in all forms influences men. The fact is that most of the women in the world do NOT look like the women in magazines and on television. Men fantasize about the unattainable women they see in *People, Sports Illustrated Swimsuit Issue, Victoria Secret* catalogues, television networks like the Playboy Channel or shows like *Girls Gone Wild.* Sadly, we also sometimes compare ourselves to these fantasy women.

Now ladies, don't get mad…just keep expanding your mind, get into your feminine power so you can change your life, and create your new *love story* from this moment on!

⚷ *If you are pissed off at men, it's no wonder you are not getting the results you desire in your relationships. These negative emotions seep into every aspect of your life and are impacting your ability to attract the right relationships.*

I bravely and lovingly represent the female perspective when I teach my live classes to men. In *Love Mechanics,* I created a *tune-up* process that opened the eyes and hearts of many men. Let's face it; we are the powerful feminine force that can change this dynamic now! This is the truth and you know it.

Today's men are expected to be confident, emotionally available and conscious of what makes women happy. Many men in our society feel pressured to be good providers, rise to the top and make big money to be able to afford a lifestyle that many women expect. This huge responsibility causes some men to fear marriage or a long-term commitment. In my *Get Real about Love* panels, a lot of misconceptions are shared and transformed. You would be shocked at all the *secrets* men reveal when they're in a safe forum.

⚷ *Men want to make us happy and proud but you must first be happy with yourself and know what you really want. A man is not your source of happiness.*

Some women have already done this inner work and get disappointed when men don't have their act together. *Wake up* sisters! If you are forty and older or a younger woman who dates older men, then the men you are dating have most likely been raised by mothers of the '50s or '60s. The roles of many women from those generations are in direct contrast to the self-sufficient, powerful and independent women of today. The dynamics have shifted and often men feel emasculated by powerful women. At the same time, women are irritated and fed up with the men who can't keep up with them. Take a look at your over-the-top expectations and *get real.*

⚡ *Many men are confused about how to deal with the new wonder woman out there who is self-sufficient, powerful, and independent. This is a paradigm shift for most men and they are learning they need our loving, feminine influence.*

Some younger men may have been raised by single mothers who have passed their *love wisdom* down to them on how to treat women properly. In addition to their wisdom, they may have subtly injected them with their bitterness and disappointments as well. This is a perfect example of how *love imprints* are unconsciously passed on.

You also need to examine the different generations, various nationalities and cultures of the men you are dating in order to understand them and how they were raised. Just like a women that has been a daddy's girl, many men are babied by their mothers and some expect the women they date to be just like their mom.

No matter which generation they were born into, most men don't have as much support as women do in the love department. Ladies, we have the power to influence men but we must first do the inner work on ourselves and understand how men are wired. This shift will take awareness, patience and communication.

Many people are being raised with less communication skills than their elders due to the "high tech-low touch" society, which is creating a completely different set of relationship challenges. Society's current obsessions with mobile devices, social networking updates and Internet porn are wreaking havoc on relationships. People aren't learning to connect face to face and are destroying what is left of their social skills.

☞ *Commit sometime every day to unplug by turning off your phone and tuning into the world around you.*

Connecting with men these days can be difficult for some women because of their high expectations of how relationships should be progressing. We worry about how our relationship status appears to our family, friends and or business associates. Women are trained from birth to find their *prince* and to help and guide each other with *matters of the heart*. Men mostly roll with the punches unless they have been fortunate enough to be blessed with great friends or strong family role models.

Generally speaking, people read books and go to support groups when they want guidance and are constantly attempting to unravel the mystery of men. In fact, women are almost drowning in information on how to find "Mr. Right" or get over "Mr. Right Now." I am a coach and confidante to men around the world who do not want to admit they need help. Have you ever been with a man who is willing to ask for directions from someone if they are lost? Thank God for GPS systems! It is truly a shame that it takes experiencing pain or the depths of alienation and loneliness for men to call for help. There are many men who need to do this inner work, and I wrote *Love Mechanics* specifically to offer these important *tune-up tools* for men.

The good news is that many men are now searching for enlightenment about what women really want as well. I'm so thrilled to offer this vital information with the men who are looking for guidance on getting back into the dating game. Luckily, the internet provides easy access for men to discreetly get these powerful healing tools and relationship coaching. You can now be a part of the solution and pass on this knowledge to the men you meet, your ex, friends or your brothers. We can lead men with our love and support instead of beating them up. By doing so, we change the path for ourselves and future generations!

Beware, there are currently many powerful online programs that are geared towards teaching men how to manipulate you to feel a love connection and get you into bed on the first or second date. On a positive note, there are also amazing programs that men are participating in that are having a huge impact. Let's be grateful that many men are waking up and taking action. I'm excited to share more secrets so that everyone can manifest *sacred love*. Pass them on!

GET REAL ♥ REFLECTIONS

- ♥   Ask yourself: Who were your primary role models for relationships? Who taught you about love? Where did you get your guidance?
- ♥   Name three ways you can convey your feminine essence as you communicate with men. Are you currently using your feminine energy to influence the men in your life? What did you assume that men learned about love? Do you have realistic expectations about the roles of men in relationships?
- ♥   Are you currently using your masculine energy to influence the women in your life? Do you have realistic expectations about the roles of women in relationships?
- ♥   Do you carry any negative emotions about men, women or love? Are you hard on yourself on a regular basis? In what ways do you see those emotions affecting your ability to attract a great partner?
- ♥   Are you happy with yourself and your life now? Do you know what you really want in a relationship?

As we go forward with this Love Design process, you will be waking up parts of yourself that may have been in hiding. You'll be replacing them with your intuitive power, insight and the clarity needed to *get ready for love* from the inside-out. Let's get started by identifying your life and love phases.

CHAPTER II
IDENTIFY YOUR LIFE & LOVE PHASES

"The unexamined life is not worth living."
– Plato

LET'S GET REAL & EXAMINE YOUR HEART

Now your journey begins! I am asking you to *get real* with your heart and identify your relationship status. This begins by taking a look at the current phase of your life, the situations that you may be experiencing right now in your relationships, and acknowledging that you are the one in control of your life.

You must be honest with yourself about what phase you are in so that you can move ahead, achieve your goals and deepen the connection to your own life and soul. Your current phase determines the necessary actions and the appropriate *tuning* needed to get you back on the road to success.

You must be clear and honest with yourself as well as the people you are dating or meeting. Otherwise, you might be led on or get hurt. At least if you know what the truth is and speak up, both parties can make a conscious choice to get involved or not. There are many life style choices out there and these next few chapters will help you determine where you are in your life right now.

�»— *Get to know your love and life phases as well as the phases a potential partner is experiencing before you get involved.*

Do you currently have a love life? Are you feeling desperate and want a mate so badly that you turn people off with your quiet desperation? Do you *take time for love?* Or, have you given up creating love in your life? Are you still single and dating unavailable people? Are you newly-single and feeling confused about getting back in the game? Are you frustrated or unfulfilled with your current relationship but too afraid to be alone? Are you married and in a funk? Are the sparks missing in your relationship? Did you recently lose your partner because of a serious illness? Are you being pressured by your family to hurry up and get hitched? When it comes to the subject of love and relationships, do you have any unresolved fears?

REALITY CHECK

It's time for a *reality check*! Take a look at where you are in your life, what your goals are now and examine all your options. I am surprised that so many people who attend my classes do not take the time to really understand themselves and their real needs before jumping into the next relationship. When I ask, "When it comes to your love life, what are you looking for right now?" I get answers that are all over the map:

- *Love? Maybe, but I'm not sure.*
- *A friend or companion.*
- *A great husband or wife to build a life with … my soul mate.*
- *A hot lover… since I just want casual sex.*
- *A monogamous life partner… but no marriage for me.*
- *I want nothing right now… dating again seems like a hassle.*
- *Relationships take too much time, so I would like to date occasionally.*
- *Marriage is not for me right now because I am building my company.*
- *I am too busy for love.*
- *My spouse is not into me and all of the romance is gone… I'm not sure what to do.*
- *I'm so confused about the new dating rules, so I will just stay in my current relationship. It's better than being alone.*

Many people are not clear on their goals in relationships, so they keep attracting situations that cause unnecessary stress in their life. Sometimes, they have no activity going on in their love life at all and they wonder why.

⚷ *People appreciate clear communication and want to know where they stand. When you send out mixed signals, you get mixed results. Send clear signals to the people you date and speak your truth.*

STOP NOW to examine your heart and soul. Ask yourself if you even know your place in the love game. Most of us go through phases where we are open, loving and creative, yet we suddenly shut down if we get disappointed. Some people become so negative and shell-shocked that no one could reach them with love even if they tried. Sometimes, you are ready to dive into the depths of passion and love from your core. At other times, you may want to be focused on yourself growing and exploring life alone. Ask yourself:

- *Where am I as a single woman or man?*
- *Am I just looking for casual sex?*
- *Do I want a friend, a life partner or a spouse?*
- *Do I know enough about what I want in a relationship?*
- *Do I want to save my marriage?*
- *Do I want to reignite my current relationship?*
- *Am I wasting my time with the person I'm with now?*
- *Am I doubting that I'll ever find love?*
- *Am I willing to look at how I create my own reality and use this wisdom to create my new love story?*

Many people are desperately seeking love, creating havoc and picking the wrong partners because they don't take time to reflect on themselves. They avoid pain with overworking, drinking, smoking, casual sex, drugs, and or shopping. Yet, they wonder why their love life is not working with their current mate or why they are still alone.

⚷ *By becoming more conscious of your current relationship status, you can design and plan the steps you are willing to take to move forward to reinvent your life.*

There will be many insights along the way to uplift and shift your patterns in relationships. By taking time to understand yourself, you will be in the driver's seat from now on. I see many different layers of growth in the three major love phases that most people are going through in the dating game. To make it easier for you to examine your heart, the next three chapters are broken down so that you can do an honest evaluation of your current love phases.

These Love Phases include:

• Healing From a Breakup

• Single Love Phases

• You're Ready for Love

As you look at your life, you will also become more aware of the phases that the people you are meeting may be experiencing. This is where many singles get off track. They are often in a phase or in phases that are different from the men or women they are dating. Frankly, it is just as important to know their phase as it is to know your own. Listen to your gut and be honest! *Get real* with yourself.

⚷ *Tune into your heart... your inner voice is speaking and guiding you!*

When there is honesty and clarity right from the start, it will keep the record straight. This way, we can all steer clear of unnecessary pain and create what we deeply desire. Some of the important values in creating a strong foundation for relationships are honesty and integrity. Many of us are not even honest with ourselves, let alone with the people we date. Utilize this information to see if you really have a clear sign to move forward and if your phases are compatible. Sometimes we don't read the signs properly and should be slowing down or just walking away.

⚷ *Muster the courage to communicate honestly with your heart and your higher self, and you will gain a better understanding of your needs and what you value most in a relationship.*

GET REAL ♥ REFLECTIONS

♥   What is your current relationship phase?

♥   Are you being honest with yourself and the people you are interested in dating or are currently dating?

♥   Are you sending clear signals and speaking your truth on dates?

Both sexes go through these life and love phases and the *secret* is to be aware, conscious and honest. As you read the next three chapters, write down or mark the phases of love and life that resonate with you. You could be in several of these phases at the same time and realize the people you are meeting are going through them as well. So, let us explore the various love phases and take note of the clues along the way.

CHAPTER III

HEALING FROM A BREAKUP

"When we live with resentment toward another our hearts close down. Letting go of our resentment frees us from placing blame on them and allows us to look toward ourselves for peace."
– Tigress Luv

"One of the most courageous decisions you'll ever make is finally letting go of what is hurting your heart and soul."
– Bridgette Nicole

We have all experienced breakups on many different levels. It could have been somebody you dated for a few months with high expectations, or a long-term relationship that suddenly ended. Below are the various phases that you may be going through during a breakup. These phases apply to both men and women.

"People come into your life for a reason, a season or a lifetime. When someone is in your life for a reason, it is usually to meet a need you have expressed. They have come to assist you through a difficulty, to provide you with guidance and support, and to aid you physically, emotionally or spiritually. They may seem like a Godsend, and truly, they are. They are there for the reason you need them to be. Then, without any wrongdoing on your part, this person will say or do something to bring the relationship to an end. What we must realize is that our need has been met, our desire fulfilled, and their work is done. The prayer you sent up has been answered and now it is time to move on. Some people come into your life for a SEASON, because your turn has come to share, grow, or learn. They bring you an experience of peace or make you laugh. They may teach you something you have never done They usually give you an unbelievable amount of joy. Believe it; it is real...but only for a season. Lifetime relationships teach you lifetime lessons—things you must build upon in order to have a solid emotional foundation. Your job is to accept the lesson, love the person, and put what you have learned to use in all other relationships and areas of your life."

– Author unknown

BREAKUP SHOCK

Are you in shock after a breakup from a long-term relationship or marriage and are suddenly single again? Are you new to the game of love? Are you all shook up about being out there on your own? Are you suddenly in a situation where your mate moved away or was transferred. Has your significant other abruptly left the relationship? Maybe you broke it off, realizing you were not a good match for a long-term relationship? Perhaps you lost your partner to an illness or accident?

This is surely a time of healing and growth and, depending on the type of separation, there is a necessary adjustment period before you are fully ready to move on to another relationship. It takes time to absorb the shock of suddenly living alone and not having that person around.

This phase can be very painful and feels like a divorce—whether it was or not. Even if you were not married, the bond was significant. Sometimes, the disappointment can tear at your heart. At other times, you may feel relieved and excited about your new status and welcome the freedom to explore new relationships.

From a new person's point of view, meeting and getting to know you in this phase could be difficult. They realize that even if you broke off the last relationship, you will still have to go through a separation period from the other person's energy as well as the old lifestyle and habits shared. Consider taking a time-out to recover instead of jumping into a rebound relationship and trying to find someone right away. Many suddenly single people go on a quest for knowledge to learn from their relationship so they do not repeat the past. I assist many singles in this phase, and I suggest that you get support so you can grow into your new life slowly with kindness and openness.

⚷ *During a breakup phase keep your heart open to receiving support and meeting new people. Take time to examine your heart now more deeply than ever before.*

Depending on how you look at it, this can be a time of difficulty and challenge, or one of excitement and transformation.

⚷ *If you meet someone new in a break up phase, communicate your circumstances honestly without telling the entire dramatic story. Most emotionally healthy people generally refrain from getting seriously involved with a person with a broken heart. However, some will hang in there if they are sexually attracted to you and may try to rescue you from your despair.*

Keep your conversations light so you can create new friendships; get to know people slowly as you heal your heart and reinvent yourself.

⚷ *Beware! When you're in a healing phase your heart is in a very vulnerable place. Some people prey on singles in this phase, so go slowly.*

This is a time for regrouping, healing and self-care as you design a new vision for your life. STAY OPEN. You are in the process of learning heart-healing tools, and you will discover many ways to recharge yourself. Take this opportunity to reflect on your core values and the lessons you've learned before you get back out there. Be thankful in advance as you reinvent your life. Take a deep breath and relax.

⚷ *Being suddenly single is usually a blessing in disguise. It's time to heal, recognize past patterns and learn lessons from your most recent relationship before seriously dating again. Don't jump into a relationship too soon out of fear of being alone.*

PASSENGER STILL REMAINING IN YOUR VEHICLE

Do you still have an ex attached to your heart? Is there someone you think of all the time, even though you are out looking for love? If so, you have a *passenger remaining in your vehicle* and the people you date can feel it! You appear to be single, but you still have a lover in your heart that you haven't quite let go of. You may have broken off the relationship and are "just friends" with your ex; or, you may still be having sex with them for fear of being alone. Perhaps your spouse passed away or you lost someone close to you from an illness or accident. You may have recently separated from your ex, but you are still living together to regroup while casually dating other people. You may consider yourself to be back on the market, but you will never be fully present for anyone else with your old lover's energy hanging around. It becomes frustrating because you can't bring dates home or feel free to date. You often hear of couples playing out this scenario while they are separating, but it isn't realistic and typically doesn't work out well.

This passenger is like having a pile of garbage in your car—no one else can take a ride until your car is cleaned out. You truly have a person remaining in your vehicle, which affects your heart and drains your life force. The space is not open and free. You haven't let go…yet!

⚷ *Having a passenger in your vehicle or someone on the sidelines can block you from opening your heart to new love.*

Dating you can be frustrating for the people you are seeing if they desire deeper intimacy and a real relationship.

⚷ *Be honest with the people you are dating about your current situation in order to grant them their fair options. Don't be selfish and use someone as you heal your heart.*

There is nothing worse than dating someone who pretends that they are over someone and doesn't tell the truth. At first, they just want to play around but then, when sex and intimate situations arise, their heartache will surface. It often stays hidden in passive aggressive and unexplained behavior. If you are dating someone like this, you may not even be aware of their lack of presence until you've dated for some time. You will sense that their energy lies somewhere else. I have had clients whose boyfriends or girlfriends were still living with old partners but they weren't informed upfront about their situation. Of course, this caused constant confusion to my clients because their dates were not totally present or being honest.

 *If you sense that something is amiss with a person you are dating, look for signs of someone else in their life: moodiness, inconsistent behavior, secret phone calls and broken plans are good indicators. Use your intuition and ask for clarity on your gut feelings.*

TRUE STORY

One of my clients fell for hard and fast for a man she was dating, named Mark. They were lovers and had an amazing connection. He moved away shortly after they met, and she never got to explore the relationship because of the distance and timing in their lives. Each time a new man came into her life, she could only be halfway in the relationship because Mark remained in her heart and thoughts. Mark would call often to keep the flame alive but they were not in a genuine, committed relationship. He was still claiming that *someday* they would be together. When she came to me for coaching, she was dating an awesome new man but had a block to overcome. She became aware that by having incomplete communication with Mark, she would never be able to move forward with any other man. She was living in the fantasy of *someday*. I informed her that she had *a passenger remaining in her vehicle.* Instead of dragging her new "friend" into a relationship that was unfulfilling, she needed to first detach from Mark or explore the fantasy long distance relationship with him once and for all. By leaving it open and unclear, her heart remained torn between two lovers. She needed to get rid of Mark's energy in her heart and soul.

Her new boyfriend came to me for coaching as well. He told me that the entire time they had been together he felt that the other man's presence was haunting and diminishing the intimacy between them. Her new man supported her in the process by giving her the time and space to let go of Mark. Once she completely moved on, she was free to truly love her new man. Now, they are together in a committed relationship that is deeper than ever. She told the truth and he gave her the space she needed to let go. It all starts with honest communication and getting real with people you date. You have to set yourself free to move on!

If you have a passenger remaining in your vehicle, it's time to drop them off at the next corner in order to create the space for real love. Let go and believe!

COMPLETE BREAKDOWN

If you are in the *complete breakdown* phase or you just went through a bad breakup, you may be a single soul who is depressed, irate, or shut down. You could possibly be experiencing all of these symptoms from time to time. You no longer *believe in love*; perhaps, you're in an emotional rut.

You constantly focus on hurts from the past. You say things like: "Why bother?" "Dating is a pain in the ass," "I am never going to love again," or "I am fed up with the games." On the flip side, you feel so desperate to find someone that you will do anything for love. You cling and hang onto the slightest glimmer of hope of a connection, even if it's a bad one. In bold print, your calling card ought to say, "Co-dependent, needy, fuel drainer." The people you date will run for the hills or, even worse, you may attract someone who's just like you...miserable.

Women and men in this phase try to fill that void by working, partying, shopping, gambling, etc. Some have chronic health problems, eating disorders, serious money challenges, or addictions to sex, alcohol, drugs, or cigarettes. They are constantly complaining and asking for help and or money. Others go into long states of depression, grieving and isolation.

If you are in this phase, you may want to get more help and join a support group, like Alcoholics Anonymous (A.A.) or Sex & Love Anonymous (S.L.A.), and utilize some of the guidelines in this book to help you find the right healing modality.

⚬━ᴣ *Begin the tune-up process by being honest with yourself. Stop being a victim. Complaining will get you nowhere. Get some supportive guidance and heal your life.*

Whatever you are doing to numb your pain, you must be willing to take responsibility for being on the merry-go-round of negative consciousness. Round and round you go with your anger, excuses and complaining— repeating the same behavior and expecting a different outcome. Your negative reactions and sour words make being around you a challenge. If you are in this phase, your gloomy energy can easily drive others away.

⚬━ᴣ *Change your state of mind and try some new activities to get you out of your dark hole. Take a seminar, walk in the woods, write a gratitude list, volunteer your time, get some personal coaching… and keep reading.*

TRUE STORY

I taught a class called "The Smart Man's Guide to Dating, Attracting & Understanding Women" at *The Learning Annex* for many years. On one memorable evening, I had a room full of single men. There was one man sitting in the back who looked exceptionally depressed. I sensed his despair and kept asking him questions during the class. He bought my book, *Love Mechanics,* and set up a number of personal coaching sessions to help get him out of this funk. He suffered from severe depression and had been rejected by many women, who were cruel to him in the past. In addition, he had a very weak support system from his family. After several coaching sessions, he shared that he had started a relationship with a special woman and was happier than ever. He told me that the class had saved his life since this relationship was the first one he had experienced in ten-years. He was very grateful and thanked me. I was touched to know that this work had made such a difference.

I had no idea until I ran into him at a Christmas party months later, that he had considered committing suicide that morning. He told me that he had already bought the ticket to come to my class and he figured before he was going to check out, he'd make one last effort to see why he was unable to achieve success with women. He wanted to confirm his reasoning for taking his own life. He felt worthless and alone.

He said that all the introspection he did after the class made him *wake up* to the good things in his life and opened his heart. He got his power back and created a new vision for his life. It was only a few weeks later that he was introduced to his new girlfriend at a party. He is now happily married and has a child on the way. He was hours away from death, only to gain a renewed outlook on life. Thank God he listened to his intuition and came to class that night. It led him to do the deeper work required to change his life for the better. I suppose it was his inner soul or his angels that guided him there that evening. I am so grateful he opened up, changed his state of mind and chose a new path that helped him finally find the love he deserved.

There is light at the end of every dark tunnel and by taking action and doing the inner work, your life will be transformed. Seek help and open up to divine guidance. Pray if you believe in a higher power. Even if you don't have religious or spiritual beliefs, you will be surprised at how asking for assistance opens doors in strange and magical ways. Be open when help and guidance show up! You may hear a song that inspires you, or you may pick up a magazine with an article that changes your perspective. A friend may show up to lend a kind ear of support and guidance. Look for the signs all around you.

☙ *Proclaim that you are ready for a change and you will be led by your new intentions. Ask for strength from your higher self and it will come pouring in. Add in a dash of faith and you can manifest miracles.*

24

SINGLE PARENT WITH TIMING ADJUSTMENTS

If you are newly-divorced or a single parent, you have various *timing adjustments* when it comes to dating. You may be feeling sad, vulnerable and perplexed about the breakup. Conversely, you may be relieved of the burden of "the ex" and excited to be moving forward. A client of mine said it was like his parole was over and he was "free at last." Realize that you now have a chance to reinvent your life. So, take your time.

⚏ *Being a newly-single mom or dad is a shock, even if it was a good decision to move on. Healing is happening whether you want to admit it or not. Having children involved increases the adjustment time and stress as you go through the transition. Some men fear dating women with kids while others are open to it.*

Being a single parent is a tremendous job, a big responsibility and the children are hugely impacted by your separation or divorce. It takes patience and communication to work out child support, custody details and schedules for the care of the children. The children's emotions and lifestyles are turned upside down, so it is very important to put their interests first. Once the new routine has been established with your former partner and the children, you can then take time to regroup and reinvent yourself.

⚏ *If you are single with no kids, realize that many people you meet over thirty could be single parents. If you get involved, you will need to consider the amount of time and energy they will need to spend with their children. Keep an open mind. There are many great singles out there in this phase who are open to love again.*

You may be dating a single parent right now and wonder, "Can I handle all this?" *Get real* about where you are at with your goals. Ask yourself, "Do I want to deal with the circumstances of dating a newly separated or soon-to-be divorced man with kids?"

⚏ *Meeting someone who is recently divorced is okay. Just slow down and don't rush into anything serious too soon. Everyone involved feels the pain of going through divorce. Many divorcees did enjoy being married and learned over time that they just didn't choose the right partner.*

Many of my clients are newly divorced, and they want to be nurtured and in love, just like you do. Just because they have kids doesn't mean they aren't open to love again. They just need to take their time! Take it slowly, build a strong foundation and get to know them, and their relationship with their children as well as their ex. Otherwise, you may end up being the healing angel who is left in the parking lot alone after the this person gets back into balance.

⚷ *There are many widowed or divorced singles who would love to be with one partner. Don't rule them out; they may be rusty in the dating game and it's all about the timing.*

Many men and women who are newly separated or suddenly single from a longtime partner show up in my classes shell-shocked. They are not in a great place to create a secure foundation with a new partner. I tell them to reach out for reinforcements and begin building a new network if they don't have friends for emotional strength. Enrolling in online coaching and seminars, or reading dating after divorce books and blogs are great places to start. In addition to your family, friends, love coach and therapist, joining groups on Meetup.com as well as other social networking groups are easy ways to rebuild your social life. Any way you slice it, being single again is not an easy adjustment and you need support. You have to separate your things, move and regroup. Money issues and custody challenges require a lot of energy and adjustment time for everyone. You may be healing from the resentment, pain or disappointment.

TRUE STORY

A newly-divorced mother with two small children joined my *Get Real about Love* seminar. She had been in an abusive marriage for many years and wanted to open her heart to love again. She seriously doubted that she would find someone who would deal with all of her drama or her kids, so we started by working on her heart. She was a stunning fitness trainer with a thriving business but she was carrying so much anger that she had developed a hard edge about men and dating. It turned out she had been brought up in an abusive family and needed to heal her *love imprints.*

After deep heart-healing work, she regained her confidence, sent out new green light signals and began attracting men like a magnet. She learned how to be happy and balanced without a man and, most importantly, reclaimed her feminine sparkle! A few months later, she met a handsome, caring and successful businessman who was divorced with two kids of his own. He courted her and asked her to be in a committed relationship within a few months. They both had healing to do, and now have the foundation and communication skills needed to make their relationship grow. Their children are all happy and will have strong role models to show them that love does work! Through mutual respect, time and working on their fears about merging families, they now are together and headed towards marriage.

The fact is that people don't want a rescue mission, so you need to present your situation in a positive light, otherwise they may be cautious about getting involved. At the same time, you are learning great life lessons. Your situation is unique to you and your particular set of circumstances. It may take some time to rebuild, so go easy on your heart and ask for support.

⊶⚓ *Many people are leery about dating a bitter, divorcee—so you may want to do some more healing or just go out casually to get back in the dating game. Do not dump your "horror" divorce stories on the men you date.*

If you are dating a man or woman who is repairing their life, especially a single parent, tell them to come back when they are legally separated and have done some healing on their own. It's important for them to resolve their custody situation as well as setting up their new living space. I know this firsthand since I tried to heal some of the men in my past that were in this phase. It's all about timing and honest communication.

⊶⚓ *Believe me, if a person with a broken heart says they aren't ready for love, you will waste your precious time and often years will go by trying to repair them.*

For all you single parents, there are thousands of divorced people looking to connect as well as singles who wouldn't mind dating someone with children. Many single parents doubt there would be people interested in them... this is not true!

☞ *If you have your life together, you have a greater chance of connecting. Your goal is to become balanced, happy and whole as a single parent to attract a perfect match for your situation.*

Many women meet men who are newly-single with children. When I met my husband, he was a single father and had been married twice before. If I had listened to all the fear and negative "crap" people warned me about dating a recently separated, soon-to-be divorced dad, I would have run for the hills. Although these facts would normally be red flags, I followed my heart and told everyone to mind their own business. Take my advice... listen to your heart, go slowly and take the relationship for a *test drive!* I loved the thought of being a step mom, but I still had some concerns. We made it work by using open communication and taking the time to build a strong foundation of friendship. I think single dads have a level of responsibility some single men do not possess because they haven't experienced being a father. You can find out a lot about a man by seeing how he deals with his kids and his ex-wife.

☞ *Don't be quick to judge if a man is a single father. Depending on how open your heart is, the timing and the circumstances—you could meet the man of your dreams.*

THE TIMING IS OFF: THE MIDDLE OF A BREAKUP OR DIVORCE

You might meet an amazing person, but they are in the middle of a complicated situation. Oftentimes, dating someone during this phase doesn't flow well. It could be their location, a job transfer, educational obligations, work requirements, family commitments, a pending divorce or a breakup. You may feel a connection, but the two of you will most likely be out of sync since the timing is off.

If you meet someone who claims that they're getting a divorce "soon" or breaking up "as soon as they get a new place, job or money," let them go through the process of legally separating, breaking up or moving out before you get involved. It's too much drama and will only cause unnecessary stress.

☛ *Love can be frustrating and painful if the person is right but the timing is off. You can't force it. Perhaps it could work in the future, but don't live your life waiting for someone else to be totally present with you when they are in the middle of a breakup.*

I meet many clients that describe the person they're dating by saying, "He (or she) is not happy with their current partner and will be moving out soon. They claim they never have sex and they're dating others, so they can date me now." My advice is, "Since both of you are feeling a strong connection and it feels so right, just slow it down and find out the real story. They could be recently separated with no intention of getting a divorce and just checking out their options on the dating scene." When I was single and dating, I met guys online who were "separated" and wanted to be "casual" while rebuilding their self-esteem. Often, they admitted that they were interested to see if they could attract women while trying to make it work with their wives. Look at the reality or you will be in the middle of a big mess. Why would you want to sneak around, never knowing when they would be free to talk or see you? Would you want to make love to a person who is living with or married to someone else? You deserve more than that in your life. Let them clean up their mess first and tell them to stop calling you until they're available. He or she is *not* ready to be committed to you right now.

☛ *Being the other woman or man and not being able to really date or talk freely is energy-draining and unhealthy for your self-esteem. You could easily waste years of your life. If this "magical connection" is meant to happen with this person, the relationship will progress naturally.*

Step out of this sticky situation until your new love interest creates an environment and a space for a real relationship. Otherwise, you will become the "other woman " (or man) and be totally frustrated. Often this timing challenge is a blessing in disguise, so trust in the timing of the universe. Until then, live life to the fullest. You can be supportive from a distance with no *secret* meetings or sexual rendezvous. Move on and date other people since they need to take care of business first!

I have had many clients call me in pain and anguish on account of being attached to an unavailable person and their needs were not being met. I always ask, "Is this painful, heart-wrenching situation really what you want in your life right now? Is it the kind of love you think you deserve?" Most often, my clients thought the "sweet heart" they were dating would be free right away and were swept away in the moment. Look at the real picture; they're cheating on someone else who may be unaware of you. Ask for the truth. How will you ever trust them when they aren't telling their partner the truth? If they can lie so easily, they may eventually lie to you too.

☙ *If the timing is off with someone you're dating, just walk away and trust in love. The fact that you have the insight to see that the timing is not right and that you can move on, shows that you have faith in yourself. By letting them go, it creates a new space for love to come in or for the other person to step up. If this love is meant to be, it will be.*

Get real, trust your gut and take the leap of faith to speak your truth. You are sending a message that you want an available partner, not one who will be dividing their time and energy between two lovers. Express from your heart, "I want to live my life with integrity and I have to honor your partners' position. I do care for you, but I don't feel right about us being together until this situation is resolved. I am a one-man woman and you are someone else's man! I don't like to share. Go take care of your business and I don't want to be involved. If you respect me, you will honor my wishes. Who knows what the future may bring and I wish you only the best. I am keeping my heart open to a person who is available to love me fully and completely."

This is a powerful affirmation... it works! If you can stand in your power, the perfect solution or situation will reveal itself. Keep the faith.

You want to be with a person who is available and create the space to build a strong foundation of trust. If someone is messing around with you and their partner doesn't know about it, you will most likely never trust their word in the future. If this love is meant to be, nothing will stop it!

TRUE STORY

This amazing story was sent in from a client who had a passenger remaining in her vehicle... and yes, he was married! Here is her story: "About five years ago, I was in the process of letting go of a ten-year, tumultuous and life consuming relationship obsession with a man. He and I did the *moth to flame* dance for years, and eventually, he married another woman. He still reached out to me and we sporadically engaged with each other for the first five years of his marriage. At one point, we had a short-lived affair. At that time, I couldn't handle the hard fact that he was not ready to leave his wife right away. I was in bed with him one night in a hotel when his wife called, and I was hit in the head with reality. I had wasted years of my life waiting!

This relationship was keeping me in a number of unhealthy situations. First, none of the men I dated during that time had a shot. I then picked men that I wasn't attracted to, who were financially unstable, or that I didn't even get along with. As long as they didn't compare to him, I was convinced that he would come back to me. I felt I had to keep myself available by not allowing another love in. I hit rock bottom. I was having panic attacks and wasn't sleeping or eating properly. I even went on an anti-everything medication for three months.

It was at this point that I went to the *Agape International Spiritual Center* as a broken and hopeless girl filled with darkness. Soon after I sat down in service, I felt a warm hand on my back touch me near my heart and she calmly said, 'Whoever he is, he is not worth all this pain... let's talk.'

I knew at that moment that God had placed a messenger in front of me to help alter the course of my life. It wasn't until later that I realized Renée had indeed peered into my soul that evening, had given me support and insightful words of wisdom that changed me forever. Renée helped me see how important it was to stand for my true values, have faith in myself, and trust that if I let my ex go and kept my heart open for someone available … it would come to pass. After working with Renée for a short time, I cut off all ties with my *prince charming*. I blocked his emails, took his name out of my phone and erased any sappy songs on my iPod that reminded me of him. I mourned and mourned. I was able to let go in a literal and figurative sense. Renée and I met several times for coaching and each time she gave me more and more inner work to do. She continued to help me out of the old thought patterns with new *love scripts* and *tune-up tools* to build my self-esteem. I felt stronger and I applied her wise advice. What I loved about working with Renée was that she was not only a spiritual guide, but she was practical and always upfront with me.

Once I was free of the self-imposed prison that I had created, I began to trust that there must be something better out there and that my *prince charming* was, in fact, not so charming after all. I came to believe that what God had in store for me was going to be magnificent. I finally started to date again.

Within a few months and through a twist of fate, I met the man I knew I was meant to spend the rest of my life with. From the first moment that I saw my now husband, I knew that he was my soul mate, life partner and the love of my life. That night I had the thought, 'Oh my God, I just met the man I am going to marry.' That was years ago, and we have been together ever since. In fact, we just celebrated our third wedding anniversary, and it was magical.

Because I was given the right tools, I was able to open my heart and soul to a man I cherish more than anything in the world. A man I may not have even met had I tried to do it all on my own. Renée, you changed my life that day! Thank you for making me see that dating a married man was empty, unful-filling and blocked the space for *real love* to come to me. I believed in myself. If I had stayed in my dismal situation, this would never have happened. Thank you for waking me up and for helping me to allow my *true love* to enter into my life. He has brought me more joy than anything I could have ever even imagined. Renée, you are my angel!"

⚊⚊ *If it's the right love at the wrong time, it will come back to you in the perfect time or the right person will show up in the meantime. Believe in yourself and in LOVE!*

Dead-End Street: You Stayed Too Long

You have been dating someone for a long time (2-10 years or more) and know for sure that you will not marry this person, or that they don't intend to marry you. You may want to breakup but you don't want to deal with the loneliness or getting back into the singles scene. You are not telling the truth about what is happening in your relationship for fear of hurting your partner and having to start over. They sense the situation, detect that you are not happy and may question you about making a commitment. You avoid discussions about the future or making marriage plans by telling them you need more time. On the flip side, your partner may make excuses and you can stay stuck, unable to move on. In most cases, you're probably filled with some fear about getting back out there. *You stayed too long!* This is a sure sign that it's time to get honest and move on for the benefit of both parties. It's time to *get real*.

⚊⚊ *Do not waste one moment in a dead-end relationship! Time is so precious and life is too short. They will be more hurt if you allow it to go on for too much longer. You will be fooling yourself to think that your partner will eventually change their mind. Your soul knows the truth. So, don't stay too long and waste years trying to make it work.*

TRUE STORY

I had a client who was getting divorced after 30+ years of marriage. She had three grown children and was reinventing her life when we met. She met a handsome new man on the internet shortly after her separation and rapidly fell in love. They had the romance, passion and chemistry but in the back of her mind, she knew she probably wouldn't marry him. They had religious differences and money issues that surfaced after a few months of dating, but the chemistry was awesome. Although she was Jewish, she knew in her heart that she wouldn't be able to live up to his expectations of becoming a strict Orthodox Jew. She thought she could convince him that they could work it out and compromise on some of the constricting Orthodox rules, but she was mistaken. She was a powerful and successful businesswoman with many passions and, since he had a flexible schedule working in real estate, he fit nicely into her busy life. He would see her a few times a week, and they would have Shabbat dinners and romantic dates. They had met each other's friends and it was a comfortable fit for a few years.

The pedal hit the metal when he wanted to get married and she was confronted with the truth. She was unsure if she could deal with his low energy as well as a few other differences in their lifestyles. In addition, she did not want to diminish her current life style by adopting his strict religious practices, which she would have to live with for the rest of her life. Dating was one thing, but committing to a life partner who wouldn't bend on this issue was a serious concern. She kept pretending that she could subscribe to his Orthodox traditions but in reality she was not getting *real* with him or herself. This further strained the relationship and he insisted that she commit to a wedding date, or he would move on. She set a date, yet as the time approached, she kept coming up with new reasons why they should wait. He patiently waited a few more months then exploded in frustration. Although he had wonderful qualities, she knew that he wasn't the *man of her dreams*.

After six years, they finally ended their relationship. She was able to let go of her fears and is now open to meeting someone more aligned with her values and life goals. She had *stayed too long* and was hanging on, hoping things would eventually change. By expanding her vision, she learned from this experience and was able to move forward in faith to meet the right person. Her ex-fiancé ended up marrying an Orthodox Jewish woman and achieved his love vision. Now, it's her turn to magnetize her perfect match by using everything she has learned from this experience and continue to be true to her heart.

⚙━🗝 *Tell the truth, listen to your gut and let go. Trust in God's plan, especially where religion is involved. Don't lead a mate or yourself down a dead-end street. By being honest, you can often remain friends and support each other to find true love.*

GET REAL ❤ REFLECTIONS

❤ What are the blessings you received from your most recent relationship? Can you identify your past relationship patterns and the lessons you've learned?

❤ Are you listening to the clear signs about the people you are dating? What are your gut feelings about the situation? Are you are honestly following your inner guidance?

❤ *Get real* with your heart. Have you stayed in a relationship for too long when you knew it wasn't right for you? Did you fear hurting your partner or having to start over? Are you aligned with your core values and what is essential for you to be happy in your current relationship?

❤ Do you believe in yourself and that you will find *real love*? Are you hanging on to the hopes of someone coming back into your life that isn't available? Are you being realistic about your current situation? Really??

Now that we've looked at the breakup phases, I hope you have gained more clarity and understand what can happen when you hang on to relationships that no longer work. Now you can move forward to create the type of relationship you deserve. Let's move on to examine the various Single Love Phases.

CHAPTER IV
SINGLE LOVE PHASES

"If you do what you've always done, you'll get what you've always got."
– Mark Twain

According to statistics, people are waiting longer to get married or to settle down. Since there are so many choices for singles out there, I wanted to illustrate several different phases that people may be experiencing. You might be in a phase where you enjoy living solo and there are a variety of these phases that we will explore! So, which one are you choosing as a single soul out there playing the dating game? Just make sure you communicate this honestly with the people you meet!

LOW PRESSURE

In the *low pressure* phase, you are either uninterested in a long-term relationship or do not have the desire to be monogamous at this time in your life. Perhaps you are new to dating or just beginning to adjust to your new single status. Maybe you have done some healing and you just want to hang out, be friends with the new people you meet and just check out your options. You enjoy dating various people, and you may or may not be sexually intimate with them. Whatever your state of mind, you do not want any pressure from dating. Truthfully, you still want to explore new adventures and new people.

☐━ᴛ *Get real with the people you are dating so they know their options and vice versa. They will respect and honor your honesty. If you are having casual sex and know that your partner wants more, you must be clear in your communication. Singles tell me that evasiveness is what drives them crazy.*

By doing this, you can save your partner a lot of heartache, and you won't have the guilt many people carry around knowing that they aren't in it for the "long haul."

Don't play with other people's hearts and souls. Building a foundation with the truth helps to avoid pain later. Men can get hurt too. Sex often bonds men, and many of my male clients experience women who just want to play around and have them around as casual lovers. Men may fall in love with a woman who told them the truth up front, but they didn't listen. Some women only want casual sex. I'd say most men don't turn down "friends with benefits" opportunities, but often their feelings can change over time. Both sexes need to open up and *get real* with each other when they feel a shift in the relationship. Don't delude yourself or lead your casual lover on—honesty is always the best policy.

⚷ *When someone you're dating tells you that they want no pressure, you need to listen, go slowly and take caution. Pay attention to the signs along the way, especially if you are in a different phase and looking for more than a casual date or sex. Listen clearly to the messages like, "Honey, I just want to keep this light and free right now," or "I am happy just being friends and lovers for now."*

Use your intuition. When both parties are clear and honest, it is surprising how many people are open to this phase. Often people just want the freedom to explore with multiple partners.

OPEN RELATIONSHIPS

People are designing all types of options these days. I have met many people who have chosen polygamy as an option. Polygamy is a marriage or commitment, which includes more than two partners. When a man is married to more than one wife at a time, there is no marriage commitment bond between the wives. When a woman is married to more than one husband at a time, it is called polyandry, and there is no marriage, commitment, or bond between the husbands. If a marriage includes multiple husbands and wives, it can be called group marriage.

Polyamory is being in love with more than one person at one time. Some *polyamorous* relationships have living arrangements in which multiple adults form one family, share the finances, care for children and share sexual access with one another. However, they do not normally form a legal marriage. The bottom line is there are many people into this open relationship lifestyle, so you need to be clear and upfront with your potential partners.

⚿ *Speak your Truth and you will attract what you ask for. There is no judgment about your lifestyle choices; only choices that help you create a relationship that works for you.*

COMFORTABLE & CONFIDENT

You have finally let go of your last relationship and are enjoying a *comfortable and confident* time in your life. You are a happy free agent and can do whatever you want, whenever you want, with no residual pain from the past. Most singles come to this place when the healing process is finished. In this phase, you've shifted gears to a new level about what you deserve; you are out again and feeling on top of your game. It's a great place to be. You are dating new people, but you are in no rush to jump into a long-term relationship at this time. You know when you go out on a date and you are clear that they're not *the one;* you are able to tactfully tell them the truth and move on.

The *comfortable and confident* phase holds an important key to creating your future. When old patterns resurface, you now know how to process through them. You are living in the now and your heart is open. So have fun and explore your new relationships, and you will consistently create new opportunities as well as connections with interesting prospects.

⚿ *When you're not needy or desperate, you will magnetize other singles in this phase. You're now in the driver's seat of your love life. When you are comfortable and empowered, magic happens!*

SERIAL MONOGAMIST: RIDING SOLO

You claim that you are looking for *real love* and want to fit someone into your life, on your terms. You may have dated many amazing people, yet you eventually find fault with all of them. Your standards may be set so high that you make it impossible for anyone to fit into your life. This could be one of your *love imprints* and an on-going pattern that keeps you shielded. You hear friends and family say, "Wow, this person is perfect for you!" Then, you pull out the list of their faults and prove why they just aren't "the one". In your heart of hearts, something is telling you that you want to be in a loving relationship, but you know yourself and can't commit to a long-term partnership.

Potential partners may say you are selfish and thinking only of yourself and your needs. Is it true? Are you a *serial monogamist*? Do you like the first few months of a relationship then find a reason to move on? Are you narcissistic? Do you make partners jump through hoops to override the barriers to your heart? Are you a commitment-phobic? Do you fear losing your independence? Or, could it be that you can't trust in love? What are you running from? Could it be that you're avoiding looking at yourself?

There is something going on deep inside of you, but rather than face the truth you look outside for a quick fix or the next "perfect" partner. Honestly, it is your fear that keeps you stuck in this pattern, and you need to take a good look at how that fear has been running your life. Half of your heart wants to go deep and the other half thinks that once a partner sees *the real you*, they may not like you at all. The first challenge is to face your fears and the reality that you are the one keeping *real love* at arm's length.

The other challenge is that you will have to change your current *modus operandi*, and you might not want to take the time. You might say you enjoy this single lifestyle, but sometimes when you are alone in bed at night those internal voices are calling you out to tell the truth! If you want to find *real love*, you will have to continue this inner work, break some habits and alter your comfortable routines. In the following chapters, we will be exploring what it takes to open your heart and moving one step closer to discovering what is blocking you. This may seem overwhelming right now and you may wonder:

- Can I ever have a real relationship and truly be happy?
- Can I honestly fit someone into my life this time?

- Do I really want to do all the work it is going to take to go deeper?
- Will I be able to share my space after being solo for so long?
- Your heart knows the truth.

☛ *The only way to shift out of the serial monogamous phase is to be honest with yourself and do the inner work with an open mind. Examine the impossible expectations you impose on potential partners. Could these just be your way of maintaining distance and control? Realize that these expectations are a symptom of your underlying fears.*

As independent people, we often have such high standards about love that we end up building huge walls of protection around our hearts.

☛ *Let go of impossible expectations and stay open to love all around you. When you become more loving and open with yourself, you will magnetically attract your perfect match.*

SECURING YOUR FOUNDATION: FOCUSED ON CAREER

You are in the foundation phase: focused on building your career, setting goals for your future and achieving them step-by-step. You may be back in school getting an advanced degree or in the process of changing jobs. You are very committed to security and may not have time to nurture a full-time relationship. You are in the process of securing and laying down the cornerstones for your life.

In my love coaching with numerous students, I hear that the challenges of school and work do not allow for much socializing face to face. Students feel that they are constantly on the run from their jobs to school to the study hall. In this day and age, thousands of us are back in school getting advanced degrees while still working full-time.

Many people are waiting longer to get married and are developing their careers before jumping into long-term commitments. Some students have great social skills, while the left-brainers, who have studied for years, need to get back into balance after school has ended. The divorce rate is high for doctors, surgeons, dentists, engineers, and lawyers. This is largely due to the high stress and long hours of required study—two factors that often eliminate time for socializing.

It can be a challenge developing people skills during those grueling hours at medical, law, engineering or business school. Many highly educated professionals attend my seminars to brush up on the people skills never taught in universities. I would observe people at my Rapid Dating and Networking events who were not comfortable meeting a new person, even for a brief 4-5 minute interaction. Learning how to build a good rapport and be a good conversationalist are invaluable skills. For most people, building confidence takes practice.

⚭ *If you are dating a student or are in school, a relationship may not be a priority for you at this time. It can be a challenge to date or connect with classmates, so it's important to take a few hours a week to consciously create time for social interaction. Communicate the truth about your situation.*

If you are a younger woman dating a man just out of college, he may still be developing his career and discovering his place in the world. This is often the first serious relationship where younger women get hurt since they spent a few years going steady with a man in school and expect it to go long-term. Once men get out of school, they may want to lock down a secure job and explore the world before settling down—this is where heart wounds are often created. Communicate!

⚭ *If you are ready for a real relationship, then you must listen and read the clear signals from potential matches to avoid heartache. They may not have the time to focus on you.*

Some people may be developing their career and still desire to have a partner and build a future together in this phase. If you meet someone who wants a relationship, it is imperative to be honest because you are simultaneously working on yourself. Let them know where the focus of your energy is going and that you don't want to feel pressured since you are busy restructuring your life and career. They may also be in a similar situation, dealing with a career change, or in the process of re-evaluating their life.

☯ *For successful, driven people, their career is often their sense of power. If you meet someone who is reinventing their career in challenging times, they may not put love first since they are busy rebuilding their foundation.*

In this crazy, ever-changing economy, we all need to be aware of our inner strengths, "keep the faith" and be open to others who are going through career changes or are back in school. Many super successful people are back to securing their vehicle and reinventing themselves after losing power positions in the corporate world. Many of my clients will say, "I have to be with a person who has a secure career." I say, "You need to see their potential and believe in them, whether they are a young rising star securing their livelihood or someone starting all over again because of the changing times."

☯ *Most often people feel that they have to be secure before they can commit to a relationship for the long haul. Money should not be the driving force to fall in love with someone.*

As a result of our lifestyle choices and fast-paced society, men still feel the pressure to be the breadwinners in the relationship, even though many women today are independent and make as much or more money as them. Relationships are a co-creation and men should not be the only source and supplier of our needs. Both sexes need to feel fulfilled and secure so that they can create a strong foundation for a relationship.

☯ *Our mates want to please us and need a supportive partner who doesn't pressure them if they are in a reinvention phase.*

Money comes and goes and can be gone in an instant! These times are forcing us all to dig a little deeper. Don't rely on anyone to be your main source of security. Many people can provide you with the emotional support you need during this important restructuring phase in your life, as long as you have clear boundaries and maintain good communication. Otherwise, you are likely to cause a lot of distress or pain from not being ready to commit since you are busy working on yourself. Planning and communicating are essential in this phase. Tune in and really listen, so you can discover if the person you meet has the time for dating.

⚷ *Being honest about where you are in life can save you anguish and frustration. If both partners understand what it takes to keep the flame going, then moving forward and co-creating a winning relationship is possible.*

A HIGH-PERFORMANCE WONDER WOMAN OR SUPER MAN

You work too much! You are an on-the-go businesswoman or man working round the clock. You have a strong commitment to your work and personal goals—you have a lot to watch over. You are already successful and have to continue to work hard to maintain your level of success.

If this describes you, you may find it challenging to get out to meet new people or date because your energy is focused on work, work, work! Because of the high-performance and steady maintenance it takes to stay on top, the men or women, in your life must be patient. Dating you can be very frustrating because you are driven by your power, passion, building as well as maintaining your business, keeping up with your competition, making money and achieving success. Usually, when powerful, highly intelligent people desire to relax and play, they seek an understanding, non-demanding partner who appreciates all their hard work, pampers and spoils them.

The problem arises when your goal-focused lifestyle clashes with the needs and desires of your significant other (if you have one), friends, family and associates in your life. You must help them all to see that it isn't personal. The fact is that you are on a quest. The people you date may be part of your support team and your inspiration, or they may be on their own path to success. This high-performance syndrome goes both ways. Times have changed and women work just as long and hard as men. Balancing work, home, kids, your family, religion, fitness, eating right and a relationship can be stressful. Even with no children, your life can get out of balance. Some busy couples may miss the chance to have kids entirely if they keep thinking "someday" it will all work out. Many high-performance people marry, share their lives and grow together. It can work as long as there is a clear understanding with good, ongoing communication and lots of appreciation on both sides.

⚭ *The romance can definitely fade when someone is too focused on their work. When this occurs, the people in their lives feel underappreciated and undernurtured.*

Hundreds of people surveyed stated that their significant other works too much and they miss the romance and quality time. They are happy for the success of their partner, but what is it all for? To live at the office. To be constantly checking emails or on the phone? To never have time to enjoy the money. Where is the sex? Romance? Passion? This is a serious challenge for many successful couples in today's society.

⚭ *If you or your partner handles your mobile devices more than each other, then you definitely have a challenge to overcome. We need to stop the insanity and focus on sacred time with our partners.*

Many of the powerful clients I coach or see at events, whether they are dating or married, often want and expect to be understood as well as pampered by the partners in their lives. However, they send mixed signals and get mixed results. Quite simply, people learn how to treat us by example. So if you want someone to cherish and adore you, it is essential to give them the love and appreciation that you want to receive in return. Most people can tell if you are coming from the heart. As you learn more about how the person you are dating receives and gives love, you can create a lasting connection.

⚭ *When you lead with your feminine energy, you are literally training your partner to love you the way that you want to be loved. It's a magical art that all women need to master.*

The men I interview often say, "Successful *wonder women* expect a lot and often don't give back what we want to receive: appreciation, affection and quality time." They add, "These busy women are controlling and demanding and most men don't feel like being manipulated or bossed around. Women need to realize that most men will not go the distance with a ball buster." You must learn to switch gears after work if you want new results. It takes practice to remove the *wonder woman* cape when you are used to running the show. You need to create daily rituals and down time to get into the "love zone" after work! Take a *get real* look at what you are producing in your life. Are you getting the results you want in your personal life? Are you really balanced and happy? Do you have any time to reflect on what's most important to you? Join me for my Love Rituals class and get into your feminine energy to learn how to magnetize your partner.

⚷ *A man is not a business deal…and men often comment that they feel like they are being fit into our lives like an appointment. Men need to feel wanted and businesswomen often send out unavailable and controlling vibes that turn men off! They do not like those vibes at all and, even if they are attracted to you, they will not tolerate your hectic schedule for very long. Instead, they will find a woman who has time for love!*

Then there is the *reality check* of having kids with a wonder woman. When you add the conversation of having a child into the mix, some couples just can't see how it will fit in the picture they have created. I hear clients say, "If movie stars can have kids after forty, so can I." Yes, it's true that many women are healthy and fertile enough to still conceive after forty, yet they often put pressure on the men they are dating since they are running out of time.

⚷ *Wake up, ladies! Your fertile eggs don't last forever. Many men freak out if you're over forty and say, "I want a few kids I can easily get in vitro fertilization… no problem." Hello!*

Most men are conditioned to want to procreate naturally. They claim they often feel pressured by bossy businesswomen who think that it's no big deal to implant their frozen eggs with sperm for $10,000-$30,000 with no guarantees.

⚷ *Men ask me and wonder, "If she has no time for me now, how will she be a good mother for our kids?" Ladies… men want women who have time for love!*

Is this you? If so, it's time to *wake up!* There will always be an important meeting, the next big deal and, of course, the promise to take a few days off soon. Don't wait until a tragedy strikes to slow down. I never expected this *wake-up* call when it hit me!

TRUE STORY

I was traveling at warp speed as my *Rapid Dating* business was expanding. I would constantly hear my mother's voice saying, "Honey, slow down so a man can catch up to you!" I was flying from city to city for my media tour, interviewing with radio and TV reporters while training people to host events. With all the growth and excitement, I was traveling and working so much that I had to squeeze in my dates whenever I could make the time. I was a *wonder woman* for sure! I was excited to be going home in May for my godmother's wedding to slow down and celebrate with my family.

My friends rarely saw me, and though they were thrilled for my success, they wished I had more time to play. I'd say, "Soon, I'll take some time off." I had promised myself that "Once I" had my company off and running, I would look seriously at my love priorities and play time. In early February I was set up on a blind date with a handsome man named Tony. I was excited since he was family-oriented and had his own business. I was only seeing him once or twice a week, so it was a slow moving romance. We did have chemistry and he claimed he was looking for a committed relationship, but I was in no rush. We had just started to get closer when this devastating tragedy happened.

Little did I know that it would take the sudden death of my mother Angela to slow me down and finally wake me up to the priorities in my life. I can assure you that losing my mother was not the way I had planned to *take time for love.*

My mom was having a simple routine heart valve procedure on May 9th and I was flying home the following week for my Aunt BeBe's wedding. I was to appear on Dick Clark's show, *The Other Half,* on the day my mom's surgery was scheduled. My mother insisted that I stay in Los Angeles to be on the show and assured me that she had enough support from our family. She said I would be there "right on time" when I flew back for the wedding, since that would give her a few days to recover. She added, "I don't want you to miss the chance to be on NBC. So keep spreading your magic, honey. I'd hate to have you miss that show just to see me sleeping in a recovery room with so many relatives in the waiting room. I know you'll be with me in your heart." I spoke to her the morning of her operation and she was in great spirits. I asked, "What if something goes wrong Mom?" She replied, "I am not going anywhere. I have places to go, people to see and things to do. I'll be at the wedding, so no need to change your ticket and spend all that money. The doctor said this is a simple procedure to put a quick stint in my heart. It should take less than an hour... it's nothing serious." The last thing she said to me was, "Just put your hand on your heart... I'm always there. I love you and I'll see you soon."

I had a bad feeling in the pit of my stomach when I hung up. I asked my dear friend Herb to come support me in the morning and we prayed for a successful surgery. A few hours passed and I knew something was seriously wrong. I called my sister's cell phone and the surgeon was announcing that there were complications. As they tried to lift her heart for the quick repair, it fell apart "like dried hamburger meat" in the surgeon's hands. They tried to repair her heart but nothing was working. The tissue was too thin to sew up and the glue wasn't holding it together. They kept her on life support, hoping to find a heart to replace hers. We had to wait to see if they could find a match.

I snapped into action to get home as soon as possible. I called Tony, told him the situation and asked if he could take me to the airport right away. He said, "I'll be there in one hour!" My friend Herb called the airlines for me as I frantically packed my bags. Herb had to leave for work and I was in a state of shock. I said, "I wish I had someone here with me right now." Just as he was getting ready to leave, my wish was granted.

I received a phone call from my dear friend Scott, who happened to be down the street visiting from Arizona. He came right over to offer moral support and I felt truly blessed to be surrounded by such incredible friends at such a sensitive time. Another hour passed as we prayed for a miracle and Scott gently rubbed my head to keep me calm. I suddenly felt my mother's presence and at the same time Scott said, "Renée your mother is here with us right now." Then, I saw her standing at the side of my bed smiling at me with a look of peace on her face. In her soft voice she said: "I love you Renée and I'll see you soon." At that very moment, the phone rang and I heard my brother Bobby's voice saying, "Renée, Mom just died. They couldn't find a new heart in time."

I heard the deep sobbing coming from my entire family and my father held the phone to her ear so that I could say goodbye. I said, "Mom, I am so sorry I wasn't there. You are with me always, I love you, and I'll see you soon. Please come visit me." I could hear all of my family saying their sad farewells. I kept hoping this was a bad dream and I couldn't believe she was really gone. I had just spoken to her a few hours ago. I was numb.

Tony showed up and whisked me off to the airport. I couldn't believe that I was on my way home for my mother's funeral. Poor Tony wasn't sure what to say or how to console me. He just held me until I had to go catch my flight. As I kissed him goodbye, a flight attendant friend of mine just so happened to pass by and asked me what was wrong. I shared the news that my mom had just passed away. She lovingly offered to escort me to my flight. By some chance, she happened to be on the same flight and had me upgraded to first class. I felt very lucky to have all the support I needed that day. It was as if a group of angels were sent right on time. As the plane took off, I was finally able to take a deep breath and began writing in my journal. In that very moment, I promised to make family, friends and love more of a priority in my life.

I arrived to a house full of family and we were all traumatized. We had to summon the strength to plan the funeral and the celebration of her life. The phones were ringing off the hook and whenever I answered, the caller would think I was my mom. I had to explain over and over that she had just passed away. For the first few days, there was a constant flow of beautiful flower arrangements and fruit baskets being delivered. People kept stopping by and most of them were crying, trying to grasp the fact that my mom was gone. It was insane! The whole family was in a daze as we planned the food, picked out the photos and put together slide shows for the luncheon the day after the funeral. Thank God my dad's chefs, family and friends brought over food… we were all exhausted. Meanwhile, my father was in a state of shock and very depressed. His wife's funeral was being held on his birthday.

All of my aunts were so helpful and loving as they helped us to pick out my mom's flowers, readings and her attire for the viewing. We all contributed to making her look gorgeous by doing her nails, makeup and hair at the funeral home. She looked like she was taking a nap before attending an elegant affair. I was the last one with her at the funeral home before the night began. I had to have a special moment with her alone before they transported her to the church. She was lying in her gorgeous white coffin that looked like a designer model with gold ornate accents that was fit for a queen. As I put the final touches on her hair, I asked her to send me clear signs and to visit me often since we'd always had a very close spiritual connection. Since she said "I'll see you soon," I was sure she would keep her promise to me and visit!

The viewing and funeral services were surreal and beyond belief. It looked like a scene from *The Godfather*; the church was filled with Italians elegantly dressed with beautifully coiffed hair and jewelry. It was a sea of black suits and sad faces. We had photos of my mom in the aisles on each the side of the church and there were hundreds of flower arrangements. Seventeen priests and the Bishop were on the altar holding vigil during her services. Since my mother had worked at the all-girl catholic school I attended, many of the students and their families came to see her. I heard amazing stories of the kindness and love she had spread over the years. Over seven hours, more than 3,000 guests poured in to pay their respects to my amazing mother. The viewing was held one day before Mother's Day, and it was the one of the largest services the church had ever seen. What a testament to her life. I am so proud to be her daughter.

This was one of the most devastating and heartbreaking *wake-up* calls of my life. The message was clear; I needed to slow down and make time for love! By the way, my mother Angela is my *earth angel*. She visits me often and sends personal messages to family members through me. She lives on in my heart forever.

So, heed my words and slow down to reflect on your life. If you aren't in a relationship now or are just too focused on work, you must carve out time to look at your goals and create your new love *action plan.*

Many *wonder women* claim they don't have enough time to find a good man and will take on a lover for fun or jump into bed with someone too fast. These women are fooling themselves when they say they're not attached to an in-between lover. Often, they waste precious years with these casual flings to fill a void. These types of lovers are, what I call, relationship *temps.*

Some of the men and women I coach have, *temps* or causal "hookups" and miss out on attracting quality people because of the sexual "quick fix" they are getting from a relationship that is heading nowhere. Many of these high-powered *wonder women* are princesses and wouldn't know a good man if he was right in front of them. Most of the time they are too busy to date and want a magical *love story* without putting in the time or the effort to create it. They are still waiting for their *prince* to show up on a white horse to sweep them off their feet. Some men are still searching for the perfect woman while they have a *temp(s)* as a "placeholder." Take time to reflect on the most important decision of your life ... choosing your life partner. Is this you? Again, ask yourself, are you:

- *Constantly busy? Working on days off?*
- *Eating on the run? Drained, irritable and short-tempered?*
- *A moving target and always rushing?*
- *Thinking about work on vacation, which you often cut short?*
- *Hearing complaints about yourself from those closest in your life?*
- *Having little or no intimacy?*
- *Feeling exhausted, restless and not sleeping well?*
- *Finding it challenging to relax because you can't cut off the mind chatter or give up control of your work responsibilities?*
- *Noticing your friends have stopped asking you to go out?*
- *Lonely but pretending you're not?*
- *Going out with a wrong person to fill a void?*
- *Having a lover, or relationship temp, who takes up most of your spare-time?*
- *Wanting to stop this insanity but are caught up in the whirlwind of work?*

Some people are so entangled in their work and don't want to deal with love issues, until they have an experience that wakes them up. It could be a breakup, a sudden accident, an illness, a death in the family or loss of a job. I have had some big *wake-up* calls that totally rocked my world. Many of the busy people I coach don't want to carve out the time and energy required to maintain a relationship or take new actions to change their circumstances. They claim, "It's too much work…let someone find me."

☞✗ *Smart and successful singles can be blindsided to the reality of what they've created. It's important to slow down and get real about your love life. If you don't, who will? Take the time to reflect, listen to and identify your deeper needs and feelings.*

Both men and women are equally as guilty of being married to their work. Maybe some of you don't see intimacy and a relationship as priorities. We get too focused and busy with our careers. Hello…*wake up* people! It is much easier for a *wonder woman* or *super man* to work, achieve, exercise, shop, eat out and numb their pain with comfort food, drinks, gambling, recreational drugs, or an occasional booty call than it is to own up to what's really going on in their hearts.

In my seminars and events, I have met many of these *wonder women* whose husbands or lovers left them for not being feminine, attentive and available. Then there are the women who leave their work-obsessed partner for another man. They were just too busy for love!

☞✗ *Hundreds of men claim they don't want to be in a relationship with a woman who is like a man: competitive, controlling, insensitive, and driven by ego or power. If a man wanted to be in a relationship with another man, he would marry his best male friend.*

The bottom line is men are simple. They desire attention, engaging conversation, appreciation and to be nurtured with food, sex and pampering. Men need to be visually attracted to you and also know that they make you happy!

☞✗ *When you take care of yourself, it shows and people will notice. When you're happy, you are a magnetic force for love!*

Women who are too busy don't have the energy or don't care to do all of that "crap." Then, they call me and still wonder why they are alone. The typical comments I hear are: "I made tons of money and never asked him for financial support... what else does he want?" or "I want a man who can handle my power and strength and get over it. He's just envious of my success."

As the author Dr. Pat Allen always says, "Girls, leave your balls at the office." You can have success and love if you can understand how you must shift gears to create a new way of managing your life and men.

☙━🗝 *I am not saying to let go of your career. Just get balanced and live a richer life. When you put your heart first for a change, your life will be more fulfilling and a lot more fun!*

If you want to end up rich and alone, that is your choice. Is that what you *really* want? When you're ready to reinvent and rebalance yourself, consider changing your routine and create a new lifestyle. Ask yourself:

- *Do I want to wake up in a year and have my love life be the same as it is right now?*
- *Am I using my accomplishments to get noticed?*
- *Am I trying to prove something to someone? (Your Father? Mother? Ex?)*
- *What motivates me to work so much?*
- *Am I working to numb my emotions or to cover insecurity or pain?*
- *Did I dig myself into a job or a situation that I can't get out of?*
- *Is there a solution in sight?*
- *Is the work I'm doing giving me the satisfaction I deserve?*
- *Am I happy and balanced in other areas of my life?*
- *Do I want a relationship now, and am I willing to take the time to open up?*
- *Can I really attend to my partner's needs, or do I want it to be on my own terms?*
- *Have I taken a good look at how I come across to others as a potential life partner?*
- *Am I afraid of real intimacy?*
- *Am I willing to slow down right now to achieve more balance?*
- *What steps can I take to reinvent my love and social life?*

* *Who will really judge me if I do slow down a bit?*
* *Can I clearly communicate what I want in a relationship?*
* *Am I trying to control my love life and scaring people away?*
* *Will I be truly happy if I keep doing what I'm doing now?*
* *Do I have the right mentors to guide me to my soul mate?*

We live in a fast-paced world, but we must maintain a balance to have some sanity in our lives. All the hectic energy and stress—for what? If a lot is coming up for you, keep writing in your journal so you can track your new alignment and make new agreements with your soul. You will see the progress soon. Once you do this work, you can't go back to pretending that you didn't get this message loud and clear. *Get real and take time for love!*

DO YOU HAVE THE "ONCE I" SYNDROME?

Some people use the "Once I" excuse, saying "Once I" get this work project completed I'll find love. This is what I call the "Once I" syndrome and it affects people from fully living life and keeps love just out of their reach! Then, years go by and they *wake up* wondering what happened to their life. My clients often say, "I forgot to get married and now I see how important love is in my life." Ask yourself now, is there an area in your life that you keep using as your "Once I" excuse? Here are some of the typical "Once I" excuses I hear all the time:

* *Once I lose 20 pounds, then I'll get new photos and try online dating.*
* *Once I move out of my place and get new furniture, then I'll start dating again.*
* *Once I get my new job, I'll feel more secure and start looking for love.*
* *Once I get my project off the ground, then I'll be ready.*
* *Once I close this deal, finish my novel, get the kids settled, get divorced…*

The list goes on and on … right?

My best friend had the "Once I" syndrome. She had such a drive to reach her goals at work that she put love on the back burner! This was my second shocking *wake-up* call that helped me put work and love into perspective and completely changed the direction of my life.

TRUE STORY
MY SECOND SHOCKING WAKE UP CALL: RHONDA'S STORY

This powerful *wake-up* call to slow down happened on January 14, 2007. My best friend, Rhonda Grayson, who was my road partner during many of my single years, called to inform me she was diagnosed with stage four bladder cancer. She was advised to handle all of her personal matters quickly, because she only had two months to live. What a shock!

She was a CNN Health News reporter, produced segments for the famous Dr. Sanjay Gupta, and a true workaholic. Despite her frantic schedule, she was one of the most generous, fun and vibrant people I have ever known. She was extremely driven and focused on moving up the CNN production ladder to spread her positive health news to the world. She had a zest for life after recovering from Hodgkin's disease in her mid-twenties. She was a deeply spiritual person with a big smile and warm energy.

Although I was numb and disoriented, I tried to stay centered. I said, "We will find a miracle, Rhonda. Stay calm." She saw her doctor calling on the other line and told me she would call me back. After we hung up, I sat in my car in total shock and cried. As I walked in to see my neighborhood printer, my friend Louis noticed that I was upset. He asked what was wrong, since I am normally cheery. I told him about Rhonda and said, "We need a miracle to keep her alive." Standing next to me was a man who overheard our conversation. He tapped my shoulder and calmly said, "I think I have the miracle you are looking for." It turns out this brilliant man had come across an alternative therapy called cesium. He had found it on a site called www.cancercoverup.com and his brother had been cured from lung cancer using this substance. He explained that this product, along with an alkaline diet, could possibly kill the cancer without chemo or at least slow its growth. I immediately called Rhonda!

I told her the news of the miraculous meeting and invited her to come and stay at our home in Marina Del Rey, California, so we could put her on this special alkaline diet and help her heal. This *angel*, an acupuncture doctor, was willing to see her and guide her through the process. I was determined and committed to using all the years of my work in the healing arts to make her well. I utilized all of my contacts with amazing health practitioners and took time off work just to be with her. My gut told me we could extend her stay on earth with love and special care. Our goal was to look at all of her options, and do whatever it took to keep her alive! With these various alternative healing techniques, the prayers from the *Angel Healing Team*, a special diet, alkaline foods and the cesium powder, her tumor shrunk in half within a few months.

She called our home "Camp Campanella" (my married name). We had fabulous times together doing her favorite activities such as shopping, manicures, pedicures, massages, walks on the beach, dinner parties with family and friends, as well as going through photos from our big hair days and dance parties. My favorite moments with her were spent talking about our crazy times, the men we had loved before, and the love lessons we had learned. I took *time for love* to help my best friend and it was an amazing, life-changing event. I got to share precious moments in time with my other *earth angel*, Rhonda. I cherished every minute I spent with her!

Rhonda passed away on December 14, 2007, in Atlanta, Georgia. With all of our love and healing, she lived a full nine months longer than the doctors predicted she would. In those last months with Rhonda, she asked me to pass on a message to all the *wonder women* and *super men* out there: "I support the powerful successful people out there, yet I don't want them to make the same 'mis-takes' I made if they want marriage and kids. I am happy I pursued my passion, yet I regret not slowing down long enough to find my life partner and have children. My work and my drive to help the world was my calling and love took a back seat. My biggest regret is not finding *true love* and now my time on earth is over."

Once she got sick, she was struck with the realization that all of the stress and striving to reach her goal of getting her own segment on CNN was actually a contributing factor to why she became ill in the first place. The pressures and competitive nature of television production left little time for love or dating. With the late hours editing, sporadic eating habits and traveling to conduct interviews, Rhonda was burned out. Although her career was exciting, it was a double-edged sword. She would always say, "Once I" get this show on the air, I promise I'll slow down." Rhonda not only had the "Once I" syndrome, she gave her love to so many people and didn't put herself first! She asked me many times, "Bunny (our nick name for each other), what is all this stressful work really for? What is success without your health or love? Please tell these workaholics the truth…none of this success or power is worth it without LOVE."

Rhonda had many wonderful suitors throughout the years, but she did not have time to devote herself to nurturing a relationship since she was so focused on her career. She had many men who wanted to marry her, but she was very particular and not sure if she wanted to settle down until she reached her goal. I always heard her say, "Once I…"

She dated and adored a hot, younger man, named Matt. She told me he wasn't "Mr. Right," but she couldn't resist their amazing chemistry when she was off work and wanted to play. They had a great connection, yet she was so focused on her career and he filled up her spare time. Then, she ran out of time!

If you want to be inspired by Rhonda's message and some of her last words of wisdom from shortly before she passed away, I invite you to go to my site and hear my interview with her at www.ReneePiane.com/podcast.com. You will see an adorable photo of her with her dog Skye. All those who love her will never forget her contagious laugh or her smile that could light up a room…I miss her so much. She is happy that I'm sharing her story with you. I got goose bumps when I was writing it.

I am passing on this story to urge you to please slow down, so that you won't need a *wake-up* call to make love a priority in your life!

O─x *Do not wait for your big career move before you find Mr. or Ms. Right. Be realistic about having kids if you want them. If you're a high-performance woman or man, you must create space and time to have love and intimacy or, in the end, your accomplishments will mean nothing to you.*

Men are attracted to women that have time for dating and romance. Being a workaholic is not an asset if you want to attract and keep a successful man happy. Stop saying, "Once I" [insert your excuse here] then I'll find love! Most people want someone to be available to love and to play with, or they will find someone who can fill that need.

O─x *Time is so precious, so take time for love! Women... switch to your feminine energy and have some fun. Men... take time out to change your routine and get some support.*

You may consider a man with more feminine energy if you want to be the masculine energy in the relationship. It's all your choice and your unique Love Design. Just *get real* about your ultimate vision.

NEW CITY: NEW ADVENTURES

You may have just moved to a new city for school, a new job, or an adventure. You are new to the area and do not know your way around. At first, you may only know co-workers or fellow students and you may be anxious to find your niche in your new home. Of course it takes time, especially in big cities. Depending on your reasons for moving and the current status of your heart, you could be having the adventure of a lifetime. If you are still healing from a relationship or are separated from your current lover, this can be challenging. You need to get into action! Go online and research the various activities and events in or around your city. Where are the great hangouts? Hot social networking groups? Exciting singles events? Join a church, synagogue, spiritual center, dance class, gym, or a local networking group to get you started.

O─x *Relocating is a new adventure and it's up to you to connect with your local community. Take Action. It's time to get familiar with your new city. Just ask the locals for the best of whatever you are searching for and go explore!*

You are in control of where you live, so choose wisely. If you want to be in the action, don't move to the boonies but find a place that suits your needs.

YOU DATE HIGH-SPEED CHASERS: BREAK THE BAD BOY/PLAY GIRL PATTERN

You seem to always date or attract people who just can't commit. These *bad boys* and *play girls* are like sports cars; they are sleek and always on the run. I call them high-speed chasers. They jump from one new deal to the next, always ready to try out the newer and slicker model. The thrill of the ride excites you because you think you can eventually change them. If you're someone who goes after high-speed chasers and think you can tame them; believe me, it doesn't work! I've given too much love to bad boys and they never turned out to be what I truly wanted in a relationship.

⌇ *Bad boys and play girls do not want attachment or commitment. If they do make a commitment to a long-term relationship, they normally don't keep their word for long.*

These *players* lease themselves out and then go for a quick trade-in when the ride gets uncomfortable, or when you ask for more of their time. The *bad boys* are like knights in shining armor riding from castle to castle. The *play girls* are promiscuous, always on the hunt for attention; they use their beauty and sexual energy to get it. These *players* don't give details, just vague and charming stories. They desire different partners for "hot sex" and love to show off their latest conquest to their friends. Both *bad boys* and *play girls* normally don't make plans and often don't know where they will end up or with whom. When they do call, it's always a last minute date. They do not keep promises and rarely make them.

Many people desire the sexy, unattainable men and women seen on covers of popular magazines, in romance movies, soaps and reality television. And to think…HE or SHE is going out with YOU?! It's a rush and a confidence booster to believe that you could be the one who ends up with this person. You feel high from the experience of them choosing you, but they continually let you down. They lure you back with their charm, false promises and great sex. Don't waste your precious time. For women, it's just the oxytocin, the hormone of love that has you addicted. Don't be fooled by that euphoric feeling, because most men do not experience the same chemical reaction or bonding as women do from having sex. For men, it's the ego boost that keeps you attracted and obsessed with an unbalanced sex kitten.

☙ *If you are using sex to get that euphoric feeling, it's time to take a deeper look at your heart and past imprints. It's time to get real about why you are attracting an unavailable player or numbing your pain.*

FIVE SURE SIGNS OF A BAD BOY OR A PLAY GIRL

• They are vague and don't make solid plans ahead of time. Bad boys and play girls like to use the word "spontaneous" so that if you say "no," they manipulate you to make it seem as if you're "no fun."

• You tell them several times that you have a special work event, wedding, or a family related celebration coming up and want them to be your escort. However, they often don't acknowledge or remember and conveniently forget that you told them. Then they apologize with a nice dinner, flowers, and a night of great sex. Because of this, you erase the disappointment and give them the benefit of the doubt. This behavior repeats over and over and you assume it's just because they need their space.

• You only see them during the week and on the weekends they disappear. Unless they work on a weekend, that is definitely not a good sign. You sense that they have other partners, but you put up with it for fear they will leave you.

• You rarely see their friends or maybe you've never met them. If they do have friends, they're vague and they will often warn you about them in a humorous way. Usually they are not joking with their casual comments like, "You never know where Alexis might show up, she is a mysterious woman and will keep you on your toes." Or, "I think I heard about you but it's hard to keep track of Big Mike. He's a lady charmer. One of these days he will settle down." This spells out trouble.

- Inevitably, a holiday or birthday comes up and you may not be included. If you have dated someone for over six months to a year and have not met their family, then it's time to run for the hills.

From the outside, their life appears glamorous. They are always on the scene, looking good, and love to show you off. This person can be very exciting yet may be damaging people along the way, including you. During this time you are having a ball, but the game playing starts to eat away at your self-esteem.

☙━☒ *You may have known they were a high-speed chaser and you didn't think you would get addicted…but you did. You believed you wouldn't get hurt as long as you didn't stay with them for too long. But now, you're afraid you will never feel the same hot chemistry again. So, you stay giving them your heart while hoping for a change or that you'll meet someone else.*

You can't seem to let go until they just stop calling or chasing you. Some *bad boys* and *play girls* will admit to being in this phase and some will never grow out of it. Deep inside, they have huge egos that need to be constantly validated. When you do meet someone new, they just don't compare. So, you discard them. You have become chemically addicted to someone who is messing with your heart.

☙━☒ *A High-Speed Chaser cannot live without the thrill, attention and false confidence that one sexual partner after another gives them. Get real! They're just a temporary fix for your self-esteem and you are not being honest about who they really are. It's time to look at the bigger picture of your life now if you want real love.*

Some singles in the early years of dating are in this phase, and they get addicted and never grow out of it. Many innocent, young men and women get wounded with this type of deception and then have trouble accepting *real love* as they get older. This is especially true in cities where there are a lot of beautiful people per capita, such as Los Angeles, New York, Miami, Atlanta, Philadelphia, Dallas, San Francisco and other big cities worldwide. If you are dating a high-speed chaser, you must realize that they won't let you know about their addiction up front. Don't get caught up in this web of deception and empower yourself to move on. These evasive *players* can cause you to distrust love in the future.

❦❉ *A bad boy's influence and power over women can cause lifelong pain and heart damage that takes years to undo and reprogram for successful relationships.*

I know this for a fact because I was drawn to *bad boys* when I was younger, and I want to warn you of this addictive pattern! This was a *love lineage* imprint I learned from observing some of the women in my family as well as my friends over the years. I wrote this book to save you from repeating the pattern of creating disappointments and years of mistrusting men and women. The good news is that these techniques will allow you to shed any past wounds so you can finally create the love you've always envisioned and deserve.

❦❉ *Why waste your energy and love on a person who may never change and most often will not give you what you really want? We all need to follow our instincts... you know the truth deep down!*

I teach men to go easy on the younger, more vulnerable women because they could become the man who creates the first love experience for her impressionable soul. *Bad boys* love beautiful women, so we must remember our feminine power and beauty as gifts to be treated with honor, respect and dignity. I have interviewed many *bad boys* on my panels TV shows and podcasts and they all admit they love to conquer attractive women. Some singles go through this vulnerable phase after a breakup and search for approval or a fix. They tend to attract *players* that temporarily fill the void of their deeper insecurities.

❦❉ *Many bad boys admitted that deep inside they felt guilty when they knew the women were falling in love with them and they had no intention of committing. They pursued those women for the thrill factor, using what they knew she wanted to hear to get her in bed.*

These men may take off for the next thrill and never look back, leaving women damaged with no explanation. I have been a spokesperson for everyone who has experienced this pain and help to enlighten men that their actions do have a powerful impact on women.

⚬━🗝 *Don't fool yourself into believing you can change a player since most of them will never change for very long. If you're a magnet for this type, get some help or years of your life could be wasted. If you're a bad boy or play girl, be responsible and let the people you date know up front that you want no commitment. If they jump into bed with you, it is their choice to get entangled in your web...you warned them!*

There are many women out there looking for the same fix as a *bad boy*. They can't live without these thrilling experiences that turn them on and make them feel beautiful. You wonder why you can't find a "good guy" to ignite that same passion. Sexual addiction and the oxytocin chemical reaction have been scientifically proven to overtake you and cause you to lose control of your senses. If you are dating a man or woman in this phase, have fun—because that is about all you will have on this fast and furious, short-lived ride. Listen to some of the hot interviews from my radio shows and my downloadable *Secrets into the Minds of Men* program about dating bad boys, so that you can learn more about how they operate.

⚬━🗝 *Don't date people you know aren't good for you, even if you think you can change them with your loving ways. It's a waste of your time and will cause many days of heartbreak, nights of tears, self-doubt and pain. Think twice before you date a bad boy or an unattainable woman!*

I live in a city full of *players*, and many claim that they will eventually settle down for the right person. After being single in Los Angeles for many years, I still see many of the same wolves and seductresses out at parties and bars, hunting for new prey. I know from experience that if you are looking for deeper intimacy, it is not worth the risk. Most of them can't control their addictions or be tamed unless they get professional help. Do you get a gut feeling he's a *bad boy* or she's a *play girl*? Listen to your intuition and senses every time!

Every woman wants to feel as though her man has claimed her. *Bad boys* often make dishonest claims to win your heart. Most women are perceptive enough to know when they are in the presence of a *bad boy* who will create heartache and pain. When you get those butterflies inside, think twice about surrendering your heart or your body to the charm and charisma of a *bad boy*. Understand that you can be truly honored by someone who genuinely wants a partner in life and not just a fling. Just take your time.

 *Bad boys and play girls are a W.O.T. (Waste of Time). Beware of giving your heart away to a bad boy if you want more than just sex. Most of them will drain your energy, and they can occupy years of your life while you're waiting for them to change.*

Bad boys rarely transform into your *prince,* and they take up the precious space needed for a good man to walk into your life. Believe me, it's not worth it. I have listened to hundreds of women who have dated the best of them and men who were blindsided by a selfish *play girl.* They have wasted many years before they learned these secrets and redesigned their plan of action. Learn from my years of experience with *bad boys*…don't go there!

TRUE STORY

As I entered the gym on New Year's Eve, I met a beautiful 42-year-old woman named Jennifer. She had been asking my husband about a dating dilemma and he wasn't sure how to advise her. He told me she had been depressed for a while because she was dating a guy who wasn't committing. We hooked up on the stretching mat for a spontaneous love coaching session. She asked me for advice and proceeded to tell me her sad story of her supposed boyfriend, whom she had not heard from that day. It was 4:00 p.m. on New Year's Eve and he had still not called to confirm their plans! They had tentative plans so she tried calling and texting him, only to have him reply that he was busy and would call her soon. So, she kept herself on hold for New Year's Eve and was feeling insecure and upset. I asked her some probing questions and she listed most of the sure signs that this man was a total *player.* She also admitted that she was addicted to their unbelievable chemistry. She had been dating and sleeping with him for almost two years, yet never met his family.

He was the ultimate *bad boy*: charming, rich, handsome, super successful and hot in bed. She was hooked!

Turns out this was his regular behavior: promising he'd have more time soon, calling at the last minute and being evasive about potential plans. I asked her if they were exclusive and she replied, "I guess so...we have never talked about it." I took in a deep breath, sat quietly, looked deeply into her sad eyes and asked in a calm voice, "Do I have permission to be frank with you, to give you my heart-to-heart observations and some *Get Real* advice?" She said, "Please, I need your help and I am not sure what to do." I said, "I look at you and see a beautiful, successful goddess who is giving away the most precious gift to a man who probably has a few women pining after him right now, wondering if *they* are going to be his date tonight! I want you to look deep into your heart and think about your future. It's going to be a new year in eight hours. Do you want to be treated this way by an unavailable man and keep experiencing these crappy feelings and insecurities this time next year?" She said, "No way!" I continued, "This man knows he can call you anytime and you will drop whatever you're doing for him...right?" She looked down and said, "Yeah, most of the time." I asked, "Have you met his family and spent the holidays with him after dating this long?" She replied, "No, not yet." I pushed on, "Does he cherish you and ever make you a priority?" She said, "Not really, but he is generous, we have fun when we go out, and he is great in bed. I hoped things would progress but he has been super busy." I replied, "Well, my friend, you are wasting your energy, time, and love on a *dead-end street* with a *player*. You need to *wake up* and see how you are giving all your love to the wrong man! He is definitely a *player* and unless you want to be sitting here next year on New Year's Eve waiting for a man who treats you like a call girl, I'd suggest you cut him loose tonight and go out to a party!" She replied with a smile, "As a matter of fact I got invited to a big party with a girlfriend tonight...so you think I should go?" I replied, "Absolutely. Get dressed up in a hot outfit and play some dance music to get you out of this mood. There are so many single men out on New Year's Eve. It's time to set your soul free from this man. He is not worth one more minute of your time, beauty or energy. I suggest you convey your true feelings to him by phone with this declaration to set a powerful intention for your new year." I role-played with her and gave her an exact *love script*, one of my favorite things to do in my coaching sessions. When he calls at 8:00 p.m. tell him, "Well, I never heard back from you, so I have made other plans tonight. I also wanted to let you know that I've enjoyed our friendship. It's been a lot of fun, but I am not going to be seeing you anymore." I told her he would reply or say something like, "Why not? What's up baby?" I suggested she reply with, "Since it's a new year, I've decided that I am keeping myself open to a man who wants a real relationship. You and I have dated long enough, and I know you aren't the man for me. I am ready to create a new *love story* this coming year, so have fun tonight. It's time for me to move on and I wish you all the best."

I added, "No more explaining, no drama, no tears, just use a powerful statement to set you free from him." What a perfect time to end that nightmare. We practiced her script a few times, and I asked her to express the qualities she really wanted in a man this coming year. I mentioned that by taking this action on the eve of a new year, she was opening the space for *real love* to come in. I told her a few inspirational love stories from other clients of mine and as I left, I said, "Soon I'll be hearing your *love story*. Learn from my 'mistakes' and don't waste another minute giving to or stressing over a *bad boy*. You have everything to offer someone special, so go out tonight, dress as if you are going to meet the love of your life and have some fun!" I also added, "It's time that you set your new intentions for a new year filled with love and an available man who adores you." She hugged me and was off.

She felt empowered and went out that night with her friends in a hot dress. She ended up magically meeting a wonderful man that night at the party who was exactly what The Love Designer ordered. Turns out, I knew him from my events and he is a special, caring man and a handsome *prince*! They have been together for nearly three years now, and she thanked me for changing her life that day. She was so glad she did not waste one more moment of her life on a *bad boy*. Sometimes one *get real* love session is all you need.

What a way to start off the New Year with a powerful love proclamation. She claims it was a miracle! She thanks and hugs me every time I see her.

☛ *As you begin to learn how to take care of your own heart and soul, you will find that you will no longer be attracted to the bad boy or play girl energy to fill that empty feeling inside.*

No Heat Combustion

In this phase, you may be dating someone who is attractive, caring and the perfect type to connect with, but there is no sexual chemistry. There's none of the magic or affection that you would like to experience long-term. Yet, at the same time, there is a deep connection. You may have been dating for a while to see if it could "heat" up, but the chemistry never progressed and you wish you could back out. You may have gotten involved romantically too soon since you were lonely or under the influence of alcohol or drugs that made you vulnerable. This phase is uncomfortable for all parties involved and honest communication is a must. Sometimes you can become friends if both of you can handle this phase with loving care and communication. Some space and time may be needed when separating to accept the phase for what it is. It is not easy to discuss this scenario, yet you must. It's the right thing for both of you to move on.

☛ *Honesty is the best policy and, as I always say, "If it ain't flowing, it ain't going." Move on so you don't end up wasting time in a dead-end relationship.*

You're in Constant Repair

In the *constant repair* phase, you are continually searching for answers from outside of yourself. Often being in the repair phase is just an excuse to not experience intimacy. You're constantly attending seminars, reading self-help books and asking your friends for feedback. Not that the search isn't great, you're reading this book, aren't you? Take time to do the inner work or you will find yourself in the same boat, floating aimlessly for years.

O—x *At some point, you must STOP looking outside yourself and actually apply the information that you have learned and work on your patterns.*

I watch many people eagerly and enthusiastically attend my seminars, then lose momentum by not creating an *action plan* or getting a coach to keep them on track. You must make a commitment to your heart first, determine which direction you want to go and then take baby steps. Once you do the inner work, you can forge ahead and achieve all of your dreams.

O—x *There are no quick fixes or temporary repairs. Take the necessary time to re-examine your heart. Be consistent with your inner work and you will get results. You are in charge of your destiny.*

OUT OF FAITH & DON'T BELIEVE IN LOVE

You have dated casually but have never gone deep into a relationship. You are just giving up on the whole idea of finding *true love* for yourself. Perhaps you have never had a real relationship or you keep attracting commitment-phobic or unavailable people. Because of past rejections or lack of connection, you may feel unworthy to have love. Maybe you feel you don't deserve it, and you never quite believed in love. You've lived out your beliefs in most of your dating scenarios. More than likely, you did not have any role models to guide you. You feel alienated and shut down. At least on the surface, you've accepted your fate: you were born alone and will stay alone. You are *out of faith.*

Nevertheless, the desire for a deep connection is buried deep inside your heart and soul. You just don't know how to find it…yet. If this is you, cheer up! There are many ways to get out of this dark phase and create a new attitude about life. This is a new territory for you…keep reading.

O—x *Keep the faith and find role models to emulate. I know deep down a part of you believes in love or you would not be reading this right now. Stay committed to this process and your life will be transformed.*

GET REAL ♥ REFLECTIONS

♥   Have you been honest with the people you've dated? Have you ever kept dating someone when you knew they wanted more? Reflect on the people you may have strung along in your past, knowing they weren't right for you. Did you ever consider their feelings? How do you feel when someone does this to *you*?

♥   Are you sending out a signal of being too busy for love? If so, examine how you are showing up. Have you ever taken a real look as to how you come across when you are asked out on a date? Do you make it impossible for them to make plans with you? Did anything come to mind when you read about the "Once I" syndrome? If so, list yours.

♥   Do you expect a man to be the primary breadwinner in the relationship? Are you open to being with a person who could be the perfect match for you but doesn't make as much money as you? How important is their financial status to you?

♥   Have you wasted time with men or women you knew were *players* and you thought you could change them? How much time did you waste hoping someone you dated would finally commit because the sex was so amazing?

♥   What three things could you do right now to create the space and take time for love?

Now that you have taken a look at all the different types of *Single Love Phases* you can experience, hopefully it has given you more clarity on how you can reach the next level and be ready for love.

CHAPTER V
You're Ready for Love

"Wake up every morning with the thought that something wonderful is about to happen."
– Flavia

Many of you have already experienced the various phases listed in the previous chapters. At this point, you may have done your inner reflection. This chapter is for those of you who know your heart and are now prepared to design your love life any way you want it.

TOP RUNNING CONDITION

The *top running condition* is the place to be. You are finally in a love zone where you accept yourself. You've defined your personal and relationship values and appreciate yourself for the gift that you are. You are fulfilled being married or single and, if you are solo, you are open to meeting others who are on a parallel path.

To be in top running condition doesn't mean that you want to be single forever. You are committed to your life purpose and to living in the moment, seeing both yourself and others with a deeper vision. You are demonstrating an inner trust within your own soul for guiding you to the perfect friendships, relationships and love in all areas of your life.

Your energy radiates joy, self-esteem and wisdom. You are fulfilled being alone as you move about your life in *top running condition*. In this phase, you have transformed yourself into the type of person you are looking to attract and are open to receiving love in your life. This is the life phase when you will magnetize your match.

LONG-TERM COMMITMENT: YOU'RE READY FOR LOVE

If you are in this phase, you have been on the solo journey long enough. You are ready to commit to a relationship and are looking for a quality long-term connection. You have explored your options and are prepared to expand on a new path with a *life partner*. You want to create a spiritual bond with that special someone and travel down the path of love. You are ready for *true love*.

You've done your inner work and have learned about your unique blueprint for love. You are ready to call in a partner to enhance and enliven your life. You know what gifts you have to share in a partnership and you understand that there will be ups and downs. You are ready to explore the world with an evolved partner and co-create a life that is unique to your united vision.

⚷ *Love is in the air. Once you make the decision that you are ready, it often happens fast. The timing of meeting your life partner could happen at any moment—anywhere you are. Get ready, love will find you!*

Relationships come in various forms and it's up to you to decide your path and design your love destiny. Not everyone chooses monogamy, marriage or raising children. You can create any kind of relationship you wish. Know thyself and express your truth so that you can have your heart's desire!

GET REAL ♥ REFLECTIONS

♥ Now that you know you are ready for love, are you clear on the type of relationship you want in your life? What is your vision for your unique love design?

Now that we have checked out your current love phases, it's time to examine what kinds of energy vibes we emit to others. Understanding these vibes is the next key to becoming consciously responsible for how you are portraying yourself in the world. This leads us to the next chapter, Energy Vibrations.

CHAPTER VI

ENERGY VIBRATIONS

"What a man thinketh, so shall he become."
– James Allen

"The first thing you have to know is yourself. A man who knows himself can step outside himself and watch his own reactions like an observer."
– Adam Smith, The Money Game

GET REAL ABOUT YOUR ENERGY VIBES: WHAT MESSAGE ARE YOU SENDING TO OTHERS?

Now that we've explored the phases you are moving through, we need to check the energy you are sending out. Some people walk around with an energy that is open and friendly, while others can give off vibes that are downright cold. Typically, it is a cloud of depression and or indifference that keeps some people from connecting.

We live in a fast-paced, modern world and we want things done quickly. We make instant connections with people by e-mail, text and cell phone, but are missing the kind of energy that can only be transmitted in person. The absence of personal connection is leaving millions of us alone with our mobile devices to check in with our friends on social networking sites. Let's face it, this evolving electronic age has incredible benefits to society, but it seems to be causing disastrous side effects. People often feel isolated and lonely because they spend too much time online or on their phone, which often replaces human interaction. Many are obsessed with the constant stimulation and can't unplug to make deeper connections. People can be anyone they want online and millions of singles are just "hooking up," or they spend hours texting and often never actually meet. Some people have so many options to choose from while others are alone, wishing for love. Just go out and connect!

Many years of scientific research has emerged related to quantum physics and the invisible exchange of energy. Regardless of your circumstances, your *energy vibe* will absolutely influence your outcome. It's important to become more aware of the energy and message you are putting out in the world. Only you know what type of vibes you are putting out there. Be brutally honest with yourself and remember that this book is not here to judge you, only to give you a *wake-up* call.

How many times have you entered an event or party and immediately scanned the room to see if anyone there was your type? If your scanner picks up a receptive energy, you are drawn in like a magnet because you can sense a vibe or energy that you want around you. Usually it is a physical type we look for, and often we don't connect because our vibrations are not in sync. If your energies are on different frequencies and you do connect, it won't be for long.

You might get a chance to meet but you will not be welcomed into their space. Even when you are in control of your energy and you send out great vibes, you may have a conversation or an experience that doesn't jive. That's how it is with *energy vibes*. You can't take it personally. Some of us aren't on the same frequency, so why waste your time. The automatic judgments and egos of some people are impossible to penetrate. They may look like your type but the frequency is way off, so move on. Who wants to be with a cold, negative-energy person in the first place?

Like everyone, there are times in your life when you feel inspired. One day you may feel like you're on top of the world and everything is going right. You are in the flow and feeling good inside. People notice you. Maybe someone you find attractive talks to you. But suddenly you begin to doubt yourself and think, "Why would he look at me?" Something is triggered inside of you and that magic feeling disappears. You regress back into your funk, and then the mind chatter begins.

"How did I get that inspiration? How can I get it again? Confidence, please come back to me." Finally, you say to yourself, "Oh well, I'm back to normal."

Being depressed and staying in that funk is not normal, yet it feels natural to many of us, right? Many single people are so used to feeling miserable that they believe that's how it's supposed to be. Who told you that lie?

You can shift from that mindset when you figure out the *energy vibes* you are sending out. You are in the driver's seat and in control. I promise that the work you do will dramatically change your life in all areas. Many of my students report instant success with others by looking inward and shifting their *energy vibes*.

⚭ *Life is what you make of it. You are in charge of changing your energy state.*

Energy is all around us in nature, music, media and the people with whom you surround yourself. If you tune in, you can sense different vibrations that either energize or drain you. These energy vibrations are everywhere, including your home environment. Regardless of where you are or whom you are with, it's all about the vibes.

In the rest of this chapter, you will become aware of what vibrations you send out. This awareness will take honesty and will positively change your relationships with lovers, friends, family, business associates and especially with yourself.

Although you have a unique vibration, you can fluctuate between types of vibrations at different times in your life. As you become aware of which vibration you send out, you can shift gears to a higher frequency and create new experiences. This process takes time and awareness.

Becoming aware of the energy you put out is the next step to shifting yourself and magnetizing or reigniting more love into your life. Let's check into your *energy vibes* and see what state you are living in now. Not only will you see the vibes you are putting out, you will also become aware of the vibes you do or don't want to attract in your life.

YOUR UNIQUE ENERGY VIBES

THE ABANDONED CHILD VIBER: This person has been hurt in the past. When you date the abandoned *child viber*, their *inner child* often surfaces on dates, and they have deep fears of their partner abandoning them. Like a scared child, they can be clingy, needy and often don't know that they are acting out.

THE ANGRY VIBER: A scowling face is the calling card of the *angry viber*. This person is filled with wrath, explosive energy and impatience. You can feel their rage and annoyance from across the room. Their movements are sharp. Watch out! They are likely to snap if the wrong thing is said.

THE BALANCED VIBER: The *balanced viber* has the ultimate balance of inner peace and harmony. Their life reflects stability, poise and balance in all areas. They radiate a sense of inner tranquility that we all strive for.

THE BISEXUAL VIBER: This is a person who has open energy and is sexually attracted to both men and women. Some people have bi-sexual tendencies, and you can sense the vibe despite the fact that they are not publicly open about it. There are many people who are not homosexual, yet they are very affectionate with both genders.

THE CODEPENDENT VIBER: This caregiver thinks of others first and can be overly loving, which impacts their relationships and quality of life. *Codependent vibers* constantly give in order to feel loved but often feel as though they are taken for granted. Giving is a tradeoff for approval and validation. This vibe can occur in any type of relationship, whether it's your family, work, friendship, or romantic interest. They have a tendency to rehash their problems on the phone and over analyze every conversation. They can be whiny and have mood swings since they are in need of constant validation. *Narcissistic vibers* are natural magnets for the *codependent viber*.

THE CONFIDENT LEADER VIBER: This person radiates confidence and power as well as a presence that others are magically drawn to. The *confident leader viber* is a self-assured, vibrant and positive viber that we all strive to emulate. A woman or man with this courageous leadership vibration is a good role model or mentor.

THE CONTROL-FREAK VIBER: Control is the name of their game. Bossy and demanding, they try to command people's time, energy and, sometimes, other people's beliefs. In their presence, people feel manipulated and insulted. *Control-freak vibers* want to take the lead, govern activities, and get upset when things don't go their way.

THE DEAD-ENGINE VIBER: A *dead engine viber* sends out no energy, is slow moving, has slumped shoulders, a monotone voice, sad eyes and is in a depressed state most of the time. Often they look like the walking dead. If this is you, check your pulse.

THE DECEPTIVE VIBER: The *deceptive viber* doesn't tell the truth and they don't keep commitments. Misleading and cunning, they don't look people straight in the eye during important conversations. They have shifty, insincere personalities and can easily deceive others with their lies.

THE HIGH VIBER: This person is usually an extrovert. They stand tall with their shoulders back, walk on air, smile a lot and connect well with others. A *high viber* is most often a leader and an entrepreneurial type. They are strong, energetic and lighthearted, but can be impatient and pushy at times. They can come across as phony to introverts and those with low energy. These vibers are often the life of the party and seem to get all the attention.

THE HIGH-STRUNG VIBER: A *high-strung viber* is a frenetic, nervous person who can rarely calm down. Being around one makes others want to jump out of their skin. They have sharp, quick movements like a free-flying electrical wire that can burn out other people's energy.

THE IMPATIENT VIBER: This person cannot sit still. They are tense, restless, and want things done now. They are impulsive and often make quick decisions. For those who have a calming energy, being in a relationship with an *impatient viber* can be challenging.

THE JEALOUS VIBER: The *jealous viber* is so possessive and domineering that you feel restricted from looking at another human when you are in their presence. They control people with their energy, which is rooted in deep insecurity and fear. They may attempt to block any person their partner speaks with or looks at. They become extremely competitive with other people who interfere or enter their territory.

THE JOKER VIBER: The *joker viber* uses humor to connect and is constantly telling stories, making zany wisecracks to get noticed and meet people. They are loud, sometimes obnoxious and attract a lot of attention. They are fun to be around, and those who love to laugh will be attracted and entertained by them. Many of these jesters wear their humor like a mask to avoid taking anything seriously. If this describes you, realize that the jokes you tell reflect your self-image and reveal your focus in life, especially when first connecting with people.

THE KIND VIBER: Warm, sparkling eyes and graceful movements are sure signs of the *kind viber*. They have an open energy and are captivating, considerate and a pleasure to be around. They exude love and glow when they enter a room.

THE LITTLE-GIRL VIBER: The playful, fun energy of the *little-girl viber* is compelling at first, but often the *little-girl viber* turns out to be needy, clingy, undependable, irresponsible and reckless. She wants to act like a child that doesn't know any better, but she's actually looking for someone to take care of her. Some women never become independent and dating a *little-girl viber* can be draining. It is great to get in touch with your *inner child* and be playful, as long as you are responsible in the other areas of your life. Often, we turn into a *little-girl viber* when we are triggered from past programming and date men who are wrong for us. Beware, is it your grown up side dating men or is it your *little-girl*? This vibe also applies to the *little boy* vibes men send out.

THE DADDY'S-GIRL VIBER: Overpowering, controlling fathers have raised some women who cannot release the hold these men have over their lives. They check in with dad or male friends for every decision and carry around guilt or shame when it comes to certain situations with men. The *daddy's-girl viber* has not let go of the attachment to her father and may have an unhealthy relationship with men because of the deep desire to recreate her father in the men she chooses. Some of these women look to be with control freaks or unavailable men and often marry someone just like dad. Some women had fathers who were very young parents that didn't give them much attention. Many of these women are looking for constant approval from men to ultimately heal the relationship with their father. This issue often causes unhealthy dating challenges until you observe the pattern. This has become prevalent in our current times due to the increased divorce rate and the fact that many children are being brought up by single parents. For men, it's the *momma's-boy viber*. The man who's constantly looking for his mothers' approval.

THE MONEY-HUNGRY VIBER: The *money-hungry viber* is spoiled. In their hunt for love, they mostly measure the worth of a potential partner by their money and social status. They are materialistic social climbers consumed with only high-ticket items. They constantly talk about what designers they wear, where they shop, eat and travel. They will ask subtle but probing questions to uncover the financial status of friends or potential partners and can pry into others' lives in a very cunning way. Usually, they are looking for a wealthy partner (a.k.a. a sugar daddy or sugar mama) to take care of them and feel entitled to have their needs met all of the time. These people often scare away potential partners from marriage. Some of my clients have been taken to the cleaners by their exes. Hopefully, they now recognize these *money hungry vibes.*

THE NARCISSISTIC VIBER: This dynamic person is vain, arrogant and has an excessive need for admiration. You don't need to ask them a question because narcissists will typically begin the conversation about themselves, and before you can even say, "How are you?" You will often hear a narcissist boasting: "Have you heard about my latest *this?*" or *"Wait* until you see my new *that.*" In most conversations, you will hear Me, Me, Me, or I, I, I. They hardly listen and rarely ask questions about you but, if they do, it's normally a springboard to bring the conversation back to them. *Narcissistic vibers* are often louder in a crowd so that they are the center of attention.

They are self-absorbed and need their ego monster stroked constantly. In relationships, most narcissists are oblivious to the wants and needs of others. They always have someone catering to their emptiness to fill the void of deep insecurities. You may feel like you are on a roller coaster of emotions because their vibes shift from moment-to-moment. These vibers are full of themselves and, typically, don't have much room for anyone else in their life.

THE NEEDY VICTIM VIBER: This person comes across as extremely needy and may be pushy because they are so desperate for love. The *needy victim viber* doesn't have a life of their own and tends to attach to people who have their lives together. They will offer their assistance while draining people's energy with their problems and a full dose of whining. This vibe can be felt in their tone of voice or in conversations when talk about their sadness, old relationships or lack thereof. They usually blame others since they haven't taken a good look in the mirror.

THE OPEN-HEART VIBER: *Open heart-vibers* love life and people. You can feel their tenderness when they interact with you. They are warm, compassionate and will maintain good eye contact. You feel your heart open around people like them. They are in their power and know who they are.

THE PEACEFUL VIBER: This *peaceful viber* is a mellow, reflective, intuitive, soft-spoken individual with a tranquil and healing effect. You will feel serene in their presence. They move with a stride of inner strength and confidence. Sometimes they seem angelic.

THE PERCEPTIVE VIBER: These people have extrasensory perception, the skills to read others and build rapport. They are in touch with their inner guidance. The *perceptive vibers* listen to the signs from their heart and gut to make clear decisions.

THE PROTECTIVE VIBER: This defensive person has a wall of protection so thick that if another individual gets too close, they might lash out at them. They're completely closed off for fear of being hurt. They tend to get very snappy and have a harsh tone in their voice. The protective *viber* is safeguarding and shielding their heart.

THE RECEPTIVE VIBER: The *receptive viber* is an interested person sending out clear signals and an open, approachable energy—a trait that most people love. From the soft look in their eyes and open body language, people immediately know that they are accessible and responsive. They smile a lot and make great eye contact. They are good at flirting and send out a clear, fun and receptive energy. People are magnetically attracted to their energy.

THE RESCUER VIBER: This person comes to the rescue of many others because they are kind and caring, but sometimes they use rescuing to avoid dealing with the challenges in their own life. Like the *codependent viber*, they feel good when saving or giving to others. Many people who fit this vibe may attract unbalanced partners. The *rescuer* thinks they can save others from despair. Quite often, the *rescuer viber* becomes resentful when they complete a mission, only to watch the now-healed and confident partner move on. I hear from both sides and, typically, *rescue vibers* attract each other. Let's face it, many women are taught that someday a handsome prince will sweep you off your feet, rescue and take care of you.

THE SAD DAMAGED VIBER: These people show visible pain in their eyes and their body posture. In a low tone of voice, they carry old, sorrowful stories from their past into most conversations, draining others with the repetition. They walk around with heavy hearts and have given up on love. This sensitive person is like a bird with a broken wing. They're in the process of healing and learning from their lessons in order to fly again. To the outside world, the *sad, damaged viber* comes across like damaged goods. This is just a temporary state of mind that can be healed with time and commitment to transform the situation.

THE SALESPERSON VIBER: This pushy *salesperson viber* is always selling you something, especially themselves. They tend to be polished, over-complimentary and definitely know how to make others feel comfortable. They may come across as bossy, but it is done in the most flattering way. They are master salespeople, open and direct, constantly trying to close the deal on you (and *they* are "the deal"). So they will sell, sell, sell. They may say things like, "We would have so much fun together at my vacation home in the mountains. I am taking you with me now." They often boast about their best attributes and oversell themselves. This vibe works on many people who love accomplished partners in the beginning, but don't be surprised if they lose interest because you may have come across as desperate and oversold yourself. You haven't left anything for them to discover because you've already shown most of your cards. Beware, they may only want you for the vacation to the islands and not truly honor your heart. This might actually lead to a risky situation. Be cautious of both men and women who sell too much!

THE SEXUAL VIBER: This viber sends out overpowering sexual signals that could knock you over from across the room. Their body language signals and the way they walk drips with sexuality. They want attention and know how to get it. If you carry this energy, you can get a lot of attention but unless your goal is sex, you may not get the long-term results you desire. On the receiving end, this sexual energy can feel both flattering and intrusive. Sexual energy is the strongest energy on earth and it can be transmitted in a pure or polluted form, depending on the thought behind it. Use your sex vibes carefully. Watch out for those *sex viber bad boys* and *play girls*. They can get you in trouble every time!

THE SHY VIBER: The *shy viber* is reserved and can come across as nervous and insecure in large groups or social situations. They are quiet, kind, usually soft-spoken, introspective and a slow starter with delicate energy. Often, they are introverted and their vibe is easy to misread. Once they get adjusted to their environment and feel out the other vibes, they open up and surprise everyone with their brilliance. Sometimes a *shy viber* could be confused with a *snob viber* or *nerd viber*.

THE SNOB VIBER: The snob is better than everyone and has an air of elite arrogance. They usually don't connect well with others because most people are below their standards. They will not give others the time of day and can make others feel like they are beneath them. The *snob viber* treats others with disrespect and can be sickening in the dating world, unless they are dating another snob. Just because they have a higher social status or may be successful in their business life doesn't mean they are better than anyone else. They only look for opportunities that will advance their lifestyle. Typically, they feel that only a few people are at their level or good enough for them.

THE SOCIALLY NERDY VIBER: The *socially nerdy* energy comes across as uncomfortable, bashful and socially challenged. Her look is often dowdy, not feminine or chic, and she looks like she could be the poster girl for constant rejection. This goes for nerdy men as well. His fashion lacks style and he normally has no sense on how to put himself together. *Social nerdy vibers* are shy, lack confidence, and are usually introverted but deep down they are very sweet. They just need some guidance and permission to bring out their inner and outer beauty and style. We all have something beautiful to share if we enhance our assets and learn people skills. Once they get a boost of confidence mixed with a little coaching and a magical makeover, watch out! Nerds can be HOT.

THE SPIRITUAL GURU HEALER VIBER: The *spiritual guru healer* uses their intuitive psychic vibrations to heal, lead and influence others by using spiritual principles to build trust. This vibration can and must be used with integrity and truth. Some people use this vibe to manipulate others with their power. Wrongly used, these actions can cause undue pain. People are very vulnerable and trust you with their heart. If you are a spiritual practitioner, body worker, massage therapist or healer, use your gift with honor and respect. Remember, what goes around comes around.

THE TICKING CLOCK VIBER: This woman is so desperate to have a baby that she comes off as rushed and anxious to get married, which scares men off. Men claim that some women seem more concerned in finding a sperm donor than finding *true love*. This woman wants to rush a relationship after realizing her eggs are getting old and going to expire soon. Perhaps she had a *wake-up* call from investing in a relationship that did not end up in marriage, and she knows her baby-making days are running out. She may not get her fantasy of being a wife and mom, so she is on a quest to find a husband fast. Let's be brutally honest, men who want kids are looking for partners that are in an age range that don't carry risks. Women who wait until after thirty-five often come across as a *ticking clock viber* to most men. So *get real* and check in if you are sending out this desperate vibe! If you want kids please start seeking a good partner sooner than later. Men hate being pushed by your ticking baby clock and wonder why you waited so long.

THE TOUGH-GIRL VIBER: This *tough-girl viber* looks like a rough chick on the outside and has a defensive scowl on her face. She sends out the vibe that she could punch your lights out if you say something to offend her. Most often, inside and underneath this tough exterior, there is a damaged woman that uses the *tough-girl* vibe to protect herself from getting hurt or being rejected. She usually sits alone and is quiet until someone breaks through the shield of energy protecting her. Beyond the shield is usually a sweetheart with a lot to give if someone can penetrate the brick wall around her heart. These qualities apply to *tough guy vibers* as well!

THE VAMPIRE VIBER: Also known as the energy-drainer, this is a needy and whiny person who worries and complains most of the time. They prey on the energy of other people and most victims feel exhausted after spending time with a *vampire viber.* Sometimes it feels like the life is sucked out of everyone when they are around. Just the sound of a *vampire viber's* voice can drain your energy. If you feel like the energy has been sucked out of you, you've been in the company of a *vampire viber*! Are you a vampire?

THE WONDER WOMAN/SUPER MAN VIBER: You are in control of your life and know what you want. You often send out vibes that you aim for perfection from yourself and others in your life. You love helping people, have a radiant vibration of confidence and are a leader in your community. Your vibes can seem masculine, controlling and over powering to some people. You might hear that you seem unapproachable or hard to get to know. These vibes can intimidate others and often make them feel uncomfortable or envious. People admire your success and may feel that you are a step above them. You may have super high standards or are too busy to have time for a relationship. On the inside, you are a combination of sensitivity and power and desire to be seen for who you really are. Deep down you're still a mixture of being a grown-up and a *little girl* or *boy*. Beware of coming across as controlling and overbearing. Some people will think you are impossible to please and may feel turned off by your energy. Change your vibes, get into your playful energy more often and have some fun.

THE WORK-TOO-MUCH VIBER: *Get real*...you work too much! You do not see how you come across to others. You are not present with people because you are always on phone or checking emails when you're on a date or out with friends. As a *work-too-much viber* you are completely unaware that you often say, "I'm so swamped," or "I'm overwhelmed right now." You are sending out unavailable vibes. People may stop calling you since you never have time for them or feel like you aren't connected at all. In your mind, you think you have time and you'll say things like, "We will hook up soon," yet your vibes push friends, co-workers and especially perspective partners away. You are short on the phone and never seem to have time to connect or make a plan. You're vague and seem flakey. I know this vibe...it used to be *me*. It's a sign to slow down and create more balance in your life to be able to recognize love when it shows up.

VIBER CHECK LIST

As I mentioned before you can be one or a combination of these *viber* types. Have a good honest heart-to-heart chat with yourself and list the top five vibes that rang true for you. The Energy Vibes You Send Out:

1. _____

2. _____

3. _____

4. _____

5. _____

After reading the list, pick out the dominant *energy vibes* that you send out to the world. This is the person you have been until now. Once you become aware of your vibes, you can begin to shift and change your patterns.

In some cases, we attract the same type of vibrations we put out. For example, workaholics often date other workaholics then complain that there is no romance. At other times, it is quite the opposite and we will avoid our type like the plague.

What about people you have dated and or were married to in the past? Can you identify what vibes they were sending? Can you see how important your vibes are in the attraction phase and in your life? If you have the courage to be honest with yourself, this awareness and insight will to empower you. Remember, your vibes affect others and vice versa. So now that we have examined all the vibes, the next question we will be answering is, "How do you change your vibes?"

⌐➤ *Awareness is the first step to change. People grow through many levels of consciousness on their quest for fulfillment in life and love. As we grow, evolve and send out our unique energy vibrations, we will magnetize people who are on the same frequency.*

Are you satisfied with the people you have attracted into your life? If not, I will show you how to work with your mind to shift into a higher vibration so you can attract people with a similar vibration. Remember that you are responsible for creating what you desire.

GET REAL ♥ REFLECTIONS

♥ Can you list the top energy vibes that you send out? Which of those may need some adjusting? Do you energize or drain others with your vibes?

♥ Are the people in your life on the same energy frequency? List the people who might be draining your energy or energizing you right now?

Now let's explore the thoughts and words that create your life experiences and your energy. Are you ready to see how easy it is to

shift? Let's check in with your inner thoughts and get them in control as we move on to examine our love imprints.

CHAPTER VII
EXAMINE YOUR LOVE IMPRINTS

"When you see a worthy person, endeavor to emulate him. When you see an unworthy person, then examine your inner self."
– **Confucius**

WHO IS STEERING YOUR THOUGHTS & CONVERSATIONS?

Now, we are investigating your inner dialogue as well as your *love imprints* to figure out who is steering your thoughts and conversations. As I mentioned in Chapter VI, if you are open and want to meet new people, you must first learn what vibes you are sending out. Then, you must shift your energy and internal states. That's what it takes...an open mental state and the internal work to back it up.

If you've experienced divorce, rejection, a lousy lover or an abusive relationship, you may start to doubt yourself. You may hear your *little boy* or *girl* whispering in your ear, "Maybe I'm not really that great. I'm not someone that people stay with for the long haul. I want to find a mate, yet don't know where to begin. I want love but I'm so busy. This process is too much effort and I'm probably going to be alone for the rest of my life. I give up!" You must get in control of your unconscious mind and realign those thoughts to correspond with your new desired outcome. You deserve love and your heart knows it.

Think back to the last few interactions you had with dating or going out socially. How were you feeling about yourself? Your appearance? Did you radiate confidence and feel attractive. Or, did you doubt yourself and feel frumpy? What about your self-worth? Were you confident and empowered or did you leave the house tired and depressed? Did you attract positive or negative people, or meet no one at all? Can you recall going out in one of your negative moods, to find your friends all happy and ready to flirt? Your energies did not match all evening and you felt irritated because they were having a great time, yet you felt invisible? Maybe you wanted to go home, crawl under the covers and never come out again. Remember, those thoughts become your vibes!

⚷ *You will meet new people, or possibly the one, when your attitude and energy equal what you are looking for. You must believe you deserve love, adjust your consciousness and don't rely only on flirting techniques. Your body language and vibes speak volumes.*

HOW MUCH DO YOU BELIEVE IN LOVE?

Ask yourself honestly: What percentage of your core believes that you deserve love, a healthy, long-term relationship or that you will meet a wonderful person to share your life with? Is it 50/50? Half of you believe it's true? Is it 70/30? Do you have more negative beliefs than positive? Or is it 30/70? Imagine how many negative thoughts are running through your mind if only 30% of your mind believes in love. That means 70% of your unconscious mind runs on autopilot, filling your mind and spirit with double doses of worry, doubt and fear.

Now is the time to identify and communicate with your inner voice to shift those percentages and change your belief systems. In all of my research with clients, most of them base their future on past experiences. If we don't shift, we will inevitably repeat our history again and again. Let's learn your belief in love percentages.

Please answer honestly from 10%-100% for each question:

- What percentage of you believes in *true love*? _____

- What percentage of you believes that you will find it? _____

- What percentage of you believes that a person will adore you and be faithful? _____

- What percentage of you believes in yourself? _____
- What percentage of you is run by your *little girl* or *boy*? _____
- What percentage of you is ready for LOVE now? _____

⚷ *What you say to yourself on a regular basis, whether out loud or in your whirling mind, affects your results.*

Now that you've looked at how much you actually believe in love, remember, your confidence can get a little tweaked when you're new at something or haven't had much success with love in the past. You have to retune your mind and stay focused in the same way you would if you were learning to speak a new language, following a new cooking recipe or taking a Latin dance class. Take it step-by-step, be patient with yourself, gentle with your heart and take risks. You'll learn new ways to create dynamic energy and build solid relationships. I guarantee it.

You are in the driver's seat. It all begins with your mental state and what you say to yourself on a daily basis. What do you say to yourself about your love phase and single status before going out into the world every day? What is the conversation you have with yourself before attending an event, party or meeting? Do you ask yourself, "Why am I still alone," or "When will it happen for me?" Do you say, "God, I am [insert your age] and still alone." Or, do you find yourself thinking, "It's not my time and it will never happen for me. I doubt I'll meet that special someone." Or say, "My last relationship was a mess, why would it be any different the next time? I am too old, too boring, too busy."

⚷ *Whatever you continuously say in your mind becomes your reality. You surely will create funky vibes with depressing thoughts.*

Are you obsessing that you are not attractive enough? Thin enough? In good enough shape to feel sexy and romantic? Smart enough? Too smart? More successful than most of the people you date. Not young enough? Interesting enough? Tall enough? Talented enough? Or, that you don't make enough money? Do you believe people are attracted to you? Or, that most men or women can't handle your power and will try to change you? If you said, "yes" to any of these questions or statements, then you were imprinted in the past and are way too hard on yourself. It's time to realign your mind. You are a unique and special person, so it's time to get your confidence back in check.

☞✶ *Your thoughts are the projector in your own Love Design movie and your life is a reflection of your thoughts. Time to shift your lens!*

Only you know what you are saying to yourself every day or what thoughts you're carrying around from your past. You know how you feel about yourself, your body, your level of intelligence and your personality. Are you constantly joking about or criticizing yourself casually in conversations? Because if you are, you will keep potential partners away, and anyone who breaks through your unconscious barriers will eventually perceive you the way you have presented yourself. In the same regard, if you present yourself with confidence, self-esteem and happiness, you will attract people like a magnet. You can count on it! Either way, you can practice moment-to-moment awareness to discover your limiting thoughts and shift them in an instant.

Work daily on your negative thoughts as they arrive in your mind. Write them down and then look at what you wrote. Where did these thoughts originate? You may find that you are not only thinking these thoughts, but you are speaking them as well. Ask yourself: "Is this emotion or thought what I want to experience in my life?" or "What is the reflection I am getting back from others and or my experiences by having these negative thoughts running through my mind?"

Write out in your journal how you would respond if you were feeling on top of your game and confident. What would people say about your new disposition? What different experiences could you see entering your life if you just changed your mind the moment you heard those negative thoughts coming? You will instantly be able to feel a new, positive surge of energy running through you.

Many of us have negative programming that we aren't even aware of in our heads. Some of these programs are like computers and have built-in operating systems that run automatically until they are deleted and new programs are installed. These unconscious messages and *imprints* were installed at a young age and are still deeply embedded in your consciousness. We have our higher and lower selves, and I have found that they both present themselves at different times in our lives. We all know when our lower self takes over, because it causes us to send out negative vibes and we feel disempowered. It's time to take control and realign our minds and hearts to receive love now. This is an inside-out job. When we send mixed signals, we get mixed results and it is caused by not being congruent with our thoughts and beliefs. As we change, the negative parts will sometimes battle with us to stay the same because it's easier than changing.

Part of the challenge is not being clear or conscious of our internal thought processes. Our goals and core beliefs from the past run us until we snap out of them and focus on a new vision. The various exercises coming up will help you *wake up*. You will begin to hear how you sound or say things, and you will get an idea of why you are or aren't having success in certain areas of your life. You should notice a distinct shift in conscious awareness after doing this work. You will become aware of the unconscious messages you send out without even knowing it. Then, you can begin to rebuild and change your life. Being unconscious of the words you speak prevents you from having loving relationships and creates energy-draining states that affect your vocal tone and energy.

THE FIRST IMPRESSION IS A LASTING ONE

Now that you are becoming aware of how powerful your old, inner beliefs are, it's time to become conscious of your conversations. Remember, this initial impression sends out the first signal for connection. If your internal conversation is still negative, you may lose contact unless you are speaking with someone on the same vibration. Many people say they felt instant chemistry on a date, but after talking with them, they pulled back and seemed distant or uninterested. What went wrong? I usually ask what they talked about, and after role-playing, I quickly discover why they exited the scene. Many singles have similar experiences that leave them perplexed. What are you saying on dates that could be sabotaging your love life?

⚬━✕ *During the first conversation, many of us communicate unconsciously and we get the opposite reaction and wonder what happened. Think before you speak.*

If we were really aware of what we said and the vibes we sent out, we would have known why our date left uninterested. To better illustrate this idea, you will realize that those internal beliefs about love, dating and the opposite sex are often exposed during casual conversations. It is crucial to be conscious of the messages we are sending out and pay attention to how we tend to over analyze every word a person says to us. Depending on which phase we are in, both men and women test and qualify each other in the first five minutes with subtle questions to see if they are a match. After watching thousands of singles go through the five-minute rapid dating process, I have observed people sending out mixed signals. Some people like to control the pace of relationships and scare potential partners away. Most of them didn't get the results they wanted because they were interrogating their dates instead of just having fun. The people with the most success had open energy and no expectations. I witnessed hundreds of couples that ordinarily wouldn't have been attracted to each other match up. They were just being themselves, living in the moment and then "magic" happened!

⚬━✕ *Become acutely aware of the things you say and the impact your words have on dates or social situations.*

What verbal signals are you sending? Too many busy businesspeople mistakenly believe that if they expose all of their successes up front, it will capture someone's interest. You might want to think twice about discussing how much you work, a big deal you just closed or how often you travel for business on the first date. You may think these things will impress them. If they're looking for a life partner to build a relationship with, your busy *wonder woman* or *super man* vibe might chase them away. It's important to be aware of how you are communicating because they may assume you have no time for love. I know this to be true because many of the men I dated told me that I sent out this busy vibe and they got turned off.

O━┳ *Keep some things about yourself a mystery so that your date can unveil you layer by layer and see you for your soul, not just your successes.*

Are your conversations leaving others with the thoughts you want them to have about you? Check out people who are around you right now. Many people you attract are often a mirror of who you are. Are they a good reflection or representation about how you feel about yourself? Do you have loyal friends who show up for you? Do they treat you the way you feel worthy of being treated? Do you give others the same type of love and respect that you want to receive? Do the people in your inner circle embody the principles that you truly deserve or desire to have in your life? If not, take a deeper look within. You will create relationships with friends and lovers that are representative of how you believe you deserve to be treated.

It's possible that you have casually used some of the comments that are listed below in your daily conversations. Some of these statements are energy-draining and can create barriers that prevent you from moving forward with your life or opening up to new social situations. Suppose you're at a party and someone asks you: "How are you doing in the dating game? How's your love life going? Why are *you* still single?" How do you normally reply to those questions?

Below are some actual answers that I've heard at my events and from coaching clients around the world. Which comments sound like your typical responses? Take notes in your journal and let's *get real* about what comes out of your mouth! Add your own responses if they aren't on the list.

CONVERSATIONS THAT CREATE BARRIERS TO LOVE

- *I'm too busy right now… love is not a priority for me.*
- *It is impossible for me to meet anyone that is my type. I'm very picky.*
- *I am just not into dating right now.*
- *Once I _____ then finding love will be on my radar.*
- *Love often pulls me off balance and I tend to get distracted from my responsibilities.*

- *Most people are intimidated by my power and confidence. That is their problem…not mine!*
- *I don't have good luck and always end up in dead-end relationships.*
- *I have a pattern of meeting unavailable men/women that just want to play.*
- *I can't find a good match on my level.*
- *I never meet anyone who fits my vision.*
- *I think I'm a great catch, but the people I meet are pathetic.*
- *When I meet someone that is too available, I quickly lose interest.*
- *I'd rather be alone than be with the wrong person.*
- *I date men, train them and then they marry the next girl.*
- *When I go out, I always seem to attract jerks.*
- *I feel invisible when I go out. Men/women don't notice or flirt with me at all.*
- *I'm no good at flirting and am never sure if a man is interested or not.*
- *Most of the people I meet are a bit damaged from their past relationships.*
- *Everyone is so unattainable when I go out to social events.*
- *I should go out, but I'm tired. I don't enjoy going out alone and I never meet anyone anyway….*
- *I don't want anyone controlling me. I like my independence!*
- *I don't believe that love lasts…so why should I bother?*
- *I will be happy once I meet someone/lose weight/work out/clean my place/feel great/look for a new job.*
- *All the good ones are taken.*
- *Most of the people I am attracted to are too young for me or just not my type.*
- *Love hurts so why bother?*
- *You cannot trust most men or women.*
- *The people I'm attracted to are not attracted to me.*
- *I am too lazy/hurt/tired or broke to meet anyone right now.*
- *Love is impossible to find at this point in my life.*

- *It's not easy for me to connect with people at parties and bars.*
- *I don't enjoy going to networking events... they are sooo boring.*
- *Men are difficult to please. They only want young, hot, sexy women.*
- *Women are difficult to please. They only want unavailable, "bad boys."*
- *I don't like dating. I'm not good at all this new online technology.*
- *It's hard to find a man who wants commitment.*
- *I'll try again once I have more time.*
- *I am not in a good space to meet my soul mate right now.*
- *I want to date but I haven't had any luck. When will it be my turn?*
- *I am so over it and am not in the mood for love right now.*
- *I cannot imagine someone loving me. I give up.*
- *I am sure that I won't attract someone, because I'm not feeling confident.*
- *Most of the men I meet are losers.*
- *Most of the women I meet are users.*
- *I don't believe in love.*
- *I've given up on love. I'm done with men/women!*

Do any of these comments sound familiar? Now that you are aware of them, you can recognize how they tend to pollute your conversations and create barriers to love. It all begins with your state of mind and the limiting beliefs that stop the flow of love in your life. I am not saying your mind is negative all the time, yet a few of those statements may make you more mindful of what you are sharing about love and dating. This part of the *get real* process is helping you to identify what you are unconsciously thinking and communicating.

Remember, as you become more aware of what automatically comes out of your mouth, you will change your conversations and the *energy vibes* you send out. The goal is clear: we want to let go of old beliefs and habits since they cause us to recreate the same experiences and attract the same type of people over and over. Let's break the patterns now!

SUBCONSCIOUS MIND AWARENESS

"Whatever the mind can conceive and believe, it can achieve."
– Napoleon Hill

Your internal thoughts are the stepping-stones to success. Say to your-self, "That was then and this is now. In this moment I am open to unlimited possibilities and great relationships in all areas of my life." It's easy to change by making it a practice to give commands to your subconscious mind, reaffirming them to yourself daily. *Act as if* you have already experienced your goals and you will begin to see a huge shift. After a while, this will become a habit and the results you'll see will encourage you to do a repeat performance. By focusing on your desired outcome and speaking with conviction and intention, you master your mind, upgrade your conversations and create your ultimate destiny.

This is where NLP, hypnotherapy and other powerful mind-shifting techniques come into play because our subconscious mind attracts experiences according to our beliefs. Our subconscious mind:

+ *Takes our language literally*
+ *Responds to our feelings*
+ *Runs our body*
+ *Is always alert and functioning*
+ *Receives directions from our conscious mind*
+ *Responds to repetition*
+ *Plays back what it receives in our life like a computer*
+ *Takes everything personally*

☞ *The subconscious mind does not know the difference between positive and negative phrases and takes your words personally and literally as do most people. Think before you speak and carefully choose the words you share about yourself with others. Keep it in mind that the people you meet only remember your last conversation; so make your dialogue memorable and upbeat.*

WHO DRIVES YOUR THOUGHTS?
LOVE IMPRINTS FROM YOUR PAST

As an adult, we can examine and reframe the *real truth* about our experiences, especially if they were not positive. We will discover when you let those limiting beliefs into your soul that have, until now, been your self-fulfilling prophecy. Once I did this work, I began healing my heart as you are right now. As you read these examples, you can see how these memories may have limited their ability to attract *real love*. Many of the people you date have their own *love imprints* as well. Here are some of my clients' true stories that created powerful *love imprints* and limiting beliefs. So tune in when asking questions about a person's family and upbringing to detect any red flags.

"My parents were inseparable and my mom was super dependent on my father for everything. I thought it was great they were so in love, yet I wanted nothing to do with that type of co-dependent lifestyle. I steered clear of marriage since I feared I would lose my independence and I didn't want someone to rely on me to take care of them."

"I was taught to take care of myself by my single mother, who raised three of us on her own. She was strong, independent and had several boyfriends, but never let men get too close to her. Although she was a great mom, she had issues trusting in love because my father cheated on her and abandoned our family. When I would meet a good person, I couldn't even accept their support or gifts since I doubted their intentions. She taught me how to survive on my own and I find it difficult to trust anyone with my heart."

"I saw how my Dad controlled my mom and I swore I would never let a man have that kind of power over me. I am a bit of a control freak and find it challenging to let men help me. Most men perceive me as bossy and demanding but, deep down, I really want let go and have a supportive partner."

"My father never noticed or spent time with me since he was always busy working. I tried to get his attention my whole life by being a super achiever and trying to please him with my accomplishments. Instead of giving me his time, he would hand me cash as my reward. I felt dismissed, like he didn't care about my

heart or my feelings. I attracted partners just like him for years. I found myself giving too much, too soon to unavailable people in order to get their approval. I kept love at a distance for many years."

"My mother was amazing and beautiful, but was mentally and physically abused by my dad for years. This showed me that it was okay to stay with men that treat you badly. My dad also verbally and sexually abused me. My mom had no way of protecting me. She never spoke up since he was so volatile. We finally escaped from his abuse when I was thirteen. I still have unhealthy dating patterns and fears of expressing my real feelings with my family and with men."

"My parents had the ultimate marriage and the most romantic relationship. I look for the perfect partner but most of them can't live up to the high standards of my parent's relationship. I find fault with the people I meet, and I expect them to know how to love me like my dad loves my mom. I am very particular about what I want and people often say I am too picky!"

"I had to look pretty and be perfect to satisfy my critical grandmother who told me I'd never find a man with the way I looked. I am hypercritical about my appearance and have always doubted that a man would fall for me. I even question if I am good enough and find it hard to accept compliments."

WHAT DID YOU LEARN ABOUT LOVE & RELATIONSHIPS GROWING UP?

"No one can make you feel inferior without your consent."
– **Eleanor Roosevelt**

As we grew up, we watched how our parents and family members interacted. We absorbed the energy vibes and words while our subconscious and conscious minds' stored the memories in the order they were experienced. Even if your parents were married for many years, their actions, conversations and behavior, whether positive or negative, etched beliefs into your mind. These experiences have now created a running theme in your life about relationships and became your unique *love imprints.*

Now, we are going to uncover memories that have been injected by people with happy or crappy programming. You might be surprised what your mind can recall when you ask it to remember. For example, I was constantly influenced by mixed signals about love and men as I was growing up. One day I would be hugging one of my uncles, and the next he would be referred to as "a cheating bastard." Then, the following week, he would be gone from the family with no explanation. I was totally confused and my innocent, precious heart received its first layer of pain—along with some bad messages that took years to uncover and heal. Here is the memory of how my love role modeling and *imprints* began.

TRUE STORY

I was upstairs playing with my Barbie and Ken dolls when I heard the doorbell ring. I was only five or six years old and up way past my bedtime. As I snuck down the stairs, I overheard my aunt hysterically crying to my mother in our kitchen saying, "What am I going to do? It's going to be so hard to raise four kids all alone, and what man will ever want to be with me and all this baggage? I feel so hurt and betrayed." My other aunts then arrived to console her, and I stayed hidden on the stairs behind the wall to listen to their conversations.

After hearing the doorbell ring a few times, my inquisitive grandmother, who had her own apartment with my grandfather downstairs, came up to see what all the fuss was about. She had great ears and overheard the crying as well as a few minutes of the conversation. As she slowly climbed the kitchen stairs, she yelled, "Men, they are all liars and bastards. You can't trust any of them!" No one knew I was hiding on the stairs that night. If they knew, I am sure they would not have shared so many disturbing details about the pain my aunt was experiencing. She had just found out her husband was having an affair with another woman. She was broken-hearted and felt betrayed.

Once that affair was exposed, I continued to hear stories from the women in my family that were experiencing the same betrayal. I saw people very close to me suffer from constant heartbreak, and then continue to stay in bad relationships for years. I swore I would never trust men until they proved themselves to me. These experiences tainted my vision of love and messed with my little heart!

Can you imagine how powerful and damaging those thoughts could be to a happy, *little girl*? One minute I was marrying off my Ken and Barbie, and the next I wasn't sure if I believed in *true love* or fairy tales at all. What ever happened to my *prince charming*? I had been injected with the fear that men would leave me, even if I was great. At that moment, I made an unconscious and limiting decision. A limiting decision is a strong statement of conviction a powerful truth that is often based on fear and conditioning anchored in your mind from a negative or traumatic experience. I remember thinking and claiming, "I will NEVER let that happen to me! I'll take care of myself." Later in my life, this translated into believing men would leave me and that I would struggle to raise kids on my own.

For years, I witnessed the financial and emotional dramas my family experienced. There were numerous divorces and scandals that added more fears about letting love into my heart. Many of our family, friends and relatives also had challenges with relationships, and they would come to our house to have treats and conversations in the kitchen.

Our house became the central hub for love therapy with my mom and aunts acting as angels, supporting each other as they raised kids through the betrayal and pain. They were strong women who survived infidelity and divorce. Ultimately, they reinvented their lives with strength, faith and determination. The good news is that they're all now happily remarried. Even after all this healing transpired in my family, the messages I heard still rang loud and clear in my mind. Marriage and kids still didn't sound like fun to me. I doubted if I would ever want to raise children of my own. I promised myself that I would never end up becoming a single mom. No thanks!

I made a commitment to become successful and knew I was capable of taking care of myself. All of my siblings ended up getting married, and my family couldn't understand why I kept attracting the wrong men. Most of them had no idea of what I had overheard or witnessed at such a young age and how those experiences shaped my early imprints.

This story was one the *first* messages I heard growing up, as well as hearing the women in my family say they would: "Turn the other cheek and keep the family together no matter what. Men 'do what they do' and we just have to deal with it … it's an Italian thing!" The men would work, strive and struggle to give their families the good life, but were often not around. My father worked non-stop to keep us all happy and in the best schools. I can't imagine the stress he endured while supporting his wife, six kids and his parents, all while managing three restaurants and a thriving catering business. However, as a *little girl*, I mostly remember him being "busy" and often missing special moments. I picked men just like him: charismatic, charming and constantly on-the-go taking care of business!

Growing up Italian is similar to being raised in other Mediterranean cultures: the women often had the "give too much" gene and the men typically ruled the house. The women worked hard and sacrificed their souls to make everyone else happy, while often falling apart inside. They were just following a path set up by their culture and the rules of previous generations. Back then my family was similar to the popular show from the late 1950s, *Leave it to Beaver…* Italian style. I knew I didn't want to live my life that way!

As I got older, I knew the men I dated could hear the hesitation in my voice when we talked about having kids. I had become so independent and self-sufficient that I sent off the vibe of not needing a man in my life. A part of me was the in-control, empowered *wonder woman*, and the other part was still a sensitive, damaged *little girl*. I always wondered why most of the men who wanted to have children never called me back. I was consistently hard on myself and wondered if I was just not the kind of woman men picked to marry. As I looked back into my old journals, I could see how conflicted my heart was all those years. Half of me wanted a husband, kids and love, while the other half didn't trust men at all.

☞ *Some of the messages you've heard, whether you were six or sixteen, can block your heart from being open to love or keep you in unhealthy relationships!*

I found myself sabotaging relationships with generous, caring men since I had trust issues and huge walls of protection around me. I wanted support, yet I was afraid of being dependent on any man. I realized one of my biggest limiting beliefs was that I had to get my business off the ground and achieve a certain level of financial success before I could find *true love*. This was one of my "Once I" syndromes. That strong belief was the block that kept love in my future instead of in the now. Could this be the culprit stopping you from finding *true love*?

More often than not, I wound up dating men just like me: half in half out with similar imprints in their lives. They were just as busy striving to achieve their goals and wanted some attention and affection. I gave away my love to a few unavailable men in order to fill a void, yet all along I instinctively knew they weren't right for me.

I pushed away some great men because I was in a constant struggle with both parts of myself. Now, I realize that it was my *little girl* choosing most of the men I dated for some temporary feeling of love, not the powerful side of me. Until this awakening, I was spinning inside and unable to achieve the inner peace I yearned for and deserved. I asked for guidance since *little Renée* had kept me safe long enough. I was ready to change my patterns and find *real love*.

I had my big breakthrough when I returned to school to become a clinical hypnotherapist and NLP practitioner. During the extensive training I became 100% conscious and gradually uncovered my patterns and *love imprints* through NLP Time Line Therapy. It amazed me how many memories surfaced that helped to me see when and where the imprints originated. Aside from being an independent *wonder woman*, I had imprints of rejection that led me to believe a part of me wasn't good enough. I realized I was in a *relationship loop* and had been dating the same type of man over and over, with similar "equipment" but different names. I still needed to address the unhealthy imprints that were influencing my life. But where did those patterns originate? The following story from my childhood came up in a Time Line session during my training.

TRUE STORY

It was Halloween day and my kindergarten class had a costume party. I vividly remember this as the day my *"men will hurt you"* belief manifested in my first experience with a boy that I had a mad crush on! Anthony was a handsome, Italian boy who used to chase me and pull my hair in class every day. This flirting ritual was a sure sign that a boy likes you at that age.

That morning, I came dressed in my animal print costume as Bamm-Bamm, from the Flinstone's and felt like I was on the top of the world. I remember my Mom saying, "You look so adorable honey." As I jumped out of the car, Anthony rushed towards me to see my costume and I was so excited by his expression he loved it! We held hands as we went into the party and shared our candy. The classroom was decorated and all the kids were wound up with all the excitement.

Then, suddenly, Anthony's head turned as one of my adorable classmates made her dramatic entrance as the perfect mini-*Cinderella*. She was a show-stopper with her long blonde hair, flowing pink gown and princess crown; Anthony was mesmerized. She smiled and it was like a light went off in his head! He instantly left my side for her and never came back to play. After feeling so special, I was suddenly replaced and felt rejected. What was wrong with me? Maybe I wasn't pretty enough? I told my mom that Anthony didn't pick me and how it made me feel so sad. I cried as she gently rubbed my hair saying, "You're a beautiful little girl and sometimes boys just want to play with other friends at school. So, let's go get some ice cream and it will make you feel better." (No wonder ice cream is one of my favorite comfort foods!) From that day on, she was his new obsession and I had no idea what happened. That first rejection was etched into my mind and made me believe that boys were not to be trusted. However, I kept trying to get Anthony's attention by bringing him candy and chasing him, but he had moved on. Once again, my storybook fantasies were shattered and another imprint was planted deep in my heart.

This innocent and somewhat comical experience may seem trivial, but it created a rejection pattern that repeated itself in many of my earlier interactions with boys. At age 12, my first teenage crush invited me to his birthday party and then snuck away with my best friend. I caught them kissing in a pickup truck with his hand up her shirt! I ran off and cried my eyes out that day. Once again, I was quickly replaced by a cute blonde, which added to my layers of self-doubt and mistrust of boys. Then, there was a friend of my brothers who would tease and flirt with me, only to dismiss me in front of his friends. His constant mixed signals left me feeling confused and insecure. Mix these *love imprints* with overhearing stories of infidelity in my family and you get one confused teenager.

Most of my clients had similar heartbreaks and experienced rejection when they were younger that left them feeling unworthy. The stories throughout this book may remind you of some of your old imprints, which could be your invisible barriers to love. Having distrust in men, believing they're all unfaithful and that I had to take care of myself were my strongest limiting beliefs. I later realized those imprints were not my truth; they were merely based on a few upsetting experiences from my childhood that were planted in my subconscious mind for years.

My life changed dramatically when I began to regularly practicing the various reprogramming techniques from my training. I realized that my *little girl* had been unconsciously running the show for many years of my life. I always believed I had to reach a certain level of accomplishment first, then I would find a man! This was the big belief that always kept love just out of my reach. It took a lot of work and patience to convince both *little Renée* and my *wonder woman* side to trust that great men were out there that would love me for all of who I am. With time, my *little girl* started to trust and believe that it

106

was possible to have a successful career as well as a wonderful relationship at the same time.

As I healed, I made new powerful agreements and aligned both parts of myself towards a new type of man: someone happy, committed, successful, family-oriented, honest and, most importantly, available and ready for love. This was when I experienced a significant shift in my life, opened my heart and set new goals for finding *true love*. Then, not only did my life change but so did the men I attracted. Suddenly, I had numerous suitors who wanted a committed relationship because both parts of me were aligned with my vision. I was safe to love and my *true love* showed up at the perfect time!

Through these amazing processes, I started passing along my wisdom to heal other hearts along the way. As my coaching business expanded, I incorporated various powerful techniques in my all of my sessions to help people *get ready for love*. The results were remarkable!

I am also grateful to have had the opportunity to work intimately with so many wonderful and successful men. In my seminars, I discovered that most men are just as sensitive as we are about *matters of the heart*. Once they began to share their old love stories from grade school through college, I would catch glimpses of the unhealed *little boy* in each of them and see their vulnerability. This helped me to realize that they have their own *love imprints* and their inner critics talking inside their minds. This gave me the opportunity to understand men in a way most women never experience. Their transparency expanded my heart, became a catalyst for my own healing and allowed me to tap into the minds of men. What a gift! This awareness was life-changing and one of the driving forces to pass this information on to the women of the world.

�━х *Guess what? Men have the same inner conflicts and imprints as women. They need us to be loving and patient with them, especially since they typically don't have as much guidance as we do in these areas. Remember, we are the powerful persuaders who influence men with our love and feminine energy.*

Now that you've read my stories, it's time to reflect and list any memories that come to mind when you think of what you may have heard, seen or experienced in regard to love as you were growing up. Do you have any similar memories surfacing right now?

These could be the limiting beliefs and powerful declarations influencing your current mindset and preventing you from opening your heart to love. Take a look at your culture and upbringing to see if there are any family patterns contributing to your unique *love imprints*. These messages often came from people you modeled after and trusted. Whether positive or negative, the messages added new layers of beliefs about love, success, sex and money that need to be examined. Otherwise, you will end up creating the same type of relationships over and over, until your *little girl* or *little boy* is healed. Don't analyze, just write down what is true for you in the exercise below.

LIST 5 MESSAGES YOU BELIEVED ABOUT YOURSELF & LOVE

1. _____
2. _____
3. _____
4. _____
5. _____

Now that you've listed some of your old messages, you can see how some of these powerful statements shattered your faith and set you up to feel unworthy of love. Many of us have stored up hard-edged memories and now- it's time to identify the original source(s) of those imprints.

Think back... perhaps it was your first crush or someone you dated that rejected you. An important role model may have broken a promise. A family member may have criticized your weight and appearance or teased you when you were young. Maybe a teacher or fellow student constantly belittled you in school. Or, a good friend sent jealous vibes in an attempt to destroy your confidence. You may have experienced a rocky divorce or a verbally abusive relationship. If you were lucky enough to get praise and adoration, you can often become obsessed with having to be perfect and keep up your faultless image. The list goes on. These are all examples of *love imprints* that can affect your entire life unless you examine and consciously heal them.

☙━☓ *The negative beliefs of your love lineage are not yours to inherit or pass on to future generations. It's time to take your power back. The pattern stops with you!*

Your mind is so powerful that it links old pictures, words and limiting decisions that can subconsciously block love and success from coming into your life. If you had a traumatic or emotional experience, you may have built a wall of protection so thick that no one can get beyond it. You could act out these patterns for years and push away some amazing opportunities, or attract people who are unavailable.

When someone new shows up, past fears or memories could resurface and cause your heart to automatically shut down. You may find yourself sabotaging the relationship for fear of getting hurt. These old memories can be triggered at unusual times: when you're holding hands with someone new, smelling a familiar scent, hearing an old song or driving by places that you visited in the past. When you think back on those experiences, you may get that familiar twinge of mixed emotions because you never had closure from a past relationship or situation.

Now that you've unlocked some of your messages about love it's important to write out the circumstance and the people involved that may have caused those beliefs. I'm sure you can recall vivid scenes and people from your past that may have clouded or damaged your heart's openness to love. You may want to reference your old journals to help uncover your previous mindsets about old relationships, dating and love. Does anything or anyone come to mind? These are the keys to unlocking your heart to finding deeper love.

You may find that you have two sides of yourself chatting in your head. Don't worry, you aren't going crazy! You are just starting to get in touch with your unhealed *little girl* or *little boy*. Once you are conscious of past *imprints*, you can begin to set new intentions and agreements to align with your new, higher self. It's important to reiterate that the unhealed and wounded parts of yourself often choose the people you date. I know this process can be challenging but it's designed to help you heal and free up space in your heart for love. Once both sides of you heal, you will be aligned and ready to receive *real love* at last! After this exercise, I will share how to integrate those parts in order to move in one direction to achieve your ultimate love vision.

Now, list the people in your life who passed on messages or imprints to you. Who comes to mind? Was it your unavailable father, critical mother, a jealous sibling, a close friend who betrayed you, a first love or someone who hurt you in some way? You know the people I am talking about ... right?

UNCOVER YOUR LOVE IMPRINTS & THE SOURCE

1. Love Imprint _____

   The Source _____

2. Love Imprint _____

   The Source _____

3. Love Imprint _____

   The Source _____

4. Love Imprint _____

   The Source _____

5. Love Imprint _____

   The Source _____

GET REAL ♥ REFLECTIONS

♥ Are your thoughts and conversations aligned with your ultimate vision of love?

♥ Have you been sending out mixed signals and getting mixed results in your relationships?

♥ What are some of those signals you may have sent in your conversations that impacted the results you got on dates or in social situations?

♥ What were the prominent messages and imprints that could be holding you back from finding *real love*?

♥   As you uncover the memories and the people who were the main sources of your imprints, just know that your heart is on its way to being free.

The next chapter is about being your own Love Investigator. I will show you how to heal, and learn the lessons from relationships in your past.

CHAPTER VIII
BE YOUR OWN LOVE INVESTIGATOR

"When we think we have been hurt by someone in the past, we build up defenses to protect ourselves from being hurt in the future. So the fearful past causes a fearful future and the past and future become one. We cannot love when we feel fear.... When we release the fearful past and forgive everyone, we will experience total love and oneness with all."
– Gerald G. Jampolsky

UNLOCK YOUR FAMILY HISTORY & SECRET LOVE IMPRINTS

This step is meant to empower you and heal your past by investigating the sources of your love and self-esteem programming. In my case, I figured if the people from my past gave me those messages, they probably had some negative imprints running in their lives as well. This work made me see even deeper into the truth of where my imprints began!

Now it is your turn to do some *heart-healing* love investigation since some of your memories could be cloudy. In the last chapter you had listed a few people who passed on their beliefs or imprinted your heart...right? Deep inside these memories, stories and mindsets are the core of the wounded parts of ourselves that want love and desire healing.

BECOME YOUR OWN LOVE INVESTIGATOR

It's time to discover more about your family history and your *love lineage* by asking for support and facts on some of these situations you remembered. Besides your family and siblings, you can also ask neighbors, old friends, co-workers, teachers or an old high school friend who may recall the situation(s). The perspective of outsiders can offer you insights and clarity on any old memories that have blocked you for so long.

As I started to investigate, I did some serious research on the love history of my family ancestry by asking lots of questions of my mom, dad and other relatives about my ancestors and extended family. I also questioned my siblings about their *love imprints* and memories. When I contacted people I'd say, "Do you mind if I ask you questions about some foggy memories that I have from my childhood? I want to clarify some facts that came up recently and I knew you might have some insights." Most people would be willing and interested to help answer my questions.

It amazed me that most of my siblings didn't have the same *imprints* about love as I did, since they did not see or hear what I saw. After discussing some of my old memories they all had different versions and interpretations based on their own experiences. We all became much closer during this process as we opened up and healed old wounds from the past. We were in gratitude for all the blessings in our family and were often amazed at some of the hidden *secrets* we learned from each other. As I further investigated, I learned that my imprints stemmed from four generations of *wonder women* in my family tree. I also discovered some family patterns that got passed from generation to generation that I would never have uncovered if I had not asked about the details.

This is where I began to see the workaholic survival pattern that many of my relatives had in my lineage. They were all immigrants from Italy arriving in the early 1900's. They struggled to make a new life since they made very little money. These men and women were brave and daring, and many of them shared their dramatic tales that made me appreciate how blessed we are today.

Since both my father and grandmother loved to tell stories, their amazing tales stirred my curiosity to dig deeper into my research. I contacted other members of the family to investigate their experiences. Some of the relatives in my bloodline opened up, others resisted. I was fortunate to discover other fascinating and shocking *secrets* and beliefs that were passed on to them from their families along the way. As my aunts and great aunts shared their stories with me about struggling to overcome adversity, I noticed that they often had stored up emotions that were able to be released and healed. It was fascinating to discover how many their children followed in their footsteps by getting married young and experienced divorce as well. There were many affairs and scandals that helped me to understand their pain as well as some happy endings to prove that love does prevail.

Turns out, these conversations were unexpected gifts for all of us. I got to see how their belief systems and hard-working ethics got injected unconsciously into my mind, as well as imprinting my siblings and extended family. Many of us learned to become workaholics and people pleasers by following in the footsteps of the generations before us. I am proud to say that our upbringing also instilled us to have a strong work ethics and we have a family that many people would be honored to be a part of. I am so grateful to have been instilled with that passion for life from my family and we are all finally waking up slowing down to appreciate the special moments in life. We were trained to "never to give up" which was one of my father's life-long mantras that we all live by. These messages have molded me into the woman I am today, and act as my compass to create balance in other areas of my life. I am on a mission to pass it on.

Once I understood I was taking on some of my relatives "old beliefs", based on their experiences as the truth for *my* life, I was determined to break the *love lineage* and my relationship patterns for good I proclaimed to myself: "I kept love at a distance long enough and I can have it all. I'm breaking the spell of their beliefs and experiences now and I'm going to design my life my own way and find *real love*."

☞ *Shining the light on the love imprints you have experienced is the key to healing your heart, as well as transcending lineage patterns passed down from generation to generation.*

So after all my love investigating and research I knew I still unconsciously carried an old theme of "All men are liars and bastards and they will leave you" running in my head. I was determined to change that belief once and for all. I decided to go to the main source of where I originally heard those statements and find out why my grandmother was so adamant about her claims. Here is one of my *love lineage* stories that changed my life:

TRUE STORY

It all began when I was visiting my family for the holidays. It was a cold Christmas morning back in 1998. My 87-year-old grandmother slowly emerged from her apartment downstairs in her blue flannel robe with her signature hairdo, a bun rolled on top of her head. My parents and my dear friend Scott all sat in the kitchen eating the delicious leftovers from our feast the night before. Scott and I began asking my grandmother questions about her life and information about when she came over from Italy. I had heard some of these stories but upon asking more probing questions about her marriage and divorce during the 1930's, some amazing *secrets* came out that I had never heard before. She said, "Oh hell, I might as well tell you the *real* truth since I am going to be gone soon enough." The stories were so detailed that it made you feel like you were there. It was like a scene out of a movie, and we were all mesmerized. This experience reminded me of the film "The Titanic" as we continued to listen to the wild journey of her life starting when she was a little girl!

This adventure turned into an intense eight-hour conversation. My grandmother finally had the chance to reveal some of her hidden, painful *secrets* and those of her mother, whose husband deserted her with four children in Virginia after moving from Italy back in the early 1900's. According to my grandmother, my great grandfather was a very jealous man. He worked hard on the docks and my great grandmother went there every day with her girls to bring him lunch. All the men would howl at her, and all heads would turn because she was so beautiful and sexy. Her husband had a bad temper and hated the men looking at her lustfully. One afternoon her husband took her out for a day in the field for a "romantic picnic" with wine, cheese and bread. That day, he told her, "Today I am going to mark you as my own I do not want any other man to want you, so you will be mine." She did not quite understand what he meant. He then grabbed her head and pulled her towards him as he attempted to cut and mark her soft beautiful face with a straight edge razor. She put up her arm just in time to block him from cutting her face, and instead he slashed the main artery near her wrist. She jumped up and began running for her life. She ran swiftly toward the street from the field with blood heavily flowing from her wrist. He was running to catch her as she screamed and she ended up near the street; people were watching her as she passed out. He came to her side and tied his shirt like a tourniquet around her arm to stop the bleeding, and he ran off saying he was going to find a doctor. He never returned.

When she woke up a few days later, she discovered he had jumped on a ship back to Italy, and he left her and the four girls abandoned in Virginia. She was alone in America with no family, very little money, and could barely speak English. Once she recovered, she went to the docks to find out more information on him and one of his friends, Dominico, who was secretly in love with her, started to bring her food, clothes and money. He wanted to support her since she was cleaning houses and doing tea leaf readings to support the girls. My great grandmother was considered a healer and a fortune-teller who eventually married my great grandfather Nepi.

So, my grandmother was abandoned by her real father, and her mother remarried. Apparently my great grandmother was a "baby-making machine" and my grandmother then became the oldest of seventeen living children. She and her other sisters, from her biological dad, became babysitters, cooks and maids to help their mother raise all the children. My great aunts claimed they never wanted to have kids since they felt like slaves all those years, yet eventually some of them did get married and raised children. These were the some of the stories I heard which left strong imprints on me about kids and men!

My grandmother told us she had sworn she would never have children, and stated, "The only way to escape my hell from having to cook, clean, and scrub diapers, the old-fashioned way, was to get married." Luckily, she fell in love at seventeen with her first Italian husband, Pete, and got married. To her surprise, a few months later she got pregnant. After she had my father, a story was going around town that her husband was having an affair, but she ignored the rumors. Unfortunately, she found out that the rumors were true. After my dad was born back in 1931, she left her husband to raise my dad alone. My father was only six months old when they moved in with her in-laws, who were very upset with their son for his infidelities and for shaming the family. She carried resentments toward Pete, and just wanted to move on. A few months later, his very pregnant girlfriend surfaced to try to find him at his mother's home. My grandmother heard a knock on the door and came face to face with her husband's mistress, who was six months pregnant, and didn't have anywhere to turn for help. While in shock, my grandmother invited her in to eat and they discussed the situation. She then discovered Pete had run away to Chicago to hide, so she kindly packed up my father's infant clothes (that he had outgrown) in a small white basket and gave the clothes to her husband's mistress. She proclaimed, "You can use these clothes, and you can have him too…the SOB." His parents shipped his mistress to Chicago where they eventually married and had five more children, my father's half brothers and sisters.

My grandmother went to the Catholic Church to ask for support, but she was a divorcee, and considered a sinner back then. She was shunned by the church. I always wondered why she hardly attended services and was very upset with the church. Now I finally understood the pain she harbored as she told us the story. Hearing the details, seeing her expressions, and feeling all of her emotions made me so much more compassionate to her situation. My veil was lifted. She made me see and understand why she was so bitter and wanted to protect me from her pain! This story also helped my siblings clear up some of their *love imprints*.

As she struggled to raise my dad on her own, while living with her ex-husband's mother; my father's godfather, Sam, brought her clothes and money to help with my dad when he visited the house. Along with Sam, other men would come to play cards, eat and drink homemade alcohol, which was made illegally in my great grandfather's basement during the prohibition. My grandmother cooked her delicious food and cleaned "to earn her keep."

Eventually, Sam asked her to marry him, and she accepted. She told me her reason for accepting was that, "He was kind to your dad, he had nice shoes and I thought he was a generous man." He offered to raise my father, and she mentioned he would be a good provider since he helped build the Blanca warplanes and had a good job. They got married and Sam adopted my father. After my parents got married, my grandparents ended up living in their own apartment with our family the rest of their lives. Sam was a kind and generous grandfather to all of us and watched us girls like a hawk. Throughout the years, she told me that she caught him being unfaithful many times, and she was heart-broken again, but stayed with him until he passed away. She claimed, "That is what Italian men do. We had to keep the family together, and accept that is how men are. We just had to shut up and live on."

Needless to say, my grandmother carried her anger and pain about love through her life. She passed on some doubts and fears to most of my siblings along the way regarding beauty, love and men. My sisters also had some healing to do, and once we all discussed her heart-breaking love stories, we were all able to see why our grandmother had so much resentment and challenges with her weight and health. She was heartbroken yet despite her circumstances was still a loving grandmother to all of us.

Once I learned these shocking facts about her experiences, (and those of many of my relatives who experienced infidelity in their lives), I told her I was so sorry that she had to go through that, and how much it helped me let go of the belief she had passed on. I was going to be the one woman in my lineage that would not let her experiences take me down a negative spiral. I decided that despite my grandmother's story, I would believe in love and trust that there are good men in the world. I made a decision I would be the example to others to dispel and heal those family patterns once and for all! I told her I was going to share her tale someday and make a movie out of it. I mentioned a few actors that might play her role on the big screen and she loved that idea.

Believe it or not, I think my grandmother was relieved to get these *secrets* off her chest and she died in peace knowing we understood her heart and did not have to live her legacy. After my grandmother passed away, we all learned so much by asking my father and other family members questions in order to get more details. Those stories were spicy for sure! There was one more hidden *secret* that I still didn't know about until after she was gone.

As it turns out, she did have a secret admirer that she confessed to having loved, named Anthony. Apparently, he wanted to take her with him to Florida in her late fifties, but she made her choice to stay with my grandfather and told him she could not leave her family. So my grandmother did find true love, and never revealed the truth to anyone until she was on her deathbed. She told my older sister, Theresa, to tell me that she did experience real love after all. I recall that time in her life very vividly when she suddenly was sad, cried and slept a lot. I always wondered what caused her states of depression, and I asked my mother about it.

My mother confirmed the year before she passed away that this man did exist. My grandmother had made the choice to not leave her six grandchildren and our family because she would never have felt right about that decision. "So, Grandmom, rest in peace, knowing that you did have love in your life, and we always knew you had loyalty towards the family. You telling the truth to Theresa freed me from the harsh words I heard about men and showed me that I can believe in love after all!" Interesting how I met my *true love* only a few years later. I had finally knocked down the walls that had been built up to protect me from opening my heart to *real love* as a young girl. This realization was extremely powerful. I finally knew the truth and my heart was free at last!

After reading the story about my lineage, I encourage you to think about your own family stories or experiences and begin to uncover them one by one. The imprints could be about sex, money, self-worth, success, love and relationships. Just think of how much space is taken up in your mind and heart from carrying your old family memories and their beliefs around with you. Some of those stories may have additional facts that you never knew. Just imagine if you have these stories running in your mind and how you may be unconsciously passing them down to your friends, children, and even to the people you date. I know that by healing your *love imprints* you will also help to heal the hearts of your relatives in your *love lineage*. They can finally rest in peace knowing the pattern has been broken forever. Your heart-healing work is a powerful example that will inspire living relatives and future generations to create healthier relationships. So, let's investigate further since there may be other relationships that have left imprints on your heart.

INVESTIGATE THE PAST: A RELATIONSHIP REVIEW

Once I did the work with my family, I added another dimension to love investigation with a *Relationship Review*. It's started by listing all the people I dated that were significant in my life. I noticed a distinct pattern of falling for the men who were not available and the ones that were too available that I pushed away. Then, I re-read all my love journals from age 22, and realized I knew what I was doing all along. I was constantly battling with both parts of myself. I also observed my close friends and clients doing the same patterns. I committed to align my parts to achieve my vision. Hmm…this was another defining *aha* moment that opened me up to see that I created what I call a *love loop* of attracting unavailable men over and over. It's like the old movie, *Ground Hog Day* or a hamster on a treadmill…going round and round and having the same experience over and over with men and my heart! Holy S#!T, I had done this to myself!

Now it's your turn to conduct your personal *Relationship Review* with the people you married, dated or had a significant relationship with. Take out your journal and add their names in order and jot down some notes about the scenarios with each person and the time frame you were together. This list will help you see if there is a pattern or a *love loop* in your life as you gather more facts and clarity on your past. Add any names that pop into your mind. It's time to *get real* and break your patterns for good.

ARE YOU IN A LOVE LOOP?

1. Name _____

   Time Spent _____

Lesson Learned _____
2. Name _____
   Time Spent _____
   Lesson Learned _____
3. Name _____
   Time Spent _____
   Lesson Learned _____

Can you see your *love loop* patterns? Did you date similar types of men or women? Attract certain type of friends or experiences over and over? Did the relationships last a certain amount of time? What was the main lesson or theme of your *love loop*?

After reviewing the entries in my journals, I highlighted a few of my old boyfriends that I wanted to contact that had left imprints on my heart. I also added a few names of men that I knew I had hurt that cared about me along the way. I was on a quest and I started looking them up online. I either spoke to them over the phone or met them live to ask questions about what it was like to date me back then. I was curious to get their view on the experience so I could learn and heal old wounds. Every one of them was happy to hear from me and it gave them an opportunity to express their feelings as well. It was easier to talk about the past than I imagined. I had some heart-to-heart conversations that washed away some past misconceptions and sadness, along with some good laughs about others fun memories. I learned a lot about how I showed up "back in the day," and I had an opportunity to apologize to a few wonderful men that still had a few battle scars left over from dating me. The whole experience was profound and it helped me to open my heart and let love in!

I also called old friends who knew me back then to get their perceptions and insights on some of my old boyfriends. I wish they had been that honest back then about what they witnessed. These powerful conversations helped me reframe the past, and made me aware that each relationship was part of my growth and healing. As I let go of those negative monsters in my mind, I rebuilt my confidence and was more loving and compassionate with myself.

These insights helped me to heal my heart and *little Renée.* Then I had a clean slate to design and reframe the vision for love in the future!

⚷ *As you open up and investigate your past, you'll see how one honest conversation from the heart could change your life forever!*

It's time to commit to do these *heart-healing rituals* since you may have resentments or old feelings surfacing from your past.

⚷ *You can only expand your heart as far as it is healed. Unlock your past imprints and be free to the unlimited supply of love.*

To help you get results from facts gathered during your love investigation, I have created a *Heart Healing List* below. As you make your *list,* it will bring issues to the surface to help you let go and unlock that heart of yours.

⚷ *An open heart is the key to finding real love. It's time for you to forgive the people who passed on their imprints so your heart can be free at last!*

Begin by naming each person you still have unresolved feelings about and the level of energy you are still carrying in your heart:

HEART HEALING LIST
(#1 Being the Lowest – #10 Being the Highest)

1. Name _____
   Level of energy you carry _____
2. Name _____
   Level of energy you carry _____
3. Name _____
   Level of energy you carry _____
4. Name _____
   Level of energy you carry _____
5. Name _____
   Level of energy you carry _____

HEART HEALING RITUALS

Now that you have your list, let's take one person at a time from the list and begin with some *heart-healing techniques*. If you're not sure which person to focus on, grab your heart stone and take a few deep breathes while you're slowly scanning the list. The name of the perfect person will seem to jump off the page to begin your healing rituals.

As you move forward with the exercises below, you will find yourself having "Aha moments" as you discover your own love imprints. At this point, you may feel the negative imprints in your heart begin to dissipate and heal.

MEMORIES & FEELINGS

Write out the memories and feelings about this person with as many details you can recall. Where were you? How old were you? Describe the exact situation. Write out the words that were said, the energy you felt, what you saw that may have caused some damage or left you with a bruised heart. Write down the words of the exact belief that you may have told yourself in that moment related to that incident. As you may recall, mine was that "All men are liars and bastards and men can't be trusted." Once I wrote out the stories of my memories, I started to connect with the *little girl* aspect of myself and I could see how she internalized that pain and wanted to protect herself. *Little Renée* felt unworthy and afraid to have someone really love her because she feared she would be abandoned. I began to communicate with this part of myself to let her know I was there to build back trust and heal her heart. I asked her how she wanted to feel and she replied, "I want to feel safe, adored, loved, happy and cherished."

As you go through your heart-healing process it's important to connect and communicate with your *little girl* or *boy* so they can help you heal these relationships. When you have opposing parts of you that are not aligned with one vision, you will continue to sabotage yourself over and over again until you choose to work together. You can see why your *little girl* or *boy* created undesirable behaviors, was fighting you to attain a goal or subtly blocked you from allowing love to come into your life. You will hear those voices inside of you fight each other as you began to change.

So, how can you build a strong relationship with your *inner child*? It takes time and patience since she has been around for a while.

GET IN TOUCH WITH YOUR LITTLE GIRL OR BOY

Get into bed or a comfortable spot with some soft lighting and play soothing music that relaxes you. Get a photo of yourself and place it next to your bed, and imagine your *inner child* there next to you. Begin talking to them gently and say, "Hi little [your name]. I'm here to connect with you and I want to know if you can hear me?" Then, listen. A familiar, or unfamiliar, little voice may pop into your mind and sound different that your regular voice. Your little child may say, "Yes. I do." Or, you may feel their presence all around you. Continue by saying, "I promise, now that I've have discovered our old patterns, to check in with you to see if we are both in agreement on future decisions about the people we date and the friends in our life. I will trust your gut feelings and listen to you. Okay? In the future, we will only have loving and supporting people in our lives. Agreed?" Hopefully, you will hear an astounding YES or some sort of positive response.

Write yourself a *heart-healing* letter or journal entry about what you've learned from these people and what actions you will commit to doing in the future to take care of yourself. You may hear two opposing voices in your head. One of these voices could be your *little girl* or *boy* speaking up, so please tune in because they may not trust you at all. Ask them what they need to feel supported in regard to trusting people, feeling worthy of love, being happy, healthy and successful in life.

Write your internal conversations down. Let all of your inner thoughts spill out onto the paper without any editing. Then, you can re-read the thoughts that are coming up and shift them into your new *language of love*! These letters will serve as proof of your inner work and will help you discover your truth and the desires of your soul. Your *little girl* or *boy* will tell you what you need to hear. You may hear them say, "I want you to take better care of yourself and listen to your heart. I want you to slow down when I tell you something doesn't feel right. I need you to pay attention to my feelings and take your time for us to go in the right directions with our work and relationships. You must take more time for love, balance and rest."

Then, add the final piece by aligning both parts of yourself to head in the same direction of your new vision. This simple technique involves visualizing your *little girl* or *boy* in your left hand and your new, empowered self in your right hand. Now, make a pact with your enlightened *little* self. Place both palms together and say, "I am so proud we are aligned in our vision to keep ourselves open to an amazing partner. We are committed to finding and opening up to *real love!* We are honoring our heart and our truth, now and forever. We are ready for love!" Stop and feel the connection with your *little girl* or *boy*; you both are committed to having an open heart and moving as one. Once both parts of you are healed and headed in one direction, you will be unstoppable!

This integration applies to all areas of our life. Do a daily heart check when you feel tempted to numb your pain and you can hear your *little girl* or *boy* attempting to speak. Ask yourself: "What's going on? Is texting Steve or Alexia for a quick booty call going to fix this feeling? Is staying in this unfulfilling job or dead-end relationship the best thing for my self-esteem? Is eating this unhealthy fried food, drinking or smoking going to fill my emptiness? Am I trying to eat away my feelings? Or, is retail therapy my favorite escape? Will buying something I don't really need make me feel any better?" Well, maybe we can let the shopping pass; it is better than wasting time with your ex!

This powerful NLP Parts Integration Technique was the turning point in my healing. I promised my *little girl* that I would always be there to support and protect her. It felt peaceful to have this new awareness and a plan to heal my past imprints. I finally had a new tool to change my patterns and let love into my life without fear. My relationship with my *little girl* got stronger over time since we were working together to achieve our goal. She began to trust me and I was happier, stronger and more committed than ever. You will see how powerful this process is when you connect with this part of yourself and work together to design your new life.

Then I knew I needed to communicate with the people who were still in my heart to clear and shift these beliefs once and for all. *Little Renée* was my guide and voice to let me know who to connect with to heal once and for all.

Now ask yourself and your *little girl* or *boy* what stories and memories come up for you? This story below was one of my love journal entries that helped me to heal.

TRUE STORY

Years ago, I had an old heart wound about Mario, a handsome 100% Italian man I once dated. I met him at a popular fitness club where I was shooting a segment about flirting for my *Love Works* TV show. After our interview he asked me out on a date. I had no intention of going out with him since I knew intuitively that he was not my type. He pursued me for weeks until I gave in. He was quite the charmer, and after dating him for six months, I discovered I had gotten involved once again with an unavailable *bad boy*. By then, I had developed quite an attachment to him and experienced three years of pain and frustration. We would break up and then make up…this went on for over three years. The last time we made up, he promised I would finally meet his family over the holidays at Christmas dinner. I thought this was progress, but still had a bad feeling in my gut. I prayed for a clear sign on my way there to know by the New Year where we were headed in our relationship. Boy, did I ever get a sign that night that he was not my match. This was the *get real* experience that jolted my heart and woke me up for good!

I went there all dressed up and brought homemade cookies, wine and gifts perfectly wrapped for him. His mother was very warm and I knew that she had been a widow for many years. He had three sisters, so he was the man of the house. He was her "baby." I went into the kitchen to help his mother with the food, and she had a photo of Mario on her refrigerator in a cream linen suit I had recently given him. He had sworn to me he would never wear it since it looked like "a fag suit." So, I mentioned it to his mom, "Did you know that I bought that suit for Mario and he told me he wouldn't be caught dead wearing it." She replied, "Hmm, he wore it to his cousin's wedding and he looked like a movie star. Everyone was surprised since he normally dresses so conservatively…but he looks good in anything since he's so gorgeous!" Her gushing was a bit sickening, yet typical of Italian mothers. I replied, "Yes, I knew he would look handsome in it, I only wish I had been there to see him." I could tell Mario was uncomfortable at that point and he looked down. I added, "He had asked me to attend that wedding, but 'something came up' and he never took me." Her face blushed and I knew he had lied to me just from her expression and his body language. Then she broke the silence and quickly replied, "Let's go eat dinner!"

This is when I unexpectedly got the clear sign I had asked for about what to do with him and our relationship. We sat down with his whole family, poured some wine and began discussing his sisters and their careers. One of them worked at MTV and we began talking about my various television shows and they were intrigued. As the conversation went back and forth Mario asked his friend to guess my age. I kicked him under the table. He was two years younger than I, and he always teased me about being "the older woman." His friend said, "I'd guess she is around thirty or so." And his sister replied, "No way…she can't be older than me, she looks so young!" Mario had been drinking wine and was a bit buzzed. He accidently said "Renée is older than all of you girls and my other girlfriend is younger then everyone here." This startling news came pouring out while we were finishing our dinner in front of his entire family. I was in shock everyone was silent as he tried to back pedal out of his comment when I asked, "Mario, what did you just say? What other girlfriend?" As he stammered to make up some lie about his cousin's relative, a cute girl from Italy, who he claimed he had mentioned to me. I replied, "No Mario, I never heard about a girlfriend! How long has this *friend* been in your life?" He said, "We have been friends for a year or so and I did tell you about her." I was speechless, and there was dead silence in the room. His sisters were all waiting for him to speak up as his mom entered the room and asked, "Anyone want some Anisette, wine or coffee?" She looked perplexed and asked, "What happened? Why is everyone so quiet I replied, "Well, Mrs.

Antonelli, I just found out about Mario's Italian *friend* tonight who I obviously never knew about. I suppose you all know her? Her eyes widened and everyone looked down as I observed their responses. I knew they all knew her! I was so embarrassed and humiliated. No one said a word. At that moment I stood up and said, "I think it is time to go now." As I saw the stunned looks on his sisters' faces, I proclaimed as tears streamed down my face, "It was lovely to meet all of you, and I wish you a Merry Christmas." Then I turned to him and said, "See this face? You will never see it again. I hope you are happy and I can't believe this is happening to me on Christmas. You are unbelievable!" I was completely blind-sided since I believed we were moving forward in our relationship. In my mind, meeting the family meant we were really committed. I felt like I was having a bad nightmare. I kept thinking, "Wake up Renée! This is not a dream, this is your reality."

I got up and got my coat and said my final goodbyes as I passed the pile of holiday gifts I had wrapped so beautifully for him in the front hallway. I wanted to take them all with me, but how tacky would that have been? I then realized, as I was attempting a rapid exit, that he had to drive me back to my car off the freeway. Holy crap, I had to ride with him, and I wanted to kill him! I was enraged as I got in his car, and I yelled at him all the way to my car. He kept saying, "I'm sorry, I swear she is only a *friend*. You know I care about you or you would not be here."

Needless to say my holidays were destroyed. I was a hot mess for a while and my heart was damaged. He was engaged to be married to his *friend* by June that next summer and married within a year. I heard that she was a young "untouched" girl from Italy and she had to have formal chaperones while they were dating. So he never believed he was cheating on me since he had never slept with her. He was an "old school" Italian, who often would court an innocent girl, and have his other women on the side while he was looking for the perfect "good girl" that he could control. He totally had a Madonna-whore complex and it was maddening. I was torn apart when I heard the news and this experience was very hard on my self-esteem. I considered myself to be a good girl, but I was a bit too independent for him. He was controlling and very judgmental of my work and my spiritual studies. As I look back now I always say, "This rejection was God's protection" since he never would have been the right choice for a life partner. God apparently had a different plan for me but at that moment, my faith in love was shattered.

As I wrote the heart-healing letters expressing my disappointments to him, and got real with myself, it came out in my writing that I knew all along he was not right for me. I discovered that I was playing out a pattern of dating men that were half available because I myself was only half available at that time. I was not following my instincts and had gotten clear signals all along that I could not trust him. I ignored these signs because of the addiction to our sexual chemistry. I thought, like many of you who have dated *players* that eventually he would come around to see how amazing I was and sweep me off my feet. I took responsibility that I had a hand in creating a situation that made my fears come true. He was a charming, low pressure man along with being a good liar and a cheater. I had given my power away to a *bad boy*, and I promised myself I would break this pattern for good!

As I went back and reread my old journals, I realized that I held onto my heartbreak and anger with him for over two years. This heart-wrenching experience stopped me from opening up to any new men, and made me doubt myself and my choices. I wondered if I could ever trust or open up to another man in my life. I know at that time my *energy vibes* were protecting me from magnetizing love into my life for sure. I wasted so much time and I only hurt myself. He had moved on!

He did call me several times, including his actual wedding day, to talk it out and see if I was ok. He said, "Hi, it's me. I'm getting ready to get married and wondering if I'm making the biggest mistake of my life right now. I wanted to hear your voice to see how you are." "Screw YOU!" I said, "I can't believe you would contact me the day of your wedding. Your fiancée would kill you if she knew you were calling me right before you walk down the aisle. I can promise you Mario, she will find out who you really are someday. Go get married, be faithful to her and never call me again!" I hung up on him and again felt the stabbing pain go through my heart. As it turns out, I later discovered that he never told her about me and after they were married she found a box of photos and love letters as they were moving into their new house. He was busted. He had to tell her the truth and that truth haunted him for years. He had lied to both of us! Karma bit him in the ass and she got to see the truth for herself.

In my letters, I realized that not only did I need to forgive him; I needed to forgive myself for staying with him for so long without asking for what I wanted. When I got real and examined the time we spent together, I realized that I was not very happy dating him. I was just got caught in his narcissistic web of lies and our toxic chemistry. My *little girl* kept trying to get his love, attention and approval because she was not healed yet. I expressed that I wished he had been more honest with me and that I had been more true to myself. I suffered way too long over a man who did not deserve one more ounce of my energy or love. After writing that letter my energy shifted and it made me more aware to listen to my gut instincts from that point on.

After writing the healing letter, which I never sent, I felt stronger and contacted him by phone. We ended up having a heart-to-heart talk, and as it turns out he felt guilty for what happened, and he asked for my forgiveness. We talked about the things we learned and appreciated about each other and then wished each other well. I felt a huge weight lifted from my heart. I forgave him and myself, and I finally felt that sense of peace that I had been longing for many years. After that, I knew I could finally move on with my life. The reason I share this particular story is because this relationship locked up my heart for years. I gave away a sacred part of myself to someone who didn't deserve my love or honor me at all. I used to carry that old story around with me and often ended up talking about it on dates and this scared many wonderful men away.

I proclaimed to Mario that one day I would share this story in a book that would help others heal. I know you might have a particular scenario that could be one of your old wounds, since I often hear these heart-breaking tales in my classes and private sessions. I meet with clients who are still carrying anger and wasting precious years suffering over someone who was just not right for them. Most of these clients have a sexual addiction to their current or former partners and can't move on. If this story triggered your heart, perfect…it's time to free your soul and to love again. Do you have a few people that pop into your mind that may have put a few dents in your heart? Write it all out now. If you're not taking care of your heart, who will? Whoever he or she was, they were a vital part of your expanded growth to love yourself more and be able to ask for what you want. Stop obsessing over the past once and for all, so you can live in the present moment and regain your power!

☞ *Remember, if you are in a relationship with hot sexual chemistry and it's still playing with your mind, take a moment to ask yourself if your partner is honoring and taking care of your heart.*

Now, after reading my imprint story with Mario, take a moment to check your heart-healing list to see if you have missed anybody. It's your turn to open your heart to find *real love!*

WRITE A HEALING LETTER

Write each person from the list a letter from your heart stating what feelings you have been carrying around with you for all these years. It can be a love or venting letter, a yelling session or just a mind dump of all your feelings and memories. Just pour out all the feelings with no editing. Often, these painful memories are embedded in our hearts because of things that were left unsaid in the past. Express what you wish you could have said, or even heard, if you had been brave enough to speak up. This will allow you to release pent up emotions and open up to healthier and more honest communication in all of your relationships.

This is a vital part of your healing process. By writing all of your feelings out on paper, you can release the emotions that have been stored in your body, and learn more lessons about yourself along the way. You may choose to either send the letter for the purpose of having a "healing" conversation or you may choose not to send the letter. Whether you send the letters or not, the energy of writing out your true feelings will make a difference. This process will help you discover what beliefs you had that could have contributed to you attracting the relationship in the first place. You will also discover how your past imprints influenced your experiences. Here are two examples of "Aha" healing moments that I uncovered as I wrote out my feelings. I faced one of my deepest imprints, which had blocked me from opening my heart until I completed this process.

⚷ *When you are honest and get real about what happened, you will see you are fully responsible for attracting the experience based on your old imprints. Expressing your truth will set your heart free!*

After that healing with Mario, I promised my *little girl* I would listen to her from now on. I then wrote a journal entry regarding my old memory from age six. I remembered that moment when I had heard that "All men were liars and cheaters!" What I came to realize, through my writing, was that the experience (of hearing my aunt cry) was just one night, and it did not mean that every man in the world would be unfaithful or hurt me.

TRUE STORY

I went to see my dear Aunt Carmella and shared these memories and writings with her. She never knew that I had overheard those conversations at such a young age. Now, she finally understood why I kept love at a distance.

Then, she shared all the stories about the love and hardships in her life. She was only 17 years old when she became pregnant and was married at a secret ceremony in the back of the church. Aunt Carmella never had self-love classes or learned how to ask for what she wanted, which made the rocky times with her husband even worse. She confessed knowing that her husband was unfaithful to her, but she was chemically addicted to and dependent on him at the time. Yet, it still broke her heart when she caught him with another woman and she guarded herself for many years after the divorce. In the following years, Carmella struggled, working three jobs to make ends meet and raised her four kids alone.

Then, in her late thirties, she met my Uncle Jimmy while she was working at my father's restaurant. He pursued her for months and she put him through the ringer to prove his devotion to her and her children. Since I was always with my cousin Carmella, I was able to witness their courtship firsthand. I still remember our "double dates" at the drive in movie theatre and becoming Uncle Jimmy's his favorite niece. It took him four long years before Aunt Carmella agreed to marry him. They were happy together for 25 years until he passed away from throat cancer. We had so many fun memories and I was lucky enough to visit him to express my love the day before he passed. He asked me to make sure that I encouraged my aunt to keep her heart open if she met another man in the future. He also gave me his wedding band to give to my future husband to carry his blessing of love. At the time, I had just broken up with Mario and he said, "If you ever go back with him or any man that isn't good to you, just know, I'll be haunting you from heaven and sending you messages. You'll know it's me!" Over the years, I've heard his voice and felt his spirit many times and listened to his warning signs.

After Jimmy passed, my sweet aunt unexpectedly found love again when she ran into an old family friend from forty years past at an Italian American Club. Frank had asked her to dance that night and she said she felt "the stirring," but was feeling guilty about her attraction. Apparently, he felt the connection and began courting her. I encouraged her to open up since he was a wonderful man. I told her to pray for a clear sign from my Uncle Jimmy that it was okay for her to see Frank. Sure enough, Jimmy sent one fast!

One morning, Carmella was alone and getting ready for work when she heard musical lovebirds singing in the kitchen window. Jimmy would wind them up every morning and she called me saying she felt his spirit in the kitchen. She wondered if this was the sign. I told her, "Your prayer was answered and the lovebirds are a sign to help you set your heart free to love again. This was Jimmy's wish." A year later, she married my Uncle Frank at the age of 63. It was a beautiful wedding ceremony and they surprised the family when they danced a romantic tango. This is just one of many amazing love stories to inspire you to believe in love at any age.

My Aunt Carmella has been like a second mother, a role model of strength and a source of unconditional love my entire life. I respect her values and adore her loving spirit. She was very proud that I was teaching women the lessons she never learned as a young woman. Being able to hear her perspective and learning more about her situation and other hidden secrets was an amazing healing opportunity for me. All of my beliefs shifted when I realized that she was just expressing her pain at a sad time in her life. These healing conversations solidified my decision that I no longer had to live out those negative imprints about love in my own life. At that point, my heart began to open up and my life transformed. Yours will too!

⚷ *Many of our parents had us when they were between 18-26 years old and were often not given any direction on raising kids or choosing the right life partners. They were children raising children. Most of their parents did not teach them many lessons on self-love and relationship skills in the "olden days." It was all kept a secret since those topics were considered taboo, therefore we learned from observing them and the way they were programmed.*

I did this heart-healing process with letters and phone calls with many of my relatives, friends and ex-boyfriends from my *Relationship Review* list. Not only did it help me let go, most of them experienced a healing in their own hearts as well. I would also suggest asking if you can meet with them to discuss some *matters of the heart* in a quiet place with no interruptions. You'll be surprised how open most people are when contacting them, yet keep in mind that some may not ever be ready to discuss old wounds.

I promise, as you communicate with people on your list, write letters and journal entries, you will understand the true heart messages that surface and see how much you have grown and healed in your life. You may discover you still have patterns and layers to dissolve and need more healing on these issues.

Go easy on yourself; you are on your way to a healed and opened heart.

Now it's time to release the person or the situation to forgive and let it go. Hold your heart stone and imagine the situation in your mind. The memories will often pop up like a movie screen and play over and over in your head. After unlocking any *imprints* and examining your heart, you write out all the memories and the feelings, infuse these letters with powerful intentions for your future.

I suggest ending the letter with a positive outcome, saying something such as, "Now that I have expressed my feelings to you from our encounter, I have chosen to let this old wound be healed, and dissolve it from my life forever. I am moving on to have the space in my heart for *true love*. I am making new choices for my life NOW, and one of them is to free myself from the ties that had me bound to you. Those old *imprints* no longer live in my heart I now release the beliefs and the energy that I carried from this experience. These ties or energetic cords are cut and dissolved from this moment on. I also release the messages you passed on to me, and create a new direction for my life. I forgive you and I forgive myself, as I release the pain from my past. I fill my life with love and peace of mind, now and forever. By letting go I am opening my mind and heart to the unlimited possibilities. I learned my lessons and I am moving on with an open heart. I bless and release you on your path and I wish only the best for you. I am grateful and thankful for this healing, now and forever and I let it be. And so it is. Amen."

Now that you have done this powerful release work, you can visualize the images of the experience shrink smaller and smaller until you can't see them any longer. The emotional charge that this person had on you will eventually be so small that it becomes nonexistent!

HEALING VISUALIZATION

Another powerful technique is to do a healing visualization with your new empowered self. Imagine yourself speaking face to face to the person who you still have feelings of attachment, resentment, anger, sadness or love towards. In your mind, see yourself strongly claiming that they no longer have power over you in this moment or from now on. See yourself receiving an apology or an acknowledgement from them, and feeling peaceful, serene and free of negative emotion. This process can also be used with those who have passed on or a person who may not be open to speaking with you directly.

If you see them fighting you in the scene in your mind, stop them when they say a negative comment. Proclaim in the moment, "STOP! Your old beliefs and negativity have no power over me, and I release them into the nothingness from where they came!" See that person stand back and walk away. You are taking a powerful stand for your soul, and your subconscious and unconscious mind will store and imprint your heart with your new powerful intentions. Breathe... feeling relieved, peaceful, and empowered.

Note: These powerful processes are best done with a trained NLP practitioner, hypnotherapist, therapist or a spiritual practitioner. Often these powerful scenes in our past have happened repeatedly, and in most cases, they cannot be erased all at once, since your mind stores the memories in the order of how they occurred. So, if you need more support, work with a trusted practitioner to do this release work. These are only a few of the transformative techniques that can help you during this process. They will help you achieve more confidence and empower you on your quest for *real love.*

⚷ *It's time to forgive yourself and the other people that may have unintentionally influenced you in the past. You can see how you may not have had the skills to communicate your fears and needs, or to defend your heart at that time.*

Now that you know you are letting go of the old stories to create a new *love story,* let's do a final *heart-healing* blessing to reignite and rebuild your faith in yourself.

⚷ *Remember, you must be patient and gentle with yourself since this healing process takes time. You are instilling yourself with renewed faith and learning new reprogramming techniques along the way. This takes practice and now you have the tools to make powerful choices in every moment.*

The blessing below will help you transmute your past experiences back to love. This will be a two-part blessing. The first part is connecting to the higher power and releasing the old memories, thoughts, and people from your past. The second part is making powerful requests to manifest your new vision of love.

Many of us have been taught we are not worthy of love and then, suddenly when asked to pray, we often beg God or the Universe for what we want. As you renew the way you pray, your unconscious mind hears this and the universe will respond accordingly.

Oᴛ⚊ᴣ *It's vital to believe that your requests will be heard and know in your heart that every word you speak, and every thought that you think, is your divine prayer to God. No begging is necessary.*

GET READY FOR LOVE BLESSING

At home or in a special location that is meaningful to you, get into a space of reflection, add music if you wish and hold your heart stone. Then begin your blessing by calling in the one power that is available anytime, anywhere you are. Some call it God, The Universe, Jesus, the Holy Spirit, Buddha, your Angels, your Higher Self, your spiritual guides, the moon, the sun, the trees. Just make requests for strength and power from this amazing force to fill your heart to overcome these old messages forever! Stop in that moment... breathe and say, "I [say your name] command and request the power of God (or whomever you want to ask) to please dissolve any negative memories, thoughts and people from my mind, heart and soul. I am now open to love, healing my heart, and connecting with my divine mate. I am letting go of any experience(s) and the doubt and fear that may have caused a blockage in my heart, NOW and forever. I am grateful for the lessons I have learned and the space that is now free in my heart to let love in. I forgive myself and move forward with more wisdom and awareness to take control of my life now!" (Breathe in again deeply; feel the strength filling you and bask in that feeling of the higher power surging in your body.) Feel your heart fill up with light and imagine the space open and ready to receive love.

Now that you've connected with a higher power, you are now making strong clear requests from the force that is everywhere and to your own soul, your higher self. Start your blessing with the name of your higher power, "God, Holy Spirit, the Universal Force, the Christ presence, etc. I [your name] am open to new, wonderful people in my life who are positive, caring and honest. These people love and adore me just as I am. I'm ready for an amazing life partner to come into my life to share joy and love with me. This special person is [add detailed description here.] I am open to love and ready to be cherished and honored in all of my relationships from this day forward. I will listen to my gut and follow my intuition. I'm ready for LOVE and a magnificent life ... so bring it on! Thank you for my new awareness, my blessings and for my amazing soul mate. I have put in my order, knowing my prayers will be heard and I am so grateful. It is done. I release this prayer in faith. And so it is."

Now that we have done this heart-healing work, you are rebuilding your faith in yourself and in a higher power by blessing any situation that shows up in your life. You may notice other old memories and *imprints* surfacing from doing these processes relating to money, your level of success, your career choices, etc. You can transform these old messages the same way with these *heart-healing rituals* and blessings. The universe is responding to your thoughts, words and prayers. It is given to you, as you believe. This is the truth that will set your heart free.

GET REAL ♥ REFLECTIONS

♥ What people from your past have come to mind to help you gain new insights as you investigate your *love imprints*?

♥ Who are those prominent people who stand out as part of your heart-healing process that you need to forgive? Who do you need to ask to forgive you from the past?

♥ After your love investigation, have you connected with the *little girl* or *boy* part of yourself? What are they saying to you now?

♥ Take your heart stone in your hand as a reminder to be gentle, kind and compassionate with yourself, as you go through this process.

♥ Mark out special times each week to do this sacred heart-healing work. Be patient knowing the healing comes in layers as you release your old imprints.

Now it's time to take a Deeper Look Inside and get to Know Thyself.

CHAPTER IX

KNOW THYSELF: A DEEPER LOOK INSIDE

"I'm starting with the man in the mirror, I'm asking him to change his ways. Take a look at yourself and then make a change."
– **Michael Jackson**

"A little reflection will show us that every belief, even the simplest and most fundamental, goes beyond experience when regarded as a guide to our actions."
– **William Kingdon Clifford**

After all this heart-healing, you may have a different perspective about your life. The next step is a deeper internal look at the various parts of your life and how you think and speak of them.

We each have areas of our lives that are going well and other areas that need refining. Take this test and write down the first number that comes to mind when you read each question. Just go for it and be honest so we know where to focus your energy.

LIFESTYLE CHECKLIST
(#1 Being the Lowest - #10 Being the Highest)

- *How happy are you with your current living space?* _____
- *Are you satisfied with your work environment?* _____
- *How fulfilling is your current job or career?* _____
- *How content are you with your personal and social life?* _____
- *Do you love and treat yourself well?* _____

- *Do you give yourself as much love and attention as you give others?* _____
- *Are you feeling organized and successful with your finances?* _____
- *What level of connection do you have with your spiritual and religious practices?* _____
- *Do you have enough vacations and play time?* _____ *Alone time?* _____ *With friends?* _____ *With a partner?* _____
- *Are you content with your spare-time activities and hobbies?* _____
- *How are you feeling about your current social network and your friends?* _____
- *What level of commitment do you have with your fitness regime?* _____ *Eating habits?* _____
- *How satisfied are you with your physical appearance* _____
- *Are you happy with your love life?* _____
- *How pleased are you with your family life?* _____

Review your answers to these questions. Highlight the questions that you rated six or below. Any number below six is an opportunity to redesign your action plan..

REALITY CHECK: KNOW THYSELF

Now that you have an overall picture of the facets of your life, it is time to do more reflective inner work and get to know yourself better. You may want to write your answers in a journal, but it is preferable to say them aloud into a tape or digital recorder. Even better, have a close friend ask you the questions and record your answers for review. I promise that this life enriching process will bring out more of the real you, especially if you are an auditory person. If you are honest, this will surely get you tuned in to your true self.

Be spontaneous and let the answers flow so that you can become aware of the messages that you unconsciously tell others. Get in contact with the inner voice which talks to you on a regular basis. In my seminars, I will often ask participants what kind of person they believe themselves to be, and why they would be a great partner. Inevitability, half the audience gets tongue-tied.

�⚷ *If you don't know why you're a good catch, how can you expect other people to believe you are? You are revealing and marketing yourself on a daily basis.*

This internal *reality check* will help you become aware of the energy you project about yourself. For most people, this exercise is a real *wake-up* call. So, be honest with your answers: express your real thoughts, your true values and your current goals. As you listen back or review your answers, you will uncover the content of your consciousness and hear the tone of your voice.

We will start with a list of belief questions. Again, you can write your answers in a journal, but recording your answers in a coaching session or with a close friend will offer added insight and reflection. If this is not possible, ask yourself the questions and record your responses. These sessions allow you to investigate how you sound and notice what energy your voice emits when answering the questions. If you do not have a recorder, buy or borrow one. It will be an invaluable tool. You will become aware of the image you project in your daily life by listening to yourself. I use a recorder for all of my sessions and important meetings. I always send my clients their recordings, so they can review the information and hear how much they've grown throughout the process.

Before doing this exercise, set up your environment to get the best results. Make sure you are relaxed and have time to complete the process. Turn off your digital devices or anything that could distract you. If you have pets, feed them and put them in another room. If you have children, send them on a play date, put them to bed or down for a nap. Make this a priority and bring any items you need into the room, such as: water, candles, snacks, your journal, nice music and your heart stone.

Nobody's keeping score here so don't bother planning your answers, just let them flow out naturally. Be as truthful and descriptive as possible. This is the deep, internal work that will clarify the areas you need to strengthen and refine. Be excited, this is a way to take back control of your life and win at love.

Some of the questions may seem repetitive. This is designed to probe deeper into the unconscious mind and uncover the core beliefs that run our lives. Beliefs are multi-layered and sometimes more than one combination of questions is needed to unlock unconscious thought patterns.

First, you will gain awareness of your core beliefs. Second, you will learn how to shift gears in order to head in the direction for more success in all areas of your life. And finally, you will be able to communicate clearly and send the right signals to others. It's time to *get real*!

Some of the questions may make you feel uncomfortable. This is a clear signal guiding you to issues that may need further attention. You will be investigating your inner conflicts and shifting them to be congruent with your future goals. The subconscious and unconscious minds take your beliefs and thoughts literally, and mixed beliefs will create mixed results. By being really honest and answering from your gut, you will uncover the basic, core beliefs that are the cause of your current situation. If a question does not relate to you just skip it and move on. No one will be reading or listening to your answers, so explore deeper.

EXPLORE YOUR THOUGHTS & CORE BELIEFS

- *Describe yourself in ten words.*
- *What do you love about yourself?*
- *What are your best qualities?*
- *Describe your best physical attributes.*
- *What are your core beliefs about being single?*
- *What is your response when someone asks why you're still single?*
- *Would you want to marry yourself right now? Why or why not?*
- *What are the qualities and values that make you who you are?*
- *Do you feel worthy to receive what you're asking for in a mate?*
- *What are your strengths?*
- *What are your weaknesses?*
- *Can you trust yourself and do you keep true to your word?*
- *Do you believe in yourself?*

- *Are you your own worst enemy? Why?*
- *Can you be too critical of yourself?*
- *Are you treating yourself the way you want to be treated?*
- *What areas of your life need more attention?*
- *What's the biggest priority in your life right now?*
- *Do you have a life mission?*
- *What is your ultimate goal in life?*
- *Do you think you have good energy vibes?*
- *Are you sensitive to other people's energy?*
- *When you get a gut feeling, where do you feel it in your body? Do you listen to these signs?*
- *Do you listen to the messages from your heart?*
- *Are you a good listener?*
- *Do you take other people's opinions personally?*
- *Are you able to communicator when things get rocky in your relationships?*
- *How do you communicate when someone hurts your feelings?*
- *Do you have a support system in your life now?*
- *Are you willing to ask for help when you need it?*
- *What does commitment mean to you?*
- *Are you open to being in a committed relationship now?*
- *Do you have any commitment issues?*
- *Are you a person that keeps your promises and commitments to others?*
- *Do you honor the commitments you make to yourself?*
- *What is your definition of love?*
- *Do you think you deserve love?*
- *Is your heart open and ready to receive love?*
- *Are you afraid that love may not happen for you?*
- *How important is having a partner in your life?*

- *Can you imagine your life with someone great who adores you? How would you describe it?*
- *How will you feel when your love vision comes true?*
- *Do you like being held or touched, receiving cards or gifts, hearing feelings in conversations or sweet words of appreciation?*
- *What attracts you first when you meet a potential mate?*
- *List some of the qualities that turn you on to a person.*
- *Which of those attributes will keep you attracted?*
- *When you are dating someone, what habits irritate you?*
- *How important is being on time to you?*
- *What excites you about being in a relationship?*
- *What scares you about being in a relationship?*
- *Where do most of your beliefs about love and relationships stem from?*
- *Are you willing to shift gears on some of the beliefs that are running you?*
- *Do you have any strong role models in relationships?*
- *What is so powerful about these role models that you would like to create for yourself?*
- *What would the experience of being in love be like for you?*
- *Are you ready for love?*

DISCOVER MORE ABOUT YOURSELF
& PROSPECTIVE PARTNERS

The next few sets of questions are the most frequently asked on dates. It's also important to ask yourself these questions, tape your answers and review them. You'll become more aware of how you sound and the vibes you send out on dates or in social situations.

At my *Rapid Dating* events, I have witnessed men and women bring out their master list of questions for prospective dates and completely turn people off. Don't ask all of these questions all at once. Remember, this is not a police interrogation. Be subtle and listen closely to what people say in response to your questions and keep it light.

☙━╍ *Asking questions in a fun, flirtatious and non-threatening way puts you in the driver's seat.*

You can save yourself a lot of time by asking the right questions on the first few dates. Now that you have a deeper understanding of yourself, you can ask your top ten questions to see if this relationship has potential. So read through the list and highlight the questions that resonate and reflect your values. I suggest asking the lighter questions on the first few dates and saving the deeper questions for later. Asking them to describe their favorite experiences will often help them reveal their passions and personality. Take your time since many people are private and open up slowly. Revealing your heart too soon can also make you feel vulnerable. What's the rush? If there is a spark, you can find out about a person over time and create a strong foundation of trust.

☙━╍ *Perhaps you have heard the saying, "You have one mouth and two ears, you should listen twice as much as you speak."*

QUESTIONS TO ASK ON DATES
(These are useful for online profiles and social media)

- *What excites you about life? What are you passionate about?*
- *When you have time off, what's your favorite thing to do?*
- *Where is your ideal place to hang out?*
- *What do you like to do to relax after you've finished work?*
- *Do you enjoy your chosen profession? Why did you choose it?*
- *What makes you happy? What are the first three things that come to mind?*
- *What experiences have brought you the most joy in your life up until now?*
- *If you could do anything that you can imagine, what would it be?*
- *When you were younger, what did you want to be when you grew up?*

- *Are you active or into sports? What is your favorite sport or outdoor activity?*
- *What are the top seven values that you live by?*
- *Tell me about your family heritage? Where did you grow up?*
- *Are you close with your family?*
- *What were you like as a child? Growing up, did you have a happy childhood?*
- *Are you fond of traditions? Do you have any special traditions that you created in your life or with your family?*
- *If you could create a new tradition for yourself, what would it be?*
- *Tell me about your mother and father. Do you have siblings? Are you close with them?*
- *Do you have any children? Do you like them? Want any children of your own?*
- *Have you ever dated someone with children? Are you open to it?*
- *What makes you smile?*
- *Do you have any mentors or role models? What is so special about them?*
- *What is your biggest life accomplishment? What was your motivation behind it?*
- *What are five adjectives that describe your personality and physicality?*
- *What are your favorite types of vacations? Where have you traveled?*
- *Where do you see yourself traveling in the future?*
- *What are the values you seek in a life mate?*
- *What is your religious background?*
- *Do you go to church or spiritual services regularly? Is that an important part of your life?*
- *Is having a spiritual partner important to you?*
- *What are your spiritual practices?*
- *Are there any charities or causes you are currently supporting or drawn to?*
- *What music gives you goose bumps? Name your top three favorite artists or bands?*
- *What are your favorite foods restaurants?*

- *Do you like to cook? What is your specialty?*
- *Are you a foodie? What are your favorite foods and restaurants?*
- *Do you have a favorite saying?*
- *What is your favorite language? Do you speak more than one?*
- *What is your favorite holiday? Do you like to celebrate birthdays and holidays? How?*
- *What is your favorite dessert? Do you have a favorite spot to buy it?*
- *Do you like to dance? What music do you like to dance to?*
- *If you had all the money in the world, what would you do with it?*
- *If you could have any wish, what would it be?*
- *Where do you see yourself in one year? Two years? Five years?*
- *Do you have a favorite story that you like to tell at parties?*
- *Tell me about your favorite Halloween as a kid. Do you like to dress up for Halloween?*
- *What were you like as a child? Where did you grow up?*
- *What were some of your favorite TV shows as a child? And now?*
- *Who is your favorite actor?*
- *What is your favorite movie?*
- *Did you have animals growing up? Do you have any pets now?*
- *What animal would you use to describe yourself?*
- *How were you perceived by others in high school?*
- *What was your wildest dating experience like back then?*
- *What subjects did you enjoy studying in school?*
- *Did you have a high school sweetheart?*
- *Who is your best friend? What makes them so special?*
- *How would your best friends describe you?*
- *What's a secret you've never told anyone about yourself?*
- *What's one thing that drives you crazy about dating?*

- *Tell me about some of your worst and your best dating experiences.*
- *Have you ever been in love?*
- *Who was the love of your life?*
- *What qualities made them so special?*
- *What was your longest relationship?*
- *What is your definition of a good relationship?*
- *What does intimacy mean to you?*
- *What stopped you from ever getting married?*
- *Do you ever see yourself getting married? Or married again?*
- *What caused your breakup separation divorce?*
- *What lessons have you learned about your relationships from your past?*
- *Tell me what activities help you handle the stresses of life?*
- *How do you feel about drinking and drugs?*
- *Are you open to having love in your life again?*
- *How important is having a partner in your life right now?*
- *Who are the most important people in your life?*
- *Do you have any odd quirks or funky habits that annoy you about yourself and others?*
- *What is your ideal first date? Your ideal romantic date?*
- *What is your relationship to money? Do you save it? Invest it? Spend it?*
- *What makes you worth knowing?*
- *What is the legacy you would like to leave behind?*
- *Is finding your life partner a priority in your life right now?*

Now that you've taken the time to reflect on the questions above, hopefully you've learned more about yourself. You will now be more prepared to communicate with your prospective dates. By listening to the key words in their answers, you'll be attuned to their primary communication style, values and their passions. Then, you will be able to quickly identify their phase in life, *energy vibes,* and know if they would complement your life as a friend or potential partner.

GET REAL ♥ REFLECTIONS

♥ After reviewing your recordings to see how you answered some of these important questions... would you want to date or marry yourself?

♥ Are you aware of the image you project in your daily life with your conversations? What is that image?

♥ Do you ask the right questions when you are on dates without making the other person feel like they are on a job interview or being interrogated?

♥ Make a list of your ten favorite questions to ask on dates. Make sure they align with your ultimate vision as they will quickly reveal your date's top values.

Now it's time to talk about another important topic that's a huge part of the dating equation. Let's talk about sex and intimacy and the effect they have on our hearts and souls. In the next chapter, we will *get real* about the topics most of us really want to discuss but rarely do.

CHAPTER X

LET'S TALK ABOUT SEX!

"Passion is the quickest to develop, and the quickest to fade. Intimacy develops more slowly, and commitment more gradually still."
– Robert Sternberg

Now let's *get real* about SEX. Everyone has their own beliefs about sex depending on their upbringing, religious beliefs and the influences all around them in the media. Sex, sex, sex...it's everywhere! Many people don't know how to talk about sex without feeling uncomfortable. Some people need to take their time to feel a deeper connection before sharing such a sacred part of themselves, while others are more open to exploring with no attachment. Since so many people are having sexual connections prior to marriage, it's important to discuss these intimate issues.

Many clients call me confused and broken-hearted after jumping into bed too soon with someone they've just met online or on a blind date. They often say they had long heart-to-heart conversations and that both parties felt this could be the match they've been searching for. Some people get intimate too quickly without knowing much about each other and then, the games begin.

⭕━🗝 *Many clients have confided in me that, secretly, they don't mind if the person they're dating asks them these questions, since many people have expectations after they have sex. Talk openly before you get naked!*

DON'T DROP YOUR PANTIES: TALK ABOUT SEX FIRST

Many of the people I coach feel pressured to have sex within the first few dates. Look at your past dating patterns. Did your last date claim that you

153

could be "the one," then start pulling back after having wild oral sex on your second date? Think about it...you probably only knew each other for less than eight hours. Some of my clients have had a two-hour lunch for a first date, then a second date over dinner and a night of hot passionate sex for dessert without even knowing their last name...right?

Most busy people want fast results and these quick sexual encounters can often leave you feeling vulnerable. Many women are dreaming of their *prince charming* fantasy and want love so badly that they often hop in the sack too soon, only to discover that man was a *high-speed chaser*. Been there, done that!

If you jump in too fast, know that some people will run from the attachment they feel after intimacy. When people casually date, having sex often changes the dynamics of the relationship and sets up the expectation that you will give it up every time. Also, sex may have different meanings for each person involved. Some women become chemically addicted to the pheromones and the oxytocin, whether their partner is into them or not. Men often claim that the woman was so cool and open the night they were intimate, but suddenly turned "psycho" after a few fun dates. They added that many women have super high expectations of them and assume they're in a committed relationship because they had intercourse or foreplay. Men will say, "She seemed so relaxed. I was just going with the flow and had no idea she would get so attached after a few dates." Some people just want to have fun! Men have confessed that they won't turn down booty if you give it up, and they normally don't bring up the commitment topic before you have sex. Having sex with someone doesn't mean you have a commitment. Don't assume anything! Ask first.

⌐╾╼ *It's up to you to take care of yourself by discussing the kind of relationship you both want before jumping in bed. I suggest that you discuss sex and safety before you rush in and drop your panties.*

It's vital to keep things real, so you should be asking personal questions and discussing topics to get clear on your values about sex and intimacy. Don't make assumptions about your partner's sexual history or beliefs about sex. We all have different issues, and it's important to discuss contraception and sexually transmitted diseases. Be safe and ask first.

Many people can have positive casual connections by being honest and upfront about not wanting any attachments. They mutually agree to share their "sexual gifts" with honor. These experiences can be positive and healing if both parties know what they are getting themselves into. I tell both men and women to speak the truth. By doing so, a fun and sexy connection can be experienced with no heartaches.

⚷ *Be honest with yourself before jumping into bed with someone. It's important to make clear agreements upfront about the experience you choose to have with your partner. Make sure you're on the same page.*

Here is a typical date night scenario: You go for dinner and drinks and your date drops you off at your place. They come in to say goodnight and the next thing you know, you're kissing on the couch and the sexual energy starts revving up. This is a good time to express your truth, manage their expectations and slow things down. First sit up, take a deep breathe, and pet their arm or cheek and use this *love script*: "I'm very attracted to you [insert their name]. This is so much fun, but it's going a little too fast for me. I'm sorry if I sent mixed signals, I just need more time to get to know you before we jump into a sexual relationship. Our chemistry is so incredible and I think we have something good here, so let's just slow down." Just speak from your heart and they will know you are worth waiting for. If he or she is the real deal, they will honor your feelings and come back to court you. Soon enough you'll know if they are sincere about wanting a real relationship or if they were just trying to get a little booty.

⚷ *If you aren't sure how your date feels about sex, ask them to be open with you. Then you'll know when the time is right. Unless you don't care and want to have some casual sex, don't pretend it means anything more than that—it's just a booty call.*

TRUE STORY

I followed my own love advice and took my time getting to know Tony before becoming romantically involved with him. I felt like he was a potential match, but I was also having gut feelings that he had unfinished business. I was getting some signs that I could not ignore. I had several reoccurring dreams about an attractive, busty, blonde-haired woman and a little boy, who looked just like him. In the dream, the woman was furious at Tony and yelling at him. I mentioned it to Tony several times saying, "Are you sure you aren't married?" Tony always replied, "No" and assured me he was single and excited about us!

It seemed like we were headed in the right direction, but I still hadn't met his friends or family. We had many deep conversations about family, sex and life and I shared that I needed to know more about him over time. We were having some make-out sessions and I made a choice to hold off on sex for a while. He was very respectful and sweet and I was happy he wasn't pushing me. I was proud that I was listening to my heart and taking my time to get to know him.

Then he asked me to go away for the weekend to a beautiful resort in Palm Springs. I think he believed that this trip was when we would finally have sex. I was excited and knew this trip would be a part of my *test drive* to see how we traveled together. It had been almost 4 months and he told me he wasn't dating anyone else and wanted to be exclusive! All was well until we went to the pool and I noticed he couldn't stop gawking at all the tall blondes with breast implants. I thought he was going to get neck strain from being such a pivot head. His immature behavior totally turned me off!

As we got dressed for dinner, I was very quiet. He sensed something was wrong and he asked me, "What's up?" I calmly mentioned over dinner that "I noticed that you have a breast obsession and your surely didn't know how to hide it very well." Then we laughed since the ice was broken. He apologized and admitted that he liked big breasts but also loved mine! I replied, "Well, I'm very perceptive and understand the minds of men. For our first romantic get-away, this experience definitely showed me what turns you on! I under-stand that many men love big boobs, but as you can see, I don't have them and I'm not planning on getting them. So, if breasts are your turn on, then I may not be the girl for you!" He laughed and told me I was being silly and that he was very attracted to me.

Even though I was exclusively dating Tony and he was very passionate, I still didn't feel like it was time to open up. I got the vibe that he was a bit of a *player* and I held back on having sex that weekend. My *little girl* was screaming, "Don't do it!" I was practicing what I preached and listening to the small signs along the way. I doubted if he was going to be the man I wanted to be with long-term. I was restless that night and that scene played over and over in my mind. My gut was still saying to wait…then I dreamed about the blonde again.

After that night, he was on his best behavior and was treating me like a queen. Tony made me a CD of love songs and took me out on fun dates. We made plans to meet his friends and he met many of mine. I was happy that he came to support me at a few of my Rapid Dating events. I even spoke to his mother and she told me that she was excited to meet me. His actions showed me that he was all in and our bond was getting stronger. So, we decided to commit to the relationship for three months to see how it would play out. I was taking him for a *test drive*! Then, two days later my mother died.

My mother's sudden passing caused me to take time to think about my deeper visions and goals. On my flight home, I was reflecting on the whole experience and thinking of all the support I had received from my friends, family and my church. I then realized that Tony never sent flowers or even a card to me or my family after my mother passed. I was disappointed since I was brought up to pay my respects to the people I cared about. I wanted to marry a family-oriented man.

After all the sadness from my mother's funeral, I was very vulnerable. When I returned home, Tony picked me up from the airport and we had a sweet reunion. He brought me flowers and was very loving. All those previous doubts were quickly swept away! I decided that if we were still dating in August, I would ask him to go with me to meet my family and attend my Aunt

BeBe's wedding that had been postponed. Then, I would confirm his level of interest and know for sure if he could handle my family.

I was in a daze for a few weeks and Tony was very supportive. It took some time before I was able to get back in the swing of work and seeing friends. I needed to laugh, so Tony took me to see *My Big Fat Greek Wedding* and it was a riot. The entire movie reminded me of my family. We laughed all night, went back to my house and as we snuggled up, I inquired if he would go back with me to meet my family. He took a deep breath and said, "Well, we need to talk about a few things." My heart skipped a beat and I got a huge knot in my stomach. I had suspected that something was up and he proceeded to say, "Renée, I've been waiting to tell you something and I know you are not going to be happy. I'm still legally married and those dreams you've been having about a blonde woman and a little boy, are actually my soon-to-be ex-wife and my 5-year-old son, Tony."

Holy S#!T! I was dating a married man. I was in shock. I proceeded to ask him, "Why did you lie to me? He replied, "Well, I never thought I would fall in love with you and was looking to numb my pain. I was casually dating a bunch of women and when you came along, I thought you would be just like the rest of them...a quick fix. I never waited so long to get intimate with any woman before in my life. Once I saw how special you are, I fell more in love with you. I felt so guilty and I knew I had to confess so we could be together. But with all your TV shows, events and traveling, there never seemed to be a good time to tell you. Your intuition was right all along and I didn't want to lose you. I was being selfish."

I sat in silence but I was fuming on the inside. He had been lying to me for months! He continued, "My wife and I were legally separated when I met you and she has already moved on. Now, we're selling our house and she's about to move in with her boyfriend. Until then, I live on the bottom floor and she lives upstairs. I was going to tell you before you left for your aunts wedding in May, but your mother suddenly passed away. I couldn't tell you then. When you told me your dreams and kept asking me questions, I was freaked out and knew I needed to be honest. I just couldn't find the perfect time to tell you.

I'm so sorry. Can you please forgive me? I really love you and want to make this work."

I was enraged and yelled, "Oh my God I can't believe this! Now you're deciding to be honest after almost five months of dating me? What kind of person can lie for this long? So, my dreams were real? Did your wife know about me? Was she the roommate you were living with? You have lied to me this whole time and expect me to take you back? Are you kidding me? You are a compulsive liar and a narcissist! How could you live with yourself?"

He was begging and pleading with me. I was already in so much pain after losing my mother and now my boyfriend was a liar and still married! All of this loss in two weeks. My head was spinning and yet, I was grateful that I hadn't gotten too deeply involved with him. Since honesty and trust were my top values, I proclaimed, "After all this time and your bullshit, I will never trust you again. You are a liar. Get out of my house and never call me again!"

I was very gentle with myself and my *little girl*. He did call me a few times wanting to talk and that old part of me wondered, "What if?" Then, he came back to drop off a few of my things before I left for the wedding. This was my defining moment, the time I knew I had healed my old pattern for good. No more taking back men that were not worthy. No more trying to fix a *bad boy*. I was in my power and had committed to my heart.

Tony showed up in my favorite shirt and jeans, smelling delicious. He had the look of love in his eyes and had beautiful flowers for me. He sincerely apologized and asked if he could have one more chance. He hugged me and said that he loved me and wanted me to meet his family. As he held me, I must admit there was that old part of me that thought, "Hmm...maybe this could work after all?" Then, I remembered that I had broken my old patterns, made a promise to my heart and was ready for *real love*. I was strong, yet vulnerable and I released his embrace and walked him to the door, saying, "Tony, I can't live out the patterns of staying with one more man that has lied to me or stay in a relationship that started out with deception. I am keeping myself open to an amazing partner, who is honest, available and ready for love. This will be the last time I ever want to see you and I hope that you can learn from this experience and *get real* with other women in the future. If you had been honest with me, things may have turned out differently. So, get out of my life and don't ever contact me again!"

I slammed the door and felt a surge of faith come over me. This was a strength that I had never felt before. I put my hands up in the air and said, "Okay God, now can you see that I have changed and believe in myself? I am ready for LOVE! I felt a twinge of sadness but then suddenly a huge wave of peace came over me. I never heard from or saw Tony again. As you read on you will see that this was the night that changed the direction of my life. If I had gotten back with Tony, I would have never met my husband because I would've gone back into my old love loop!

Many people think that they owe their partner sex if they do nice things for them: taking them on a trip, out to fancy dinners, buying nice things, etc. You are not obligated to do anything sexual, even if they're ready to jump in bed. Just keep appreciating them and you will know when the time is right. Look for the signs and listen to your gut. Remember, it takes time to determine if they're a real candidate for love!

Granted, many people could care less about your feelings and will take sex any time, not thinking twice about it. They'll often claim they share your love vision and goals, only to disappear after a few spicy dates. Many of my male clients tell me, "Wow, Renée this girl was wild and I had a blast, and now she is moving way too fast for me. I wonder if she gets this wild and crazy with other guys. Is she always this easy? She's a lot of fun, but not wife material."

It is tough for pushy *wonder women* and *super men* to slow down the process in order to reveal whether the person they are seeing will honor and cherish them. I hear it all the time, "I know this one is going to work out Renée, I swear. We have that special connection, our chemistry was hot and I could not resist the feeling! So, who cares … I'll take my chances and go for it." I normally respond, "It's all your choice, you're a big girl/boy." However, if you have a pattern of high-speed romances and haven't gotten the results you desire from this approach, you may want to try a new *action plan.*

☜⚷ *Stop pretending that sex doesn't bond you to someone who isn't worthy of your love. Don't give away a piece of your soul in an attempt to heal your heart or numb your pain. Your soul knows the truth, honor it!*

You may find your *little girl* or *boy* speaking up when someone comes on too strong. Check in with them by putting your hand on your heart before you share such a sacred gift with someone you hardly know!" Ask yourself, "Is this how you really want to start out a new relationship? Will this fast, sexual encounter be the best thing for me right now?" Then, listen to your heart for the answer and speak your truth.

☜⚷ *In my two decades of research, most of the men I interviewed and observed at social events admitted they have double standards about women who are "too easy." Don't get mad about it… be smart and think before you get naked. Many men unconsciously judge, whether they admit it or not. If you treat the act of sex sacredly, your partners will follow your lead.*

What's the hurry if you know your sexual side can attract people like a magnet? You may find yourself wondering if they will stick around after the initial romantic rush passes. You slept with them after a few dates and then they suddenly get busy with work, stop communicating as much, or tell you that they "aren't ready for a relationship right now, but you are amazing!"

Often, their dates will say that they'll be in touch when they have more time. My clients ask me, "They said they had fun and would call me soon. What happened to our connection?" *Get real,* you may have felt a deep connection in the moment but, more than likely, it was just an attraction and some fun sex. Sorry, but they probably moved on to their next conquest since there was no solid foundation for a relationship. Or, they may call you for a last minute "hook up," since they assume you'll say yes.

Many clients have pretended to be open to casual sex or a part-time lover, thinking they wouldn't get attached. Often, these encounters came back to bite them in the butt and affected their self-esteem. A lot of people will stay with someone because they are sexually addicted and waste their time trying to make it work with a person who isn't a good match. This includes dating *players* or married people that claim they're "separated" and can waste precious years of your life.

� *Once you are aware of your soul's deepest desires to find true love, don't fool yourself by sleeping with someone you hardly know. It's like giving pieces of your heart and soul away to someone who doesn't honor the gift. Let's admit that having a casual fling can make you feel a bit vulnerable especially when you know your actions are not aligned with your deeper intentions.*

Check in and be honest with yourself. Look into the depths of your heart if you think you are wasting your time or maybe just afraid to be alone. In the past, I stayed too long with men that were not going to go the distance. I called them a *W.O.T. (Waste of Time)*. I prevented myself from being honored and respected by some good men who wanted to date me because I was busy with a *player* and missed out. This was one of my biggest "mis-takes" and I want you to learn from it so you can avoid years of heartache and disappointment.

Are you wasting time with a *high-speed chaser* or someone your gut knows isn't right for you? Can you recall anyone that you jumped into bed with that you knew was wrong for you or unavailable? You may have ignored your *little girl* or *boy* and were just numbing your pain. List any names that come to mind in your journal that you knew were unsuitable partners or a *W.O.T.*

� *There is no judgment if you only want casual sex; just be honest with yourself if you've gotten hurt in the past and make sure that "casual" is what you're really looking for. Be real with your heart and speak your truth! By scattering your sexual energy you are sending mixed signals and will continually get mixed results. Be honest with your heart.*

I have interviewed thousands of men who claim they love the chase and respect when a woman wants to wait to have sex. These interviews inspired me to host hot-man panels, seminars called *The Secrets into the Minds of Men*, which offers direct insight from men regarding flirting, sex, and commitment issues.

Women are always amazed at the revealing secrets the men share in my seminars. Even in these crazy times of people "hooking up," men still have imprints and double standards about *good girls* and *bad girls*. Don't assume your relationship will be exclusive if you have sex. I would suggest asking the people you're dating some of the questions below before jumping in bed too soon. However, please understand that some of these questions shouldn't be asked on a first date. Many of them are intense and take some thought and time to answer. We're all big boys and girls, so it's important to *get real* about sex.

So, how and when can you talk openly about intimacy and sex? It's good to ask these questions when the chemistry starts to get fired up, but you aren't quite ready to have sex. Check in with yourself and get in your power first. The timing of this discussion and the tone of your voice are equally important when talking about sex. You need to be relaxed and confident.

It's your right to slow down the process and speak your truth before you have sex. Keep the conversation light, be playful and ask questions so you know the real deal before you get naked. Once you open up this conversation, you will discover what true beliefs you and the people you date have about sex.

LET'S TALK ABOUT SEX! QUESTIONS WE ALL WANT TO ASK BUT RARELY DO

- *Would you mind if we talk about sex before we fool around?*
- *Do you assume you're in a relationship when you have sex with someone?*
- *What are your thoughts about waiting until you commit before becoming sexually involved?*
- *Does having sex make you feel committed?*
- *How important is sex to you in a relationship?*
- *What makes you decide that it's the right time to connect deeper sexually?*
- *Are you okay with waiting to have sex until there is sexual exclusivity?*
- *Where did you learn about sex?*
- *Did your religious beliefs have an influence on you regarding sex as you grew up?*
- *Are you someone who desires to wait until after marriage to make love?*

- *What are your thoughts on being monogamous? Are you capable of being monogamous?*
- *Are you looking for a real relationship with one partner?*
- *What's your distinction between making love and having sex?*
- *What do you consider sex? Kissing, touching body parts, massage, oral sex, tantric practices, intercourse?*
- *What's your status on birth control or STD's?*
- *Who do you think should take responsibility for contraception?*
- *What if we got pregnant? Then what?*
- *How often do you enjoy having sex? Are you a morning, daytime or evening lover?*
- *What are your favorite body parts?*
- *What about me attracted you?*
- *What is your favorite place to make love?*
- *How do you feel when someone asks you for or initiates sex?*
- *Will I hear from you after we have sex?*
- *Will you judge me if we have sex too soon? What is your definition of "too soon"?*
- *Do you see us building a committed, emotional and physical relationship at some point?*
- *What makes you grow in love with someone?*
- *Is it important for you to keep your promises? Are you a person of your word?*
- *What is your description of an attentive lover?*
- *Do you have hang-ups about sex? What are they?*
- *Is kissing important to you? What makes someone a good kisser?*
- *What are your thoughts on dating a sexually aware person?*
- *What are your fantasies? What turns you on?*
- *Are you into porn? Sex toys Swapping Swinger parties? Voyeurism? If so, how often?*

This work will help you to become clear in your communication about sex and intimacy. I encourage you to come back and do these important exercises as needed and ask any other questions that may come up. You may hear your *little girl* or *boy* speak up, so please listen to their voice and your gut feeling if your mate is not communicating clearly about sex. You must know yourself first, and be honest with this sacred gift. This is the key to breaking your patterns and creating a new love story with a happy ending.

By answering the questions and listening to your responses, you may discover new topics and subjects that change how you view life, love and sex. You are getting in touch with a deeper side of yourself and accessing the emotions attached to these topics. Overtime, you will uncover the values that are important to you and in the people you date. You can use your responses to create your ideal Love Design list and for the "Manifesting Love Exercises & Rituals" in Chapter XII.

GET REAL ♥ REFLECTIONS

♥ Are you being honest with yourself about sex? Do you get attached after being intimate?

♥ What did you learn from your past relationships that you can use in your next dating experience?

♥ Do you feel comfortable talking to a potential partners about sex?

♥ List all of the partners you've been intimate with. Can you see a pattern or a *love loop*?

♥ Check in with yourself and your *little girl* or *boy* before jumping into a sexual encounter by putting your hand on your heart and listening to your gut instincts.

Next on our Love Design list is your unique sound effect. Let's explore how you sound and what you tell others about yourself in conversations about your life and love.

CHAPTER XI

YOUR UNIQUE SOUND EFFECT

"What kills a skunk is the publicity it gives itself."
– Abraham Lincoln

"Every waking moment we talk to ourselves about the things we experience. Our self-talk, the thoughts we communicate to ourselves, in turn control the way we feel and act."
– John Lembo

Now that you've answered the questions from the last few chapters on a recorder, you are undoubtedly more aware of the tone and words that automatically come out of your mouth in conversations, as well as the thoughts that created them. It's an eye-opener, isn't it?

I'd suggest that you review the recordings again to gain some additional insight. How does your voice sound? Pay attention to resonance, tone and the vibration when you are speaking. Are your conversations engaging or boring? Are you an attentive listener when you're in a conversation? Are you aware of the statements you make about love and relationships? Do you use words that send out different signals than what you thought you were sending?

UP-LEVEL YOUR THOUGHTS & CONVERSATIONS

It's empowering to know that we can have control over our thoughts, words and conversations, which leave a lasting impression on others. It takes consistency and awareness to create new conversation skills and transform our belief patterns. Begin by using more positive sentence starters and become aware of the tone and speed of your voice.

This daily practice will begin to pave the way towards the life you are creating, which is a major component of your Love Design plan. The next time a friend or family member asks about your love life, consider doing this process: stop, breathe and remember that you are sending out a new signal to the people in your life as well the universe. You have looked back at your old *love imprints*, and now you get to put your new awareness into practice. It's all done in that moment of choice. Once you start doing this process, it gets easier and more fun!

Here is the story of a woman who had serious imprints and how she transformed her old family patterns and her love life. She used all of these *secrets* and created her new *love story*.

TRUE STORY

A beautiful Armenian client of mine, named Ada, had some relatives who would constantly interrogate her about being alone and still single after a bad divorce. It affected her so badly that she found herself eating her feelings away on Sunday visits with her very traditional family. Ada called me for sessions in despair, believing that she would never find love again. She was a vibrant and successful woman but had lost her confidence and didn't feel supported by her family or her friends. She had a girlfriend who was divorced and was very jealous of her bubbly personality and would constantly say things to belittle Ada's lack of success with relationships. Ada was curvy, sexy and very stunning but had gained thirty pounds from the stress of a recent breakup. Her ex was a *bad boy* who wouldn't commit and kept coming back for casual sex. We began the heart-healing process and worked on her self-esteem. She had those internal monsters that were not positive or supportive of her new goals. She committed to do this inner work and finally began taking control of her life. She addressed why she gave so much of herself to undeserving people. Ada spoke up to her *bad boy* and stated that she deserved better and broke up with him for good. Then, she looked at her *imprints* and realized that she needed to heal her heart from her family's control patterns, guilt trips and opinions. There had also been a lot of infidelity in her family and she didn't have many good role models. She let them all know she was designing her new *get ready for love* plan!

Ada was committed to not let the negative past of her *love lineage* affect her future. After doing some love investigating, she discovered that she had unresolved issues with her dad about his cheating. He had been caught having multiple affairs with women and had lied to the family throughout the years. He was not always there for her and rarely told her how proud he was of her. Ada saw that she was seeking approval from men and would try to win their affection by giving too much and opening up sexually too soon. She continued her heart-healing process and worked with her little girl, which helped her heal the relationship with her father. She then dealt with her family and how they were dragging her down with their opinions. Once Ada learned these new skills on how to change her negative language by making powerful statements to her family and the new men she met, her life rapidly transformed.

She stood up for herself for the first time ever and told her family that she didn't appreciate the negativity she felt every week when visiting. She also had men from her past calling and told them she was not interested in hearing from them anymore about casual dating or last-minute booty calls. She proclaimed she was looking for a real relationship.

Ada stopped going out to bars with her negative friend, went on a healthy diet and worked out regularly. She got some new hot dating clothes along with a new attitude. She committed to her heart and created a powerful vision board with her clear love vision. She was amazed at how fast men were magnetized towards her. She was being courted by several men and eventually met her match. She is now married to a wonderful man who adores and worships her. Her family is elated, and she claims that her new positive attitude is rubbing off on them. They saw her dramatic changes and now they want to learn how she achieved her goals. She feels confident, healthy and in love with her new husband and even has a baby on the way. You go girl!

Your friends and family will be shocked when they ask the same old questions and hear these new statements coming from your mouth.

RE-ALIGN YOUR THOUGHTS & REIGNITE YOUR FAITH

Before you go to see the people that triggered your heart in the past, prepare yourself in advance by meditating or saying a little blessing. Call in your new higher-self for the strength to deal with their negativity, which often comes from their past programming or previous generations. Be compassionate and stay centered. Imagine being surrounded by a glowing, white light or a magical energy shield of protection. Keep repeating to yourself, "I am in my power now! No one has any power or control over me from this moment on."

Then, begin by repeating these new statements to yourself about love and realign your thoughts. Before you go out, practice saying these powerful declarations out loud while looking in the mirror. Post up your favorites and write them down in your journal. You will feel the difference in your body and spirit.

POWERFUL DECLARATIONS TO IGNITE YOUR HEART

- *I am embarking on a whole new plan for my life. Something great is coming my way.*
- *I am ready for my amazing partner to come into my life now.*
- *I treat myself the way I want to be treated in all of my relationships.*
- *I am open to extraordinary love… since I am extraordinary!*
- *I am receptive to the clear love signs and I listen to my gut feelings.*
- *I know there are great partners out there and I am magnetizing my match.*
- *I am changing how I communicate about myself, love and relationships.*
- *I am creating miracles and magic in my life every day.*
- *I am letting go of my past and designing the life I have always imagined.*

- *I've learned great lessons from my relationship and grow from my "mis-takes."*
- *I am gentle with myself and the little girl or boy inside me.*
- *I promise to listen to the messages from my heart that will lead me to my ultimate vision.*
- *I am in balance with my body, mind and spirit.*
- *I'm taking time for love in my life now.*
- *I am a magnetic force of love wherever I go.*
- *I am in the most amazing relationship with myself and all is well.*
- *I open my heart to the love all around me.*
- *I am lucky in love.*
- *I am attracting people that are supportive and loving in my life.*
- *I have strong faith during this heart-healing process.*
- *Love is a choice and I choose love now!*
- *It's my turn to have real love.*
- *I am expanding my heart to greater dimensions of love.*
- *My little girl or boy trusts me to make the right choices when it comes to love.*
- *I set my intentions and call forth my divine mate now.*
- *I feel my soul mate in my heart and I am excited to meet them.*
- *I am open to new and exciting opportunities and people that are aligned with my lifestyle.*
- *Love comes easily and effortlessly to me.*
- *I know my amazing life partner is searching for me now.*
- *I trust in God's plan for me.*
- *I know that my future relationship will inspire others to believe in real love.*
- *I am ready for LOVE.*

Realize that you will always attract what's in your mind and heart. You are that powerful, and through this shift in your inner conversations, you are attracting circumstances that lead you towards (or away) from success. Again, to get your desired outcome, you must first open yourself up and believe that you deserve it. Say or write out this mantra: "I deserve only the best in all of my relationships. Love comes easily and effortlessly to me. I am safe to open my heart to *real love*."

Occasionally your *little girl* or *boy* may speak up when you're alone and feeling down. You may hear them doubt you and your new way of thinking. When negative voices surface, STOP, put your hand on your heart and say, "I command these thoughts to leave my mind. I know the truth about myself." Then, in that moment, replace that negative thought with the opposite—a new power statement. "I am opening my heart to *real love* now! I promise you I am changing my patterns and will listen to your needs." Then, take a moment and close your eyes and imagine how you would feel, what you might hear, see, taste, or smell and begin visualizing your new outcome. Then say, "We are fearless and free to manifest love now." Breathe and relax. You're now in the driver's seat and in control of your mind. Practice your new *language of love* everywhere you go.

Continue to use the declarations from the list to lift your spirits and shift yourself out of those feelings. Then, replace them with elevated words to reframe your mind until this becomes a daily practice. I also recommend using these affirmations in your online profiles as well as in the various love visioning processes in the next chapter. These steps are all part of your new *action plan*, which sets these intentions in motion by speaking your new *language of love*. You will be surprised at the results.

○━━ *Prepare in advance to answer the most frequently asked questions that normally cause you to spiral down a negative mind path. Learn how to instantly switch the energy with your new language of love.*

Your friends and family will be shocked when they ask the same old questions and hear these new statements coming from your mouth. They may ask questions, which in the past may have triggered a negative reaction. Such as: How is your love life going? Have you met anyone lately? Are you planning on ever getting married? Are you just too picky to settle down?

When I would visit home, my favorite comments came from my grand-mother and aunts. They would not-so-subtly say, "You'd better hurry up and meet someone soon, honey. Your eggs are getting old and no man will ever want you once you get too old!" Those comments always made my visits so *special*. Who wouldn't get triggered being interrogated by a loud, Italian family or any family? I surely use to get angry and hurt until I took charge. So, I changed my mindset and my reaction every time it happened, and so can you.

What can you do to stay in your power when this scenario or conversation comes up on a visit or holiday? When asked the same old questions, use your new *language of love*. "Thanks for asking" and use up-leveled statements, or your own lingo in your conversations. You can change your world by changing your words. Here are some powerful statements you can practice saying when people ask questions that trigger you.

ELEVATE YOUR NEW LANGUAGE OF LOVE

- *I am totally open and excited about having an extraordinary relationship.*
- *I am doing great and I've been working on a plan to meet my match.*
- *I am asking for my family and friends to support me by believing in love for me.*
- *I am committed to having only the best for myself in all my relationships.*
- *I am now attracting the most amazing people in my life and my soul mate is on their way!*
- *I am ready for real love and I'm asking for your prayers to support my vision.*
- *I am heading in the direction of success in all areas of my life. Meeting my true love is on the top of my list.*
- *I am prepared to meet the perfect person for me. I am ready for love now!*
- *I am clear about my intentions, I sent in my order and my partner is coming into my life at the perfect time.*
- *I have faith in love and I know it's my turn. I trust in God's plan.*
- *I am clear and open to meet someone special. If you know anyone special for me... let me know.*

- *My intention is to have the kind of relationship that is an example of real love.*
- *I am 100% focused on achieving my goal to create wonderful relationships this year.*
- *I am open and prepared to meet my amazing husband or wife and create our life together.*
- *I am happy to report that my life is going well, and I am achieving my life visions.*
- *I have opened my heart to receive sacred love by doing this healing work.*
- *I've chosen to recreate my inner thoughts about love and partnership... will you support me in my new vision for love now?*
- *I am manifesting love now with ease and grace.*
- *I believe in love, and I know that love will find me in the most extraordinary way.*
- *I am ready to meet my divine partner and I'm sure he or she will be amazing.*
- *I believe that I deserve only the best in all areas of my life.*
- *I know that there is an abundance of available people who will adore me just the way I am.*
- *I am sure my soul mate is searching for me and I am knowing they will show up in the perfect time.*
- *I am free from my past and open to having extraordinary love. I feel it from the depths of my heart.*
- *I love my life and am ready to create an amazing lifestyle with my soul mate.*
- *I am a magnet for a passionate partner who wants real love and commitment.*
- *I have designed my love plan, and I am ready for true love that works.*
- *I have renewed my faith in love and my heart is open like never before.*
- *I am ready for the best life has to offer. I am here and ready to meet my true love now!*

After a short while, you will find that doing this conscious shifting exercise will become your new routine. The results you will see in your energy and life experiences will encourage you to maintain this habit. Be in charge of your daily thoughts and conversations while influencing other people in your life along the way. You will begin to integrate your *little girl* or *boy* with your new realigned energy and develop a new level of trust and faith in yourself.

☞ *In every moment you can make a new choice. It's easy to change those thoughts by giving new commands to your subconscious mind on a regular basis. ACT AS IF you've already experienced your love goals and visions, and they'll appear into your life, like magic!*

Can you feel, see and hear the difference in these statements when you shift your language and are aware of what comes out of your mouth? By becoming clearer with your voice tonality, vision and words, you will open up many new experiences and attract different people into your life. Just try it! It absolutely works.

Now let's practice using our new *language of love* and finish these statements below:

PRACTICE YOUR NEW LANGUAGE OF LOVE

* *I'd make the best partner because…*
* *My vision for my love life is…*
* *I know that I deserve…*
* *I have the greatest relationship. It is amazing because…*
* *I will surely create the kind of love that is…*
* *One of the unlimited possibilities for my life is…*
* *I am committed to manifesting…*
* *I imagine my soul mate will be…*
* *I am open and prepared to meet my amazing partner. They will be…*

Did you notice that you changed your answers by revising your *language of love*? Please note that you'll be tested by people in your life that may be pessimistic of your new ways because they aren't used to you being so positive. What do you do with negative energies that come your way now that you've changed some of your old conversations?

⌘━🗝 *Remember…your life force and energy vibes are affected by what you say and hear in most of your conversations; stay true to your new language of love.*

TRANSMUTING OPINIONS & NEGATIVITY

"The image that concerns most people is the reflection
they see in other people's minds."
– Edward De Bono

Many of us are powerfully influenced by other people's negativity and opinions. If you're affected by what others say or think about you and your current love status, remember that their views and opinions stem from their deeper beliefs and fears. What can you do in the moment when someone says something negative to you? How can you transform these opinions?

First, listen to what they say and ask yourself if this opinion or belief is true for you. Replace the negative belief in that moment with what you desire to feel and experience instead. If someone spews negativity in your direction, say silently to yourself, "No, I refuse to let this person's opinions and thoughts penetrate me. Cancel! Cancel! I cancel this thought now." Set boundaries and then say to yourself, "I dissolve that energy-draining thought from this inter-action and cancel it now. It's only an opinion based on their personal beliefs and experiences."

For example, a friend or family member might tease you and say, "You're unlucky in love these days. I bet you want to just give up on this whole dating game with these uncommitted people. Why bother?" You might reply, "Thank you for your concern about my love life. That might be your opinion but those statements aren't true for me. I have faith in love and I'd appreciate if you kept your opinions to yourself from now on. I could use your support to see me successful in my relationships."

Then say to yourself, "My mind is free from others' opinions. The doubt and fear are now dissolved." Introduce new beliefs in the moment: "I attract positive people in my life that love and appreciate me for who I am. My heart is open and ready for love!" Erase their negative opinions in the moment. Do this until it becomes a habit and then ignore or rid yourself of the people who aren't supporting your growth or *love vision.*

⌖ *Keep your mind free of polluted, negative words and become an example for others to follow. Rid yourself of the negativity and the pessimistic people bringing you down. Their opinions have no power over you, unless you allow it.*

If this quick exercise doesn't work, you may want to go deeper. Many times your feelings are triggered from stored memories and may still need healing. Write out what's going on for you after being set off by someone else's opinion. What thoughts creep in? Write out what you believe you deserve and observe the mind and the energy-draining chatter that comes to the surface. Then, realize that the chatter is an automatic response that you can change in the moment. Are the comments that disturbed you truthful? Use this feedback to deal with issues, not hide behind them. Do some of their comments contain a grain of truth? Why does their opinion set you off balance? Write out the thoughts that show up as you process your new way of being. You'll start to see progress as you expand your awareness and get real with yourself like never before. You may find this experience will repeat itself until the emotional charge is erased and reprogrammed for good.

How can you tell if a person influences you in an energy-draining way? Put your hand on your heart or where your intuitive feelings come from, and ask yourself the questions below to realign your thoughts. Your body and intuition will give you the answer when asked the right questions.

⌖ *Listen to your gut and your heart…they know the truth. Then, look at the lives of those who are giving you their opinions.*

REALIGNMENT EXERCISE

Ask yourself:

- *Are the beliefs of this person what I desire to experience?*
- *Is this person's life one I would like to lead?*
- *Does this conversation increase or decrease my energy level?*

177

• *On a scale of one to ten (with ten being the highest), how much energy is this conversation taking away or adding to my life and goals?*

• *Is this amount of energy helping to solve my challenges now?*

• *Is this person's energy one you want to emulate or be around?*

• *What thought(s) would be the better choice right now?*

• *Is this person supporting my life vision and growth?*

• *Why should I take their beliefs so seriously?*

• *Are these comments and opinions draining or empowering me?*

• *What conversations, feelings or beliefs would be more beneficial to me now?*

⚷ *Become the new you without talking about it to anyone who isn't on your side or drains your energy. Without saying a word, they will see the transformation and results in your life. You will be a living example and a powerful influence in the world.*

Take the time to pay closer attention to others and the statements they use in conversations. Slow yourself down and listen more intently to the people you meet to see if there is a value match. Go deeper inside, open up and sense if they would enhance your life or drain it. Don't bother wasting one minute of your time or energy on negative people.

⚷ *Tune in and you will have a stronger intuitive sense that reveals who you should let into your life or not. Your life is sacred, so don't waste your precious time on anyone draining your energy.*

Whatever you constantly think about is the issue that's calling for your attention now. A huge shift will happen if you get to the root of the matter once and for all. Forgive yourself for allowing those beliefs or draining people to set you off course. This will help you take control of your life and focus on your dreams and intentions. You are now your own Love Designer. You will elevate to a new level, be renewed and strengthened from the deepest place in your inner core.

SHARE YOUR VISIONS WISELY

It's important that you only share your visions, *secrets* and challenges with sacred people that you can trust with your heart. Be aware that there will be a few unsupportive people who may attempt to sabotage you. If you know who those people are, don't bother mentioning your vision or goals to them. Keep your new sacred vision to yourself. Continue your inner work and don't react to the negativity coming from *vampire vibers*. It's a waste of words and time to try convincing negative people to change. Clear them from your mind and focus on your new life vision.

⌦ *Your family and the people you socialize with will only remember the last thing you told them. Often they will pass on your latest updates and your secrets in casual conversations. Be sure to only share personal information you don't mind having repeated and spread. People love to gossip and often stories get distorted.*

When people ask how you are, just state "I'm doing well, reinventing myself and making great changes in my life." Even if you are going through a challenging time, just say, "I am grateful and focused on moving forward in a new direction. I am excited about living life to the fullest." This is an effective technique to change their perception of you and influence them with your newfound, positive approach to life. People will remember your attitude, what you say and how you say it. Choose words that empower you and show your true character. If they ask for details, tell them the truth about your inner heart work and ask for their support without sharing too much information.

Your friends and family may think you are crazy at first, and they may not back you up because they aren't comfortable with the dynamics of change in their own lives. So, as a result, they may project their discomfort on to you. You may discover that you want to connect with new friends because you will grow from this process and no longer feel connected to their *energy vibes*. Now that you have this information, you can't pretend not to know the truth. As you change, you could be an influential mentor role-model and ignite their hearts to change as well. What an awesome feeling! Here is a story of how I asked my family to support my love visions.

TRUE STORY

One of my most powerful moments happened after I had done my inner work. I had healed my heart from the past and finally let go of my limiting beliefs that men could not be trusted. I was ready to find a husband, life partner and soul mate—no more noncommittal men or *bad boys* for me! I was excited to share my *love vision* with my family and let them know I wanted their support. I knew this news would shock them all!

It was Christmas Eve, the year before my mom died, when I made the decision that it was time to try my powerful *language of love* techniques on my own family. I flew into Philadelphia every year before Christmas to celebrate the holidays, and we sure knew how to celebrate. Since we come from a family of chefs and my dad was the nation's first five-star caterer, we were known for having amazing feasts at our house. We celebrated Christmas with home-made, traditional Italian food like you see in the movies; it was over the top. The room was filled with fifty or more of my East Coast relatives from three generations. When you're Italian, it's all about food and family! My grand-mother cooked all the traditional dishes, including the seven fishes and her special desserts. The house smelled heavenly between the baking, garlic and spaghetti sauces. Remember, I was the only unmarried one out of six children and knew I was going to be interrogated, once again, by my big, passionate, opinionated family. I was constantly teased about being in the love business for many years, yet alone on Christmas Eve without a husband or special man by my side.

The first question asked by my great aunt and grandmother was, "Are you dating anyone seriously right now?" I'd say, "Yes, but it's too soon to bring this one home to this crazy family!" Sometimes the nuns from my high school or old family friends would stop by and ask the big question, "Why are you still single? I think you are just too picky, Renée. You should just meet a nice guy and get married!" Then, as each one of my sisters and brothers (and their spouses) would show up, I'd hear comments like: "What's up with a dating guru with no boyfriend?" or "Renée will probably never get married at this point…she's never going to settle down in Hollywood!" Eventually, my grandmother would chime in, "That's the city of fruits and nuts; the people are crazy out there, and most of the men are gigolos that want to shack up with rich women. I saw it on Oprah."

So, I told the nuns my intentions and asked them to keep me in their prayers and told the others I would keep them posted. That night, I knew it was time for me to speak up, so I made a plan to share my *love vision* with my family and to practice what I preach. I was done with their teasing and negativity and wanted them to support me.

As the entire family sat at our very long table, we would all gather to say a prayer before dinner and toast to the holidays. Finally, with everyone there, this was my chance to speak up. As I stood up to make a toast, I could hear whispers, "I wonder if she has a new man now? "Hmm, what's this all about?" I said, "May I have your attention please? I want to propose a toast, but before I do, I need to say I love all of you, and this year I need to make a request that you stop asking me about why I'm alone and stop bugging me about not coming home with a man! I am very aware that I don't have a husband yet, and I pay a lot of money to come here to spend the holidays with all of you. Frankly, I want to request that you all stop teasing me about not being married. I don't think you all know how hurtful your jokes are to me. I have lots of love in my life, and I am actually happy and fantastic on my own. After all these years in the love business, I am sure God has someone special for me. Instead of beating me up when I come home, I'd like you all to see me in a happy, committed relationship with a great guy who fits into this loud, crazy family and will love me for who I am. Hopefully, he can deal with all of you in his face."

I continued, "I teach so many people how to manifest love, and I know if God created me with this passion for my life and my work that he also created a man who could handle being with me and support my mission to spread the love. I want my partner to be a kind, giving man who cares about others, is family-oriented, happy with his work, and passionate about life like I am.

When people see us they'll see *love in form*, and together we'll make a contribution to the world. So, I am requesting that all of you, from this moment on, as I pointed and looked each person in their eyes, see me as happy, fulfilled and finding an amazing life partner. Instead of worrying about me, use that energy to see me healthy and successful in life and love. I want you all to hold this vision in your hearts and pray for me, knowing that I am finding my *true love*! Mark my words, one day very soon I will walk into this house with my man and you will say, "Oh my God that is him, the man Renée described and the one we prayed for."

I stopped and looked around the room with an intense stare. Everyone was silent, and I said, "Do you all promise you will do this for me, please? It would really make me happy to know that you *believe in love* for me." My brother, Bobby, had tears in his eyes since he could feel my conviction, and my mom smiled at me with her gentle look of love. She believed in me for sure!

Everyone else seemed to be in shock and agreed to my request with nods and smiles. I raised my glass and said, "Let's toast to my future husband, my amazing man, wherever he might be! Here's to us finding each other and creating an amazing life together! I am ready for LOVE. Hear, hear! And so it is!"

We all toasted and, after that night, I was never teased again. That was Christmas Eve 2001 and I met my husband nine months later on August 10th. He met most of my family on Labor Day weekend that year when my dad invited a huge group over. They loved Joe from the first time they met him. My request was heard and my vision came in God's perfect time.

I made my claim that Christmas Eve, and it's time to make yours. I had put in my order to God and the powers that be and asked for my family to support my *love vision*. Now, it's your turn to ask for support from the people you love and to communicate clearly about what you need. My family still talks about that night when I took a stand for my heart. It was a magical moment in my life.

I hope this story inspires you to speak up and practice your new *language of love* the next time you see your family and friends. You will be surprised at how amazing it feels to speak up and how it can change the way your family and friends perceive you from now on!

GET REAL ♥ REFLECTIONS

♥ Practice up-leveling your thoughts and conversations. Name the top three conversations that you could adjust right now to help you create your new love vision.

♥ Are you comfortable speaking your new *language of love*? Practice saying some of those powerful lines out loud in the mirror or to friends and family regularly so those new declarations flow easily off your tongue.

♥ List the sacred people that you can trust with your heart and *love vision*.

♥ Rehearse how you would express your new love vision to your family and friends. Would it change the way that they perceive you and your old love patterns?

Now, you will take this powerful knowledge and create the vision for your dream relationship...it's time to create your manifesting love list!

CHAPTER XII
ALIGN YOUR VISION

"Once a man has made a commitment to a way of life, he puts the greatest strength in the world behind him. It's something we call heart power. Once a man has made this commitment, nothing will stop him short of success."
– *Vince Lombardi*

"If one advances confidently in the direction of his dreams, and endeavors to live the life which he has imagined, he will meet with success unexpected in common hours."
– *Henry David Thoreau*

ALIGN YOUR VISION TO MANIFEST LOVE

Now that you have done so much inner reflection and opened your heart, it's time to activate your imagination and envision your future. The next step in the Love Design process is becoming clear on what type of partner you want, no matter what phase of life you are in right now. Get out your *love journal* and jot down your thoughts as you go along using your new *language of love*. We will create your *Manifesting Love List*! What kind of partner do you desire? What qualities do they possess that are most important to you? Have you ever described your ideal mate and the kind of lifestyle you want to experience in writing? Have you ever shared the vision of your ideal relationship with anyone? People spend years working on marketing plans in business or searching for the perfect home or car, yet many of us rarely think deeply about the type of person we want as a life partner. It's essential to examine if there is a value match when designing your ideal lifestyle with someone. It is vital to communicate about these topics before getting married. If you ignore these important issues and just expect them to be resolved after you meet, they can cause challenges in the future.

Let your imagination run free, and write down your heart's desires in detail. It's important for you to stretch yourself and go beyond your normal comfort zone. Now is your chance to use your expanded awareness, imagination along with the answers from the list of questions from the previous chapters This will help direct you towards your new *love vision*. After reading the following questions, review the list of adjectives in this chapter. As you begin implementing the techniques and rituals into your daily practices, you will develop more clarity and understanding. Dream big as you create your love vision.

MANIFESTING LOVE LIST: DESCRIBE YOUR IDEAL MATE

Physical attraction is usually the first step in bringing people together, so answer the following questions:

HOW DO YOU DESCRIBE YOUR IDEAL MAN: What parts of a man attracts you? His sparkling eyes, a nice smile, the way he walks, his hands, his broad shoulders, his dimples, his behind, or his baby soft face and skin? How would you describe his style? Is he the earthy hippy type, the casual jeans and t-shirts man, the business professional, the conservative preppy, the sporty jock, the trendy artist, the classic European style, the ruggedly handsome look, or the chiseled model type? What is his body type? Is he stocky and strong, fit, athletic and toned, a lean build, or a muscular body builder type? Or do you prefer a big and burly man who is the "teddy bear" type? Does his height matter to you? If so, how tall is he? What preference do you have for hair color, hair length, facial hair and eye color? Get descriptive!

HOW DO YOU DESCRIBE YOUR IDEAL WOMAN: What does your ideal woman look like? What parts of a woman attract you? The glow in her eyes, her warm smile, the way she walks, her soft skin, pretty hands or cute feet, her curves, breasts, legs, facial expressions? How would you describe her style? Is she the simple elegant type, the casual, yet classy type, the natural girl next door, the earthy bohemian type, athletic and sporty, the business professional, the fashion forward trend setter, the sparkle glamour girl, or the sexy model? How would you describe her body type? Is she, curvy, voluptuous, athletic, lean and toned? Do you prefer a taller or petite woman? What preference do you have for hair color and the length of her hair? Get descriptive!

CAREER CHOICE: What is your ideal partner's career path or profession? Describe your ideal scenario. Do they work in the corporate world, the legal or medical fields? Are they an engineer or designer? Do you want to be with a partner who is powerful, driven and with a solid career? Do you want someone who is the artist/creative type, like a musician, chef or writer? How about someone who is now retired at home doing their own thing? Does the entrepreneurial partner who loves to create new businesses work for you? What about someone who followed in the footsteps of their family's business? Do you want a natural country boy or girl, a partner in uniform, a stay at home parent or someone who works part-time? How important is their financial stability to you? Describe their work ethic.

EDUCATION LEVEL: How important is their level of education? Do they have to be on the same level as you? Is it important to you that they have an advanced degree? Are you worried that they may be more or less educated than you? If they are currently in school, is that okay with you?

PERSONALITY TYPE: How would you describe their personality? Do they have an open, extroverted and friendly personality? Do they have charisma? Are they a little more introverted, subdued, quiet, or soft-spoken? Are they the intellectual type? How do they act with you alone or in groups? How do they treat strangers? Are they a family oriented person? What about their demeanor makes them special? List the character traits your ideal partner would possess.

HOW YOU FEEL WHEN YOU ARE WITH YOUR MATE: Write out a detailed description of how you will feel when you're with your mate. For example, "I feel so protected, nurtured and loved in their presence. We are connected and can really open up and communicate about our life goals.

I feel supported to be myself and we encourage each other's creativity and dreams. I trust them and feel safe since they keep their word. I feel grateful since we appreciate each other and welcomed into their life. They are so caring and responsive, and they honor our relationship. We have so much fun together and I'm so proud to have them in my life."

LIFE STYLE AND DAY-TO-DAY LIVING: Describe a typical day with your ideal mate. How do you envision starting and ending your day? What will life be like during the week? The weekend? What kind of common activities do you share with your mate at home? Describe the type of lifestyle are you co-creating. How will you handle daily activities like cleaning the house, cooking, laundry, errands, kids, animals and food shopping? Are you super organized and scheduled, or do you go with the flow? Is there one of you that delegates roles and responsibilities? Or, do you decide things together? If you are a busy person, do you want an equally busy partner? What are your expectations from your partner if you work more than they do? When you come home, do you want them waiting for you with dinner prepared or vice versa? Maybe you would prefer that they work full time, so you can stay home and take care of the kids. Many people work from home these days. If you both worked from home, would you be okay with being around your mate 24/7? How much interdependence or independence are you looking for?

FAMILY: You marry into a person's family, so what is your ideal family scenario? What if they are very close to their family and you are not into the family scene? How would that play out? What if they detest your family and don't want to participate in family gatherings or holidays? How important is this family issue to you? Is this a deal-breaker?

SEX/INTIMACY: Your beliefs around sex are vital in a long-term relationship. Answering the questions at the end of Chapter X will clarify your values about these important issues. When it comes to sex and intimacy, what kind of person do you envision yourself with? Do you believe in sex before marriage? Are you into kissing, lovemaking and sensuality? Do you mind if your partner is experienced sexually? What if your partner has been more sexually active than you? Are you in touch with your values on this issue? How open are you to talking about sex and what turns you on? Do you want your partner to tell you what they desire from you sexually? Have you studied the art of sex and sensuality? Are you open to learning how to please your mate?

ROMANCE: Is your partner romantic? What is your unique definition of romance? How do you romance your mate? How do you like to be romanced? Describe a romantic evening with your ideal mate. Do you want a person who plans romantic dates and surprises you with love notes and gifts?

RELIGION/SPIRITUAL PRACTICES: Religious beliefs are very important in relationships, especially to people from specific religious cultures. Does your mate need to have the same religious background? Is religion a deal-breaker for you? Do you want to attend religious services and expect your mate to join you? Is prayer a part of your life? How about meditation or other spiritual practices? Are you an atheist and not into religious practices? Are you open to having a mate on a spiritual path? If you are not on the same spiritual path, is it possible for you to accept their faith to be together? If you are from different faiths, will your families accept this and be comfortable with it? We all have the right to our own beliefs. Can you *get real* and share that you want to pray and practice the rituals of your chosen religion? What would you do if your mate is not interested or supportive?

EATING HABITS: Does your mate need to have similar eating habits? How important is this issue to you? Are you a vegetarian? Vegan? A meat eater? A healthy eater? Or, a junk-food junkie? Describe your food preferences. Do you have any special food restrictions or allergies? Are table manners important to you?

PHYSICAL FITNESS: How important is regular exercise to you? Does your mate have to have a similar workout levels or schedule? Do you care if they don't work out at all? What would you do if your mate claimed they were a fitness type and a healthy eater then suddenly stopped working out? If your mate was a skier, hiker, biker, runner, golfer or tri-athlete and you aren't at the same level athletically, will that work for you long term?

ALCOHOL & MIND-ALTERING SUBSTANCES: Does your mate drink a lot, smoke marijuana everyday, or use other recreational drugs? Would it bother you if your mate took prescription drugs, sleeping pills, anti-anxiety medicine or anti-depressants to maintain mood balance? What if your mate was in a twelve step program or rehab? Does that matter to you?

MONEY: Money issues and spending habits are critical issues to discuss. Do you know how you'll handle bills? Spending? Organizing and saving money? Would you feel comfortable supporting your mate if they weren't the main provider? Do you want the relationship to be an equal partnership, where money and spending are concerned? Do you need a prenuptial agreement before you marry? Do financial challenges sway you from being interested in a partner long-term? Are you in debt and afraid to be honest about your financial situation? Do you see yourself being the provider in the relationship? How does being the breadwinner feel to you in your day-to-day life? What if your partner doesn't work? Would you be able to take care of most of the bills? In these challenging times, money status can change in an instant. Are you able to accept that fact? A partner can be wealthy today and broke tomorrow.

CHILDREN: Do you like kids? Do you want to have your own children? Do you have a timeline in mind? Does a partner with children fit into your picture? Do you see yourself being a stepparent and helping raise someone else's children? Are you concerned that you may have to deal with your partner's ex? Is having a child or not a deal breaker for you? Are you ready for the responsibility and the financial realities of having children? Are you aware of the level of commitment and time that it takes to raise children?

ANIMALS: Are you an animal lover? If you are not, but your partner has animals, is that a deal breaker? If you are allergic to certain animals, will that be an issue? If you love your partner, will you bend on this issue?

What if you have animals and your partner is allergic? What would you do? Would you give your pet away to accommodate your partner's health? Would you be willing to search for a solution with homeopathic remedies or medications?

SLEEPING HABITS: If your mate is a night owl and you are an early morning riser, is this a concern? Are you a heavy snorer? Does snoring keep you awake? Can you wear earplugs? Are you into snuggling or do you like your space? Some people don't want anybody touching them when they sleep. Do you sleep with windows open or closed at night? Do you sleep naked or with PJs? Can you sleep with the television on, a fan swirling, or music in the background? Do you like a dark room or sunlight? Sleeping habits are adjustable, yet we all have our own routines. What are your sleeping habits and those of your ideal mate?

PUBLIC BEHAVIOR: How does your partner treat you in public? Are you proud to be seen with them? Are you into being affectionate in public or are you more private? How do you expect them to treat you when you are out with friends and family? Are they respectful to waiters and valets? Are they polite to others? How would you describe their public behavior in general?

FRIENDS: Does your partner have nice friends? Describe them. How do you feel about them? Do they like you? Are your partner's friends a good reflection of them? Could you enjoy hanging out with "the gang" if they are a big part of your partner's life? Do they have a lot of friends of the opposite sex? Do you mind if they are still friends with an ex-spouse or a former flame? Would you be jealous if they had friends of the opposite sex? Would it matter if your friends liked your partner? How would your partner act towards your friends if you had them over for a fun get together? Do you even want your partner around your friends? Or, will you be proud to introduce them?

HOBBIES: Write out your favorite hobbies. Is it important to have similar hobbies as your partner? If so, what hobbies or activities would you enjoy sharing with your mate? Are you more into having separate interests?

These hobbies could include: participating in or watching sports, nature hikes, traveling, dancing, hosting parties, visiting museums or art galleries, listening to music or going to concerts, reading, writing, continued education, card games, board games, theatre, movies, or exploring food and wine. The list of creative ideas goes on and on!

COMMITMENT ISSUES: Do you know how your partner feels about marriage and commitment? What is your definition of a committed relationship? Are you comfortable bringing up the topic? Do you believe that making love means that you're committed to someone? Do you assume you are committed after dating for a certain amount of time? Do you expect your partner to ask for a committed relationship? What actions are you anticipating from your partner to show you that you are in a committed relationship? How important is commitment or marriage to you? How long do you think you should date before you commit to a relationship?

HOLIDAYS CELEBRATIONS: What is your ideal vision for how you and your mate will celebrate holidays and special occasions? Do holidays, birthdays and celebrations carry a lot of meaning to you? Are you sentimental? Does your mate have to be involved in all of the family activities you participate in? Can you deal with a partner who is not sentimental? Do you expect your partner to make a big deal about holidays like your birthday and Valentine's Day, or could you care less?

VALUES: What are your strongest core values? Which values are most important for your partner to possess? Do they have to match yours totally? What are your top seven values? Are you a true representation of these values?

PARTNERSHIP: What would make you happy in a partnership? What is your definition of a good partner? How would you describe your perfect partner? What do you want your marriage or partnership to represent in the world?

TRAVEL & PASSIONS: What types of trips and vacations will you take? What passions will you share? Describe them in detail.

It's very important to write down goals for your life and focus on the values and attributes that mean the most to you. Once you have listed your most important values, you can then ask potential partners questions that will let you know if there is a match. Listen carefully to the words people use in their answers and to your gut instincts as well.

Now that these thoughts are fresh in your mind, let's quickly write the seven most important values you wish for in your ultimate life partner.

TOP VALUE LIST FOR YOUR IDEAL PARTNER

- ♥ _____
- ♥ _____
- ♥ _____
- ♥ _____
- ♥ _____
- ♥ _____
- ♥ _____

Ask questions of yourself as well as your dates and listen to the answers carefully. This way, you can save yourself time and energy if there isn't a match. I often hear women say in sessions: "I knew he hated animals and was unsure about having kids." Or, "What was I thinking to continue dating him and waste my precious time when I knew he wasn't for me?"

Other important questions to ask yourself: "What would I be doing right now if the love of my life was going to be delivered in thirty days? How would I be acting? What steps would I be taking to get ready? How would I be feeling?" In my classes people often say, "When I am in a relationship, then I'll feel like cleaning my place, working out, taking a cooking class, getting a new couch, buying new lingerie, taking better care of my body, etc." Get the picture? How will you treat yourself when you are in love? Do those things now! Treat yourself the way you want to be treated and you will discover that love will show up in all areas of your life. List the top five things you would be doing today if you knew that your *true love* was going to be delivered to your door in a month.

GET READY FOR LOVE TO-DO LIST!

♥ _____

♥ _____

♥ _____

♥ _____

♥ _____

Now, it's time to take action and *get ready for love*. Do this work in a joyful state with confidence and believe that love is on its way.

☞ *First, become what you are asking to receive. Then, act as if you have already received the love you envisioned and it will come right on time. Be grateful for your life now!*

MANIFESTING LOVE EXERCISES & RITUALS

I have practiced many techniques for manifesting love and success. Now that you are clear on your vision, let's get you moving with few powerful exercises to help you call in divine love. After you have written out your unique goals in your journal, you can then easily program into your subconscious mind all the feelings that these descriptions represent to you. In order for you to attract a partner, you must first imagine these goals and then believe they are attainable. You must be willing to receive love and know that you deserve a great relationship. It's just like visualizing your business succeeding: in your mind, create a clear picture of your ideal relationship entering your life. Here are some rituals to practice as often as possible to create new habits that will assist you in attracting your soul mate. You'll become a magnetic force for love.

NIGHT TIME RITUAL

Before sleeping, meditating or relaxing, consciously create in your body the sensations associated with the descriptions you wrote about your ideal mate. As you do this ritual, either put your hand over your heart or hold your heart stone as a way of expanding your love vibration. Now, play soft music and get relaxed. Take a few deep breaths. Breathe in for a count of four seconds, hold for four seconds, and release the air for four seconds. Repeat this four times. Listen to special music that creates a romantic feeling inside of your body. Every time you hear this music, it will anchor you into a state of being loved and connected.

Allow the feelings of being totally loved by a wonderful partner to enter your mind and body. Use your senses. How will they smell and feel in your arms? Where do you see yourself with them? What is the ambiance of the environment, including the lighting, scent, sounds and food? How are you dressed? How do they look? If you are snuggling in bed, how does it feel to be in their embrace? What will they be saying to you about your relationship? How does their voice sound? How does their skin feel against yours? How will it feel to make love to them, massage each other, kiss, hug and sleep together? Feel the joy surging through you while you imagine connecting passionately.

Visualize living with your partner and how you will co-create your living space and the environment for your home together. Where do you see yourself traveling and taking vacations? What will your lifestyle be like together? What foods will you prepare and eat together? What is it like sharing a life of friends, family and spiritual practices with this special partner? How will you treat your lover? Imagine how much ecstasy and passion you create in your communication and lovemaking. Hear the music, see yourself laughing, feel the closeness and passion enveloped in the scent of their body and embrace.

Playing music that creates emotions of connection, passion, romance and love while you are visualizing really adds to the experience. Every time you hear this music, you will be associating and creating the vision of the relationship of your unique design in your mind. It is a simple technique that you can use to get yourself accustomed to the feeling of being loved. This technique is called an "Anchor" in NLP (Neuro-Linguistic Programming). Every time you repeat this ritual, it will put you in an *energy vibe* that is receptive to love.

When you use this technique and are in a heightened state, touch a spot on your body that you can easily access. Squeeze your wrist, touch your heart, tap the back of your hand gently three times, snap your fingers, or use your heart stone to bring you back to this moment. By touching that spot over and over, you are creating an anchor for that feeling in the future. Each time you touch that spot or hold your heart stone, you will feel the emotions and sensations of this love in your heart and in your life.

By doing this exercise regularly, you will create a new internal message. This message becomes an amplified vibration that sends out a new signal, attracting men with the similar vibes. You will find yourself magnetizing potential partners or perhaps your soul mate and it will seem magical. I know this ritual to be very powerful and it works.

IMAGINE YOUR PARTNER IS THERE WHEN YOU GET HOME

I know it might sound silly, but I suggest doing a fun ritual when you come home each day. As you approach your place and get ready to open the front door, imagine that your partner is inside waiting for you. You can get into this feeling by saying, "Hi honey, I'm home." I found that I got a jolt of excitement every time I did this ritual, knowing that one day soon my vision would become a reality. The first time I came home and Joe was waiting for me with open arms...I cried. Imagine how you will feel if it's been a while since you've had a lover around. It may sound ridiculous to people who are married, but for those of us who aren't, it's a good thing to say aloud, affirm, imagine, and play with. Your neighbors may think you are a bit "out there" since they may never see anyone there with you. I came up with this ritual one night in a dream and thought it would be a fun exercise. Try it, it will make your heart smile and you will feel great. I promise your partner will appear soon enough and you will be saying, "Hi honey, I'm home" for real.

LOVE LETTERS TO YOUR BELOVED

Some of my clients don't like to write out their "ideal mate list." So, I suggest that you write love letters or gather romantic cards as if you've already met your soul mate. These letters helps create the consciousness of having your desire now. When I read my personal journals, I found that I had at least a dozen letters and poems that expressed my emotions as if I had already met my soul mate. I also had purchased a dozen romantic cards with sayings that moved me to give to my lover someday. After I finally met Joe, I sent him a few of the cards and I read him the letters. He was amazed by what I expressed to him in writing prior to actually meeting him. The words I wrote were identical to how we both felt. It was as if I had magically created him. He fit the description of everything I imagined and had written down. These letters are a direct request to the universe or your prayer to God. Here is an excerpt from one of the letters:

My Sweet Beloved,

I am here, ready and open to meet you, my love. I can feel you in my heart and soul. Your smile warms me and your embrace makes me feel so protected and safe. Your kisses melt me! I know you are out there looking for me, and we will know each other when we magically meet. I am ready to adore you and be adored by you. Our lives will just fit because we are a match made in heaven. I see us as being an example of "love in form", like two peas in a pod. When others see us, they want to know our love story and how they can achieve such love. They see and feel our connection and want what we have—divine love. We have a beautiful home that is our sacred space and people love to come celebrate life with us. We have friends with like-minded souls who are like our extended family. We are blessed with health, abundance and joy. Our families love each other, and we take time to share special moments with those we love. I can be myself with you. We allow each other the space to express our gifts to the world and support each other's life goals and dreams. I am here waiting for you and want to grow old with you. You are my angel man, and I feel you in my soul. I am ready for love. I love you, and I call you into my life NOW!

Try it. What do you have to gain? *Love. Passion. Magic.* It may seem corny to some, but it is a powerful exercise and in the near future you can read it to your partner.

You can use your Love Design journal to write letters, prayers and poetry. After writing out your dream partner list, read it before going to bed to program these feelings into your heart and your subconscious mind while you sleep. You can also write down or recite the statements from *Your New Language of Love* section. Make some post-it notes and place them in special spots to keep the affirmations fresh in your mind. Pray with conviction that you are *Ready for Love* and request assistance from your angels, God or the powers that be, to lead you to your perfect partner. Then after you have put in your order, trust and let go.

Only you know what your heart desires, so keep in touch with your heart every day. You can achieve your ultimate vision if you align your thoughts, *energy vibes* and believe you truly deserve *sacred love*. Like a magnet, this alignment creates an invisible signal that attracts what you truly want. You will get results and love will magically find you at the perfect time.

The descriptive words listed in this chapter are also useful in creating a winning profile for online dating sites, matchmaking services, online video and personal ads and social media sites. Using these adjectives will also enhance your love letters, new love language, vision board and help you on dates. Not only does the written word influence your subconscious mind in creating and manifesting your desires, but it also influences anyone reading your profile or asking you questions on dates. Express yourself with passion and honesty. Others can feel your energy in the statements and the stories you use to describe yourself.

DESIGN YOUR VISION BOARD

I have been using vision boards and designing vision journals for over 20 years. Many people know what vision boards are, but most don't know how amazingly powerful they can be. Many companies and athletes use visioning to achieve remarkable success. It is also a powerful tool to help you find love and meet your own personal goals.

Vision boards can be simple or intricate. It's all up to you. By taking time to cut words, pictures and power statements from magazines or other sources, it programs your subconscious and conscious minds to give you what you see and feel! Your unique vision board represents your lifestyle, your heart's desire and often helps you clarify your vision by doing this creative exercise. Here are a few steps to help you prepare to design your amazing vision.

Get organized and make it fun. From this moment on, be on the lookout for words and pictures that inspire your heart and tuck them a love vision file or in a zip lock bag until you are ready to create your board. You can find photos of attractive people and happy couples that resemble your type in magazines and on dating sites. Save them on your computer and print them. Pick up free publications at health food stores and grocery stores if you don't get magazines sent to your home.

Start gathering photos of yourself, your family, travel destinations and couples engaged in activities like watching the sun set, dancing, snuggling, laughing, getting married and celebrating with family. Add pictures of your ideal home, animals, furniture, cars, artwork, love symbols, clothing, jewelry, money, business logo, the title of a new book you want to write or a career vision. As you flip through magazines words will pop out! Add other things you'd like to enjoy. Success, great health, financial freedom, a new home, etc. Cut out powerful words or phrases that describe the qualities and characteristics of your ideal mate. You can create your own words on the computer in different colors or fonts and get photos of many things you can't find in print. Check out free photo websites and Pinterest.

Get all your supplies ready to go. Gather a variety of magazines from friends, family and co-workers if your collection is limited. Organize glue sticks, poster board paper or core boards, good scissors, fun colored construction paper for backgrounds and fun decorations. I have a cool collection of sparkle paper, stickers, crystals, and hearts that I'm constantly adding to my craft collection. Use your imagination and I also suggest designing sections with different themes.

Put all of the words and pictures that you've collected into different sections using different colored boards or a journal, depending on the theme. Different vision board themes include:

- Health and fitness, beauty and body image
- Travel, hobbies and activities
- Love, romance and weddings
- Family photos, babies and animals
- Homes, living spaces and furniture

- Success, abundance and ideal employment

- Legacy and goals

Create a special event to make your vision board alone, with friends, or join a vision board class. It's a process, so plan on three hours plus cleanup time. Set up the environment to create your love vision with music, candles and snacks. It's a fun, creative project and it's amazing how many things will start to magically show up in your life! I suggest taking your time when laying out the power words and photos that represent your future vision in all parts of your life. This board is your unique piece of art. Take your time and don't glue too quickly. Play with the words and the pictures. These powerful vision boards work with your unconscious and subconscious mind, and help you to clarify your vision. If you don't get it all done in one session, no problem. Just store your extra words and set another date to complete it. After teaching hundreds of clients my vision board process, many of them report that their visions have come true. Now it's your turn, so dream big and have fun with it. Here are a few success stories.

TRUE STORIES

VISION BOARD SUCCESS STORIES

Victoria is a 62-year-old, beautiful and energetic graphic artist who had challenges finding men she was attracted to. She came to my vision class to manifest love and success. She doubted she would find a man who could keep up with her energy level and passion for life. She was looking for an intelligent, romantic man who could make her laugh, was spiritual, sexually active, loved to travel, still had a full head of hair and a sense of style. She envisioned him to look like Jeff Bridges, so we created a cool vision board for her with a picture of him on it. We added descriptive words, a photo of *The Kiss* by the artist Gustav Klimt, a wedding ceremony and couples in love. At the time, Victoria had been dating a nice man named James and she thought they were "just movie buddies" for months. After she added romantic words and photos of a couple kissing to her vision board, James suddenly landed a hot kiss on her and she was shocked. They realized they had built a strong foundation for a loving relationship and they also had amazing chemistry. She called me to pass on the news that her vision board had worked! She is now married to James, who is a spitting image of Jeff Bridges and has all the qualities and characteristics she added to her board. They are very happy and deeply in love! Check them out on my site.

Mohammed, my very sweet and shy client from Algeria, created his vision board with my help over Skype. He collected pictures of a beautiful home, furniture, a man and woman with two children, and wedding scenes with photos of a Mediterranean island that he envisioned for his honeymoon. He also used numerous power words to describe his love vision. He added a picture of an attractive woman with sparking eyes, brown hair, a fit body and a beautiful smile. Being a Muslim living in Algeria, it was rare for Mohammed to meet someone from his culture without a formal introduction. He had left Jordan because his family was trying to force him to marry a girl he did not love. He was committed to finding *real love* and letting go of the imprints from his lineage. A few months after Mohammed created his vision board and completed his heart-healing process, he was introduced to a girl that looked exactly like the girl from his vision board. He called me in shock to share the joyous news, saying he met a beautiful girl who looked like the one on his vision board through his best friend's family! They were married in September 2013 and moved into place with all of his new furniture. They even called me from Santorini, Greece on their month long honeymoon. They are now expecting their first child. His vision of love came true and you can hear his love story on my website under radio shows.

You must conceive and *believe in love* before you see it. Most of my visions came to fruition after I created my vision boards, including meeting my amazing husband and finding my adorable dog, Buddy, on my birthday. I am sure you will be amazed at the magic that happens when you create yours! My amazing visions were featured in an article in *The Huffington Post* about the power of vision boards.

I am honored to be one of the contributing love-vision-board artists and certified vision board coaches based on the bestselling book, *The Vision Board Book* by Joyce Schwartz. My theme was *Take Time for Love*, which was a very powerful message that represented the balance between work, love and home life. Now, I have created my new vision board to include all parts of my life with my husband, spreading my message with this book series and expanding my *get real* heart-healing work worldwide. Shortly after this board was created, I was partnered with various dating companies and won the 2014 Top International Dating Coach Award at iDate! My vision board also includes opening the hearts of people worldwide by turning this book of secrets and true stories, especially my own my love story, into an inspiring, blockbuster movie. So, please visualize that dream for me. I see the film coming to a theatre near you and becoming the love story everyone wants to see!

⚷ *Sharing your vision with others can help speed up the process, even though some people may not believe in the power of vision boards. Who cares what people think? Do it any way!*

As you continue redesigning your life, you can update your existing vision board or create new ones. Then, when you meet your match, you can create one together. I suggest taking a photo of your vision board and putting a small version of it in your journal and appointment books. I also have mine stored on my iPad and cell phone to share with clients. Keep your board in a special place that you see every day and watch the magic happen.

ROLE MODELS OF LOVE

Now that love is on your radar, you may notice couples in love all around you. When you see people that have the type of relationship you want to manifest, I would encourage you to go ask them how they met. When I was single, this was one of the most powerful exercises I practiced to keep me inspired as I searched for my soulmate. I found that most of the couples I spoke to were flattered and excited to share their love story. These stories will help you keep the faith while you're looking for love. Look out for some of these inspiring love stories on my website.

CREATE YOUR VARIOUS ONLINE PROFILES

The Internet connects millions of singles worldwide. As part of my services, I help people create their online love profiles that *get real* results. After all of this inner reflection and becoming clear on who you are, what you have to offer and want to receive, you can use these descriptive adjectives and create vision statements for the Internet. Remember, the words and phrases you use to describe yourself are paired with others profiles on dating sites by complex algorithms. Every time you update and refresh your profile with new pictures and words, you will find that you suddenly have more matches. In addition to your online dating profiles, people are also searching for you on Facebook, LinkedIn and other popular social networks. Make sure that your professional online networks are aligned with your personal dating profiles and that your love vision statements are sending the right signals. Be aware that online you are being asked questions all the time and the words used in your replies are the initial connection. Also, the words and descriptions of your business and your social life are also being reviewed. It's like being marketed on multiple platforms.

HOW ARE YOU MARKETING & BRANDING YOURSELF?

Your written description is the first *energy vibe* a person notices about your character. According to the BBC News, females are far more interested in the written information on a page, spending 50% longer reading through the text on profile pages than men.[2] So, men listen up: Women will pay more attention to what you write! Put some feeling into your answers and use fun photos of yourself in different situations that show your personality. Share a funny story or experience that makes people want to continue reading. This shows that you are open to a relationship and took time to articulate your visions.

---

2 "Searching for Cupid's Algorithm." *BBC News*. BBC, 13 Feb. 2012. Web. 01 Sept. 2014.

If your online dating profile sends out one message with racy party photos with various partners but your business profile presents you as a conservative businesswoman, you may get mixed responses.

Your online photos are also a very important component of the process of "getting yourself back in the game." So make sure you have someone take nice, updated photos of you so that potential matches get a good representation of the *real* you. When I do profile updates for my clients, they often bring photos with a mysterious person who has been cut out of the shot, obviously an ex. I also see selfies taken with cell phones. How tacky is that? Spring for some new photos that make you look approachable and open. Wear clothing that makes you confident, radiant and sexy.

Use photos that express your personality and your lifestyle. The BBC News also noted that men spend 65% longer looking at pictures of prospective dates than females and lose their interest quickly when viewing unappealing photos.[3] There are online companies like www.DatingHeadshots.com that will help you look your best. Most importantly…remember to smile for your pictures!

Your online dating profiles are equally as important as your professional resume. The difference is that your dating profile is the blueprint for attracting a life partner aligned with your vision. You must take your time if you want to create a winning profile that gets results. So send out the right signals online and in person. Most of the profiles I review are stale and have no passion. Many people write too much about their work and accomplishments, which sends the signal that you are too busy and unavailable. If you are not getting any action online, it could be time to *tune-up* that profile!

⚷ *Remember, choosing your life partner is one of the most important decisions of your life. Take your time to consciously choose the messages you send out to the world and potential mates because—first impressions are lasting ones!*

I have helped thousands of people redesign their personal profiles in order to generate more positive responses with potential matches online. Words are

---

3   "Searching for Cupid's Algorithm." *BBC News*. BBC, 13 Feb. 2012. Web. 01 Sept. 2014.

powerful, so use them wisely online and in person on your dates. I suggest writing these qualities out and continually revising your list as you grow and change. You will soon see your partner manifest in your life. First, ask yourself, "Are you what you are asking for in a life partner?" Secondly, does your profile send the right signals to attract great partners or just *players*?

Magnetize your match by adding some sizzle to your profile and expressing yourself. I used these principles on several sites when I was single and still use them in coaching sessions. Use these words and add your own unique adjectives for your online profiles, letters and vision boards. Save all of your profiles on your computer in case you want to put yourself on multiple sites. It can save you a lot of time and energy with the ever-changing dating platforms.

DESCRIPTIVE ADJECTIVES TO SPICE THINGS UP

accomplished	athletic	cerebral	creative
active	attentive	charming	cultured
adorable	audacious	chatty	curvaceous
adventurous	balanced	charismatic	dainty
ample	bashful	cheerful	daring
agreeable	bawdy	chivalrous	dashing
ambitious	bewitching	classy	debonair
amiable	boisterous	communicative	delicate
animated	bold	compassionate	deliberate
appealing	brawny	complex	delightful
ardent	brazen	congenial	demure
amusing	bright	conscientious	dependable
aristocratic	broad-minded	conservative	devilish
articulate	burly	considerate	dignified
artistic	buxom	convivial	diligent
assertive	candid	cosmopolitan	direct
assured	captivating	courteous	discerning
astute	career-oriented	crazy	distinguished

down-to-earth	gifted	lively	polished
earnest	glamorous	loyal	positive
earthy	good-natured	mature	practical
easygoing	gracious	maverick	pretty
eccentric	graceful	mellow	prosperous
educated	gregarious	merry	rambunctious
elegant	giving	mischievous	rebellious
empathetic	happy	modest	refined
enchanting	hip	multi-faceted	reflective
energetic	homebody	natural	relaxed
enterprising	honesty	new age	reliable
ethical	humanitarian	nonconformist	reserved
even-tempered	humorous	observant	responsible
exquisite	husky	old-fashioned	responsive
extraordinary	idealistic	open-minded	reticent
extroverted	idiosyncratic	opinionated	risqué
exuberant	impish	optimistic	robust
faithful	impulsive	original	roguish
fascinating	independent	outrageous	rowdy
fearless	individualistic	opulent	rugged
fiery	intelligent	outgoing	saucy
finicky	intense	outspoken	seasoned
flamboyant	introspective	particular	secure
flexible	intuitive	patient	self-assured
frank	inventive	peppy	sensible
frisky	jovial	perceptive	sensitive
fun-loving	kooky	personable	sensual
funny	laid-back	petite	sexy
gallant	liberal	playful	serene
gentle	lighthearted	plump	serious
genuine	literate	poised	shapely

sharp	steady	talkative	vibrant
skillful	stout	tenacious	vigorous
sociable	strapping	tender	vivacious
sophisticated	strong	thoughtful	voluptuous
spicy	stylish	timid	vulnerable
spirited	substantial	tolerant	well-rounded
spiritual	sultry	traditional	whimsical
spontaneous	sunny	tranquil	willowy
spry	supportive	trustworthy	wise
stable	tactful	unconventional	witty
stately	talented	universal	wonderful

These words will help you make more online "magic!" This heart-healing work is guiding you to *get ready for love* and elevates the message you're sending out to the world. My intention is that, as you continue the journey to prepare your heart, you will soon be manifesting your own *true love story*. I know that people are inspired by *true love* stories, so let me share my magical love story. This story proves that love is possible when you least expect it. It's sure to awaken your heart and help you to *believe in true love*. It warms my heart to finally know that dreams do come true!

MY TRUE LOVE STORY

I returned to the East Coast in early August for my Aunt Bebe's wedding celebration, which had been postponed due to my mother's recent passing. Aunt Bebe was 60 years old and marrying for the first time. We all had a blast at her wedding and I, as the flower girl, was no doubt the oldest one in history!

During this trip, I launched *Rapid Dating* events in Delaware. There was a great deal of media buzz with radio and television coverage since this was my hometown. My photo and the event were also featured prominently in the local newspaper, *The News Journal*.

With Aunt BeBe's wedding and my work events behind me, it was time to take a break and be with my family. I was scheduled to stay at my Uncle Bill's beach house with my cousin Gina for a couple nights. Their house was located just outside Dewey Beach, Delaware at a place called Pot's Net. I had vacationed there before and I have fond memories of jet skiing, laughing and great meals with my family. My mother's death had been a loud and clear *wake-up* call that I needed to practice what I preached by *taking time for love.*

Since I had recently broken up with Tony, I was free to date. I was so proud that I had made a commitment to my heart to not go back to him, even though I was very vulnerable after losing my mother. Tony called constantly and it wasn't easy to say no, but I didn't want to date a liar after all the work I had done on my heart. I kept the faith and was ready for *real love!*

Surprisingly, while I was in town, I was asked out by a successful businessman with an ocean-front home in Rehoboth Beach. I had just taken a strong stand for myself and thought it was a sure sign that I was heading in the right direction. Since I was going to the beach anyway, I thought, "Why not?" I had met him once before and he seemed like a nice guy.

My cousin Gina was driving me to the beach and offered to drop me off to meet him for lunch. He called and said that he was running late and asked if my cousin could drop me off at his beach house a few hours later. I told him that plan wouldn't work since they would all be busy jet skiing and I had no means of transportation. I suggested that he pick me up on his way because I was only ten minutes off the main road. He seemed very annoyed that I couldn't get a ride and asked where I was staying. I replied, "Pot's Net," which is a charming community. When I mentioned the location, he said, "I can't believe a girl like you is staying in place like that since it's a trailer park! Just think, you can stay with me in my big mansion." I was so disgusted by his cocky behavior.

Again, he requested that I get dropped off, which didn't make me feel cherished or happy. I recognized the big *red flags* and I wasn't going to waste my time with a *narcissistic viber!* I couldn't believe he was being so rude and told him that I didn't want to meet him because I already knew it wouldn't work out. So, I cancelled the date and mentioned to him that I didn't appreciate him insulting my family. I also added that if ten minutes was out of his way, then 3,000 miles to California would be a stretch. So, why bother?

With that said, I hung up. My Italian roots run deep and one thing you don't do is insult my family! He didn't give up and called me back. Again, the *red flags* could not have been any clearer. My mother's recent death taught me that time is precious and there is no time to waste. So, I told him again that it was obvious that he and I would not get along and that I didn't appreciate him being rude and disrespectful. "Have a great day," were my parting words to him. I hung up once again.

That night, after dinner with my family, my cousin Gina and I decided to go out for a drink. The moon was full and breathtaking. As it turns out, it was a rare, magical blue moon. As we drove near one of my old stomping grounds, The Rusty Rudder in Dewey Beach, my heart leaped, skipping a beat. I insisted to Gina that we stop there because I had an intuitive gut feeling that I would run into someone that night. She was resisting because it was a busy summer night with large crowds and horrendous parking. Despite her unwillingness, my persistence won. To this day, I bless my heart for listening to my intuition. It changed the course of my life forever.

After manifesting a parking space right out front, I bought us both drinks. Within minutes, we were revisiting my old *lucky spot* on the top upper deck. Since I am only 5'2", I used to stand in that spot because it has a bird's eye view of the crowd and all the single men. When I lived there, my old friends could count on exactly where to find me. As I turned the corner to go to my lookout point, I noticed a handsome man that I recognized from the past. Gina also knew him. It was Joe Campanella. She had previously done his wife's nails and mentioned that she wasn't there with him that night. As we walked towards him I said, "I bet his wife is in the ladies room and will be coming out in a few minutes. He is so gorgeous!" She agreed.

The connection was instant magic. I had previously met Joe in my early twenties at his cousin Mary Ellen's wedding. I was one of her bridesmaids and we had shaken hands as he went through the receiving line. I remember as he took my hand and I looked up into his beautiful eyes, thinking to myself as he smiled at me, "Wow, I think I am going to marry that man someday."

As we reconnected that night, we smiled, hugged and realized that the chemistry was definitely still there. We locked arms and could not stop smiling at each other. We both expressed our attraction from the past and in that moment. According to Joe, he had asked my older brother about me years ago but Bobby had told him that I was engaged. So, Joe had assumed I was on my way down the aisle. Shortly after that wedding, I broke up with my high school sweetheart of eight years and cancelled the wedding. A few years later, I left for California.

Gina blatantly asked about his wife and Joe held up his left hand to show us there was no ring on his finger and he replied, "No more wife! We are legally separated and getting a divorce." The good news for me was that he wasn't married. The bad news was that he lived in Delaware and I was in California. Oh no, a LDR (long-distance relationship) was not something I wished for in my life. So, I was living in the moment and we continued our fun flirtation.

Joe told me that he had seen my picture in the newspaper earlier that week and had wanted to attend my event, but couldn't because he was vacationing with his son, Joey, for his birthday. Originally, they were supposed to be white water rafting in the Grand Canyon but had changed plans the previous week. Joe had snuck his handsome son, who loved music, onto the deck to listen to the band. After 9:00 p.m. no kids under 21 were allowed on the deck. Joey was only sixteen and it was 9:15 p.m. Minutes later, a big burly bouncer came by and noticed Joey. We were asked to "take it to the parking lot" if we wanted to talk. I asked if he could give us a few minutes since we were having "a love connection" and he powerfully said, "No lady! Again, take it outside now!"

Joe and I went out into the parking lot (with Joey and Gina in tow) to finish our conversation. I mentioned that I was originally supposed to be on a date with another man that night and told him the story. It turns out that my rude date was in the same grade and went to high school with Joe. Apparently, they were friends and athletic competitors back then; it's small world when you live in Delaware. We took a photo together, hugged and made a date to meet for coffee in the morning before I left for the West Coast.

In hindsight, had I not taken time out to relax on the East Coast after the wedding, broken things off with Tony, gone to the beach with Gina, cancelled my date and followed my intuition to go to the Rusty Rudder at that exact moment, Joe and I may have never connected. It was that moment in time when the stars aligned and my life was changed forever. I did indeed meet my soul mate that night and after all the work I had done, it was my turn to have *real love*!

I was exhilarated, joyous and ecstatic. I could barely sleep that night! I wrote it all down in my journal. Joe lived 3,000 miles away and a long-distance romance would have been the last thing on my *manifesting love list*. I immediately understood the reality of his being in the grips of a messy divorce. His job also had him traveling around the world and I was sure he had women in every port. I was smart enough to know that, given his circumstances, he might not be looking for a serious relationship at this moment in time. We met in the morning for coffee and we still felt the magic. I was excited and hesitant at the same time because long distance relationships usually don't work. I did not want to fall for a man so far away. I had tried this scenario before and it was heart-wrenching. I was trying to be realistic and yet, I was still interested. I was totally attracted to him.

Joe was quick to tell me what a great feeling he had about us, and I expressed my honest concerns about his situation. He was making points that made my heart skip a beat. He wanted to "get to know me from the inside-out" and "date the old-fashioned way." I was thrilled when he asked me out for a date the following Thursday, August 14, 2002. Joe worked for Oracle at the time and they had offices on the West Coast. He had a week full of meetings in San Francisco starting the following Monday. He told me he could fly to Los Angeles on Thursday and stay on the West Coast instead of flying back East. It was more cost-effective for his company to have him stay out West. Thank God! He flew into Los Angeles and stayed at the Loew's Hotel in Santa Monica, just a few minutes from where I lived. Only five days later, we had our first date. Imagine that. Coincidentally, this location was where I hosted my

Rapid Dating events and I knew the entire hotel staff. We had a 3½-day first date and talked for hours. (Yes, we only talked.)

The dating process was wonderful and dreamlike. We took it slowly and I was glad I had given Joe my first book *Love Mechanics*, so he could learn more about me. The experiences and conversations we shared were extremely helpful for us during our courtship. We talked and opened up about all of the values and issues that couples face. We discussed all the questions you have just read in this book to see if our lifestyles were aligned. It was awesome to put my *secret love tools* to the ultimate test with my own heart.

In that first week, I discovered that Joe was casually seeing three other women from different parts of the world. Since I also had men pursuing me, I totally understood and supported him to do whatever he wanted with no pressure from me. I just told him, "I'm a one-man woman and perhaps the timing isn't right because we're in different phases." I was ready for love and he was in the middle of a divorce. A few weeks later, he let me know that he told the other women that he had met someone special and wanted to explore our relationship exclusively. Then, Joe asked me to be his girlfriend.

Since marriage wasn't on his mind, I agreed to make an exclusive three-month *love contract* to take our relationship for a *test drive*. This took the pressure off of both of us. I designed this *love contract* process to help clients discover if they were a match without pressuring dates or wasting years of their lives. I practiced what I preach to successfully screen out the *players* and it really worked. Check out the *Love Contract* CD on my website!

Our *love story* kept expanding with miracles each day. We saw each other most weekends. We texted, emailed, spoke daily and were both committed to our budding relationship. After a month of getting to know each other and exploring our hearts, we knew we were soul mates. This epiphany was euphoric.

He came to visit for my birthday just as our three-month *love contract* was coming to an end. He surprised me with plane tickets for Thanksgiving and Christmas, so we could be together back East with our families. I teased him saying, "You took a chance buying these tickets without a renewed *love contract.* I could have traded you in!" He loved that I wasn't giving him ultimatums or pressure like the other women he had met. Our relationship was getting stronger and then a few weeks before the Christmas holidays, another traumatic event came to pass.

On December 11th, I received an urgent call from my brother Bobby requesting that I come home right away. My father had just had a severe heart attack and was admitted to the hospital for open-heart quintuple bypass surgery. The doctors gave my father less than a 20% chance to survive. I wasn't going to miss seeing him in case he passed away. My adrenaline was pumping and I experienced a déjà vu. I sensed my mother's presence as I packed my clothes. I could hear her voice and she gave me a message for my father as well as clear directions to rub his head. I felt that sinking feeling in my heart and rushed to the airport.

Joe flew in from San Francisco and met me at the Philadelphia airport late that night after my connecting flight was delayed for three hours because of an ice storm. I was lucky to get there in time and we rushed to the hospital to see my father. As I entered the room, I saw my father hooked up to breathing tubes, IVs and wires all over him. A Catholic priest from our church was there anointing my father with oil and giving him his last rights. My younger sister Angel was recording my father's last messages for the whole family.

He was very weak and tired. I asked for everyone to leave us for a few minutes so that I could give him the message from my mother. I gently rubbed his hair and told him to relax and take a few deep breaths. He asked softly, "Did you know your mother used to rub my head like that at every night?" I said, "Daddy, I didn't know that but she told me to rub your head, so shhhh." I kept petting him and told him to close his eyes as I began sharing her message: "Daddy Bear, it's time for you to live on and let go of the past. You need to be strong now. It's not your time to go, you have more love work to do! Trust in God's plan. I love you and I am always with you." He cried and told me about how bad he felt for always working so much and not always being there. I said, "Daddy, Mom and all of us love you so much and we need you to get well. You have your children and nine grandchildren to live for and we want you to be around for a long time. I'm praying that you will stay alive to give me away at my big Italian wedding." His eyes opened wide. I continued, "I am the only of your kids that has not had a wedding, so please promise you will stay alive to walk me down the aisle. I finally found my perfect match so you can't die now." I looked deep into his eyes and said, "Daddy, Joe is my husband and I need you to be alive to see me get married. Do you think you can hang in there for me?" He said with a grin "So, you think he's 'the one'?" I smiled, nodded and with tears streaming down my face replied, "Yes I do, so please don't die now Daddy!" He smiled and gave me a high five. I knew he was excited. He survived the surgery and had so many visitors that the hospital staff teased us that he must have been famous or from a mafia family. They had never seen so many Italians in one place.

The amazing thing was Joe was there to help me and my family support my dad through his healing process. My dad's heart needed time to heal since he was so weak and was still grieving from the loss of his wife of almost fifty years. While Dad was still recovering in the hospital, we had a bad storm that caused a sewage flood that filled our basement and spare room of our house with a foot of dirty, smelly sewage! All of my mother's clothes were stored in the basement so we had to trudge through sewage to save them. The house reeked and my dad was coming home in just a few days to recover. Joe took charge and got the flood crew to sanitize and restructure the rooms. The house was completely cleaned up and ready in time for my dad's arrival home.

Wow, Joe sure came to the rescue and my family loved him. I thought to myself, "If he could handle all this 'crap', he was *definitely* my man." It was amazing. I knew my prince had finally arrived. I would tell my family and friends, "This man is husbandly!"

I fell even more deeply in love with him as he cared for my dad at home with me for three weeks. He bought walkie-talkies so that my dad, a stocky man, could call him for help getting in and out of bed, the shower and bathroom. Joe organized all of his meds and helped him walk to get his daily exercise. We cooked and cleaned the house together and were surrounded by family. We spent a joyous holiday feeding the homeless in the rain on Christmas Eve for

The Salvation Army. I recall looking over at him as he led the groups of volunteers to deliver food and thinking that this man was a leader and my husband for sure! My heart just knew. Then, we had a huge traditional dinner, the Feast of the Seven Fishes, with my family. We all prayed and thanked God my dad was home in time to celebrate with us. Once my dad was stable, we left to go back to Los Angeles to ring in the New Year with some friends.

Our second day into the New Year brought another shock. Joe's company dissolved the division he was working for at Oracle. We weren't sure how we could continue seeing each other as often since his division shut down and he had no plans of flying out to San Francisco. We stayed in faith and tried to relax knowing nothing could stop this love connection. Little did we know how fast our prayers would be answered. A few days later, on January 6, 2003, Joe was offered a new position in the health care division at Oracle in Southern California, only seven blocks from my house! Was this fate, a miracle or just destiny for us to be together? I'm convinced that it was my mother watching over me and that she had somehow orchestrated this miracle from up above.

Joe and I began to build a life together and things were moving along smoothly. We worked through a few bumps in the road, including dealing with his divorce proceedings and the job transfer. Dating a man in the middle of a divorce was a challenging experience. That's why I started my personalized coaching program geared towards dating after divorce. As we shared many special moments along with life's trials and tribulations, I knew deep down in my heart that Joe was my *true love*. With open communication and a clear vision, we went step-by-step to build a foundation of trust and *sacred love*. After applying and living the lessons I wrote about in my book and taught in my love seminars, I had finally manifested my dream man. Two years later, on September 18, 2004, after attending the 50th wedding anniversary party of his parents, Joe proposed to me with my mother's engagement ring. He had gotten the ring three days earlier from my dad, after formally asking for my hand in marriage. He got down on one knee, (the old-fashioned way) and asked me to marry him. I said, "Yes, I would be honored to marry you!"

We were married on September 4, 2005 and designed our "Dreams Do

Come True" Goddess themed celebration, which was held at my beautiful childhood home. During our wedding ceremony, surrounded by 250 of our family and friends, a large white butterfly flew above the pergola my father had built for me in our back yard. It circled above our heads as we exchanged our sacred vows. Once I said, "I do", the butterfly cheerfully whisked off into the garden. All of our guests gasped as it left the tent. My mother surely made a grand appearance that day, and she rang the chimes on the porch all afternoon. You could feel her there and I knew she was happy that I found true love at last!

It took my mother's death to slow me down long enough to *take time for love*. Joe and I thank God every day for finding each other, and I truly believe my *angel* mother sent Joe to me. Thanks, Mom! This story proves that love is possible at any time and when you least expect it. All my internal work paid off and I finally manifested the love of my life that magical night. Since I was in the love business, I always dreamed of having my own inspirational *love story* to share. Our chance meeting was like a scene from a Hollywood movie and it happened "once in a blue moon." It warms my heart to finally know that *dreams do come true*!

I always remember my mother saying, "God's timing is always perfect. Trust in God's plan." Hopefully, you can see what a gift each moment is without having to lose a loved one to teach you how to slow down and look at what is most important in your life. LOVE!

GET REAL ❤ REFLECTIONS

❤   List the top five things you would be doing if you knew your *true love* was being delivered to your door in 30 days.

❤   Write out your *Get Ready for Love* to-do list.

❤   Carve out time each day to practice your love exercises and rituals while acting as if the love of your life is already there.

❤   RELAX and live in joy. Bask in the feeling of being loved, focus daily on your love vision and believe that love is on its way!

Now that your heart is open, you're on your way to manifesting the love of your life. I believe in love for you and I am here to support you on your path in this wild world of dating. In this first book of the series, you have explored the internal part of your life and you are in action to connect with great people. It's only a matter of time before *real love* happens for you. This inner reflective work is a part of the foundation that will be forever woven into the fabric of your soul. You now have the secrets and tools to change the meaning of the messages that were installed into your heart from your *love lineage* and open yourself up to *sacred love*.

○┿х *Remember, by living your life with an open heart… anything is possible!*

You must keep the faith and continue your daily commitment of connecting with your heart and nurturing your soul. You can never turn back now that you know this information, so be kind and true to yourself. Keep the vows you took as you began this *Get Real about Love* process and treat your heart sacredly. Take time out to complete the *Manifesting Love Rituals* and practicing your new *Language of Love*. Always take care of your *little girl* or *boy* and I promise that your life will be forever changed. Each moment of your life is so precious, so set your intentions and stay in gratitude. You are the creator of your own *love story*. Be the love you are searching for and love will show up when you least expect it. That is the *secret*!

THE FINAL WORD

Thank you for trusting me with your heart! Whatever you do, don't give up! Learning about relationships is a life-long process and I have so many more secrets to share in my *Get Real about Love* series of books and CDs. I'm confident I can reinvent your love life. I help people open their hearts around the world. I look forward to meeting you, hearing your story and helping you find *true love*. You can get continued support with my various services listed below. I am consulting with many international companies and collaborating with many of the top experts and coaches in the world, so I am sure I can assist you. I am also training heart-centered coaches to be on my Love Designer Team to help spread my love work worldwide. If you are interested please let me know.

When You're Serious About Finding Love
Work with Renée Piane
Voted Top International Dating Coach

Calling all busy men and women who are ready to find real love! Let's Design your Personal Love Action Plan and Create Your New Love Story.
Not someday but... NOW!

If You Are:

- **Suddenly single?** Still single and **frustrated?**
- Getting back in the **dating game** after a **heartbreak** or **divorce?**
- **Not getting any results** with online dating or at all?
- **Ready** to make a shift in your love life?

Renée, The Love Designer, offers a variety of services and a very personalized approach to relationship coaching to support you to achieve your love vision. You can work Renée NOW in-person, by Skype or by telephone!

Personalized Coaching Packages • Interactive Classes
Heart Healing Sessions • Cocktail Mixers
Get Real Panels and More...

Get ready for love and commit to a change NOW!

WORK WITH RENÉE AS YOUR COACH
Single Men, Women & Couples Welcome!
www.ReneePiane.com/coaching

"GET REAL ABOUT LOVE" EVENTS
CLASSES, COCKTAIL MIXERS & PANELS

Are you a single wonder women or super man looking to find the love of your life? These events are interactive, heart-opening and always an enlightening experience! Who knows who you might meet?

RAPID COCKTAIL MIXERS: The most time efficient & fun way to connect with tons of great people fast! These parties offer busy, single professionals a social experience with music & food at upscale, lively locations.

HOT MAN PANELS: *Learn the Secrets into the Minds of Men*
An evening with a panel of men, both married & single, who open their hearts & share stories about dating, attraction, love, commitment & sex. Ask questions & gain insights. Learn that great men really DO exist!

CREATE YOUR VISION BOARD: Learn how to design a powerful Vision Board to make your personal & professional dreams come true with a fun, interactive group. We provide all of the supplies & the inspiration.

FLIRTING CLASSES: Learn flirting & body language techniques, how to dress to impress & where to go to meet great singles. At this co-ed event get direct feedback from role playing to master the art of flirting.

LOVE RITUAL CLASSES: Learn self-love & heart-healing rituals to stay balanced on your quest to find a meaningful relationship. Discover & align the parts of you that may be sabotaging love in your life.

EXPERIENCE RENÉE'S EVENTS
Single Men, Women & Couples Welcome!
www.ReneePiane.com/events

CLAIM YOUR FREE GIFTS FROM
THE LOVE DESIGNER

It is my passion to offer my years of wisdom and experience in the love and dating field to help you achieve your personal love goals! I hope you enjoy these free gifts and I'm looking forward to hearing from you.

Go to: www.ReneePiane.com/freegift

Enter your information online & receive your free gifts:

♥ **"THE 5 TRADE SECRETS TO MAGNETIZING THE LOVE OF YOUR LIFE"**
(MP3 audio download)

♥ **A COMPLIMENTARY 20-MINUTE LOVE COACHING SESSION**

GET IN TOUCH WITH RENÉE
www.ReneePiane.com
Office 310-827-1100

www.youtube.com/user/ReneePiane

www.facebook.com/renee.piane

www.twitter.com/reneepiane

www.linkedin.com/in/reneepiane

www.reneepiane.com/podcast

TO ORDER ADDITIONAL COPIES OF "GET REAL ABOUT LOVE"

Telephone orders to: **(310)827-1100**

Online ordering at **www.ReneePiane.com**

Renée Piane, the Love Designer, lives happily in Marina del Rey, California with her husband Joe and their amazing dog Buddy. You'll find her out daily "making magic" and truly living her passion spreading love on the planet. Renée is looking forward to hearing your new love story.

Keep your heart open and remember... Love is all around you!

Renée Piane

THE LOVE DESIGNER

Made in the USA
San Bernardino, CA
25 January 2017